Designing and Assessing Courses and Curricula

ROBERT M. DIAMOND

Designing and Assessing Courses and Curricula

A Practical Guide

Revised Edition

JOSSEY-BASS PUBLISHERS ▪ San Francisco

Substantial discounts on bulk quantities of Jossey-Bass books are available to corporations, professional associations, and other organizations. For details and discount information, contact the special sales department at Jossey-Bass Inc., Publishers (415) 433-1740; Fax (800) 605-2665.

For sales outside the United States, please contact your local Simon & Schuster International Office.

Jossey-Bass Web address: http://www.josseybass.com

Manufactured in the United States of America.

Library of Congress Cataloging-in-Publication Data

Diamond, Robert M.
    Designing and assessing courses and curricula : a practical guide
/ Robert M. Diamond — 2nd ed.
        p.   cm. — (The Jossey-Bass higher and adult education series)
    Rev. ed. of: Designing and improving courses and curricula in
higher education. 1st ed. © 1989.
    Includes bibliographical references and index.
    ISBN 0-7879-1030-9 (alk. paper)
    1. Universities and colleges—United States—Curricula.
2. Curriculum planning—United States.   3. Curriculum evaluation—
United States.   I. Diamond, Robert M.   Designing and improving
courses and curricula in higher education.   II. Title.   III. Series.
LB2361.5.D5   1997
378.1'99'0973—dc21   97-17599

PB Printing   10 9 8 7 6 5 4 3 2 1   SECOND EDITION

The Jossey-Bass
Higher and Adult Education Series

CONTENTS

PREFACE

It is not an easy time to be a faculty member at an American college
or university. Hours are long, responsibilities are expanding, and
classes are increasingly diverse and challenging. Critics express concern with the quality of our teaching, with our curricula, and with
our priorities, which are perceived to be more focused on personal
agendas of research and publication (so as to ensure tenure and promotion) than on the teaching and learning of our students. In his
1995 report for the Education Commission of the States, Roy Romer,
governor of Colorado and chair of the commission, observed, "For
all its rich history, there are too many signs that higher education is
not taking seriously its responsibility to maintain a strong commitment to undergraduate learning; to be accountable for products that
are relevant, effective and of demonstrable quality; and to provide
society with the full benefits from investments in research and public service" (Romer, 1995, p. 1).

Ernest Boyer (1987, p. 6), in his earlier study of twenty-nine
institutions, reported "a disturbing gap between the college and
larger world, . . . a parochialism that seems to penetrate many higher
education institutions, an intellectual and social isolation that reduces
the effectiveness of the college and limits the vision of the student."
Boyer also reported a lost sense of mission, disciplinary fragmentation, divided loyalties, and competing priorities.

National studies sponsored by such agencies as the National
Endowment for the Humanities, the National Institute of Education,
the Association of American Colleges and Universities, and the
Carnegie Foundation for the Advancement of Teaching have all identified significant systemic problems. Their findings point to a need
to create orderly, effective change in curricula, set new priorities for
faculty, establish systems for evaluating and rewarding success in

teaching, and create healthy, vital environments in which students can learn.

This book is concerned with the need to reexamine curricula and make appropriate changes. The Association of American Colleges and Universities (1985) identified essential content and skills for which higher education programs should assume responsibility:

- Inquiry: abstract and logical thinking and critical analysis
- Literacy: writing, reading, speaking, and listening
- An understanding of numerical data
- Historical consciousness
- An ability to distinguish science from other kinds of inquiry
- A sense of values: the ability to make choices and to accept responsibility for them
- Appreciation of and experiences in the arts
- International and multicultural experience

Similarly, in his chapter "General Education: The Integrated Core," Boyer (1987) called for an "integrated core curriculum" leading from "essential knowledge" through interdisciplinary connections that facilitate "developments and integrate community service, political participation, [and] application of knowledge to life beyond the campus" (p. 91). Institutions, he said, need to have clear mission statements and to reflect in their programs the value they place on teaching and research. He recommended orientation programs that introduce entering students to the values and traditions of higher education and to courses that provide a strong, integrated core, including attention to the communication skills cited in the Association of American Colleges and Universities report cited above.

The National Endowment for the Humanities report *To Reclaim a Legacy* (Bennett, 1984) called for an undergraduate curriculum that provides a strong core in the humanities and values teaching, a curriculum characterized by cooperation between administrators and faculty as they move toward constructive change in their programs. Although the twenty-seven specific recommendations of the National Institute of Education (1984) report *Involvement in Learning* focus on similar categories of change, they emphasize the need to show demonstrable improvement in students' knowledge, capacities, skills, and attitudes between entrance and graduation. The report stresses further that these demonstrable improvements should be based on established, clearly expressed, and publicly announced standards of performance, and directs the colleges toward efficient, cost-effective use of student and institutional resources of time, effort, and money.

John Abbott questions the very structure of higher education when he observes that "we continue to get graduates who think narrowly, are teacher-dependent, and who have too little ability to tackle challenges or embrace change"; he suggests that "the need may be less for 'reform' than for fundamental redesign of the system" (1996, p. 4). Accrediting agencies increasingly press us to provide assessment models and to specify measurable outcomes for our courses and curricula.

These reports present a clear call for imaginative planning, with faculty, administrators, and students working together toward change. They look toward curricula that take advantage of technological developments and include community service, political participation, and other opportunities for civic involvement. Although they call for changes in content and pedagogy, they do not describe how these changes might be made.

Often institutions, departments, or instructors recognize significant problems in the content and design of curricula or courses, but efforts to change are hampered by uncertainty about how to make orderly changes, where to begin, what outcomes to target, and what roles faculty, curriculum committees, and administrators should play. This book provides a model for change that answers these questions.

Attempts to change curricula are not new. Major projects in developing core curricula were undertaken in the 1920s and again in the 1940s. But each of these efforts foundered as it attempted to build in more flexibility and greater student choice. This trend was even more in evidence in the early 1970s, when requirements, structure, and sequence of programs and courses almost disappeared from many campuses. The key, as Joan Stark and Lisa Lattuca point out in their major review of curriculum innovation, is "to find the balance that will provide choice while preserving culture, one that will provide exposure to alternative perspectives while avoiding fragmentation" (1997, pp. 354–355). No easy challenge.

In their study of college and university productivity, William Massey and Andrea Wilger observed that the primary losers in recent budgeting shifts have been the curriculum, the quality of teaching, and the quality of advising, mentoring, and tutoring. Most of the increases have gone toward reducing teaching loads and supporting an increased emphasis on research and faculty specialization (1992).

Diane Halpern, in her book on changing demands in higher education, identified both internal and external forces that, when combined, are creating a demand for change that must be met. "Students in college now will face changes and advances in the workplace

[and] in the world-at-large that we cannot even guess at today. It is thus more important than ever to switch from an emphasis on rote knowledge of content, which is quickly outdated, to an emphasis on the processes of thinking, learning, and questioning. This switch from content to process is required . . . if [students] are to succeed at a time when the only certainty is the rapidly accelerating rate of change." She also points out changes in the students: more then half are now women and "increasing numbers of students [are] from ethnic minorities and recent immigrant groups, resulting in a change, quite literally, in the complexion of higher education" (Halpern and Associates, 1994, p. 2).

Although the problems we face are significant, this is also an exciting time to be a faculty member at a college or university. Increased attention is being paid to teaching and learning. Many institutions are rethinking their goals and priorities, their curricula, and the way learning takes place. Numerous examples will be found throughout these pages. The promotion and tenure system is also beginning to undergo major transformation. Many of the disciplinary associations are actively facilitating the improvement of teaching and making teaching more important in the faculty reward system.

The Disciplines Speak (Diamond and Adam, 1995) includes fourteen statements from disciplinary associations that list teaching as a scholarly/professional activity under appropriate conditions. Additional associations have since completed similar statements. The American Sociological Association has long had a special office that provides materials on the teaching of sociology. The "ADE Statement of Good Practice" (1996) called for the effective teaching of English. Statements and initiatives of this type are becoming the rule rather than the exception.

We also have available to us technological innovations such as e-mail and the World Wide Web that open up opportunities that can significantly increase faculty access to course and curricular information and also improve the quality and scope of our students' learning experience. As we move from being presenters of information to being facilitators of learning, our courses can expand far beyond the four walls of the classroom, conference room, or laboratory. Thomas Angelo, one of the leaders in the movement to change how we think about our students' learning, describes what is now going on in higher education as a basic "shift in the academic culture," including a shift from "largely unexamined assumptions to one of assessment and evidence," "a shift from focusing . . . on teaching and teachers to a focus on learning and learners," "from a culture which ignores what is known about human learning to one which applies relevant knowledge to improve practice," and from a "narrow, exclusive definition of scholarship to a broader, inclusive vision" (Angelo, 1966). The combination of all these elements will help us develop the effective learning environments necessary for higher education to be successful in producing skilled and knowledgeable learners and engaged faculty.

Course and Curriculum Design and Assessment

Designing and Assessing Courses and Curricula responds to the questions of faculty who recognize a need for change but are unsure of how to reach their goals. The book is also designed to answer questions raised by administrators and chairs who support faculty efforts in these activities. The chapters focus on an approach that has been used at institutions with very different profiles—private and public, large and small—and with varying budgets. It offers a practical approach to systemic change. The book shows how to move from concept to actualization, from theory to practice. Case studies illustrate the model's adaptability to broad curricular change and to course and program design; it works with equal success in both areas.

Unlike the earlier edition, this one is written primarily for faculty rather than those who support them in improving the quality of instruction. Although the model described is the same, the content is different. References to related research have been highlighted, and other references that provide an in-depth look at specific areas have been added. The book reflects the increased focus on student learning rather than on teaching a body of content.

In their study of the contextual influences on faculty as they design their courses, Stark and Lattuca observed that less than one-third of those teaching general education courses reported that books and articles on teaching and learning were an influence in their course planning (1997, pp. 224–225). To successfully revise a course or curriculum, you need up-to-date knowledge about learning and the various ways to facilitate it. Without this knowledge efforts to improve student learning are unlikely to succeed.

New sections have been added on curriculum design, goals, assessment, and the design of programs that have complex goals like multicultural diversity and critical thinking. Case studies have also been expanded to include examples from a broader range of institutions. A major attempt was made to provide useful references and a summary of relevant research findings in teaching and learning. As noted, the primary constant is the model itself, which has been retained because it works.

Furthermore, several factors make this model particularly relevant. Programs that have been developed using it meet the goals identified in the major reports on educational change referred to earlier. Compared with other approaches, it is cost-effective and provides visible results in the shortest possible time.

Experience has simplified it and made the model easier to use. These changes have reduced the time needed for implementation. Program assessment is now a part of the process. The measurement of outcomes is ongoing, ensuring continuous improvement and the accountability demanded by state, regional, and national agencies.

Several additional characteristics significantly affect the model's success: the use of an expert from outside the content area and the initial focus on the "ideal" are unique and successful innovations. Furthermore, the process is data-driven, using information from a wide range of sources to help determine scope, content, effectiveness, and efficiency. This systems model places technology in perspective, using it where and when it is appropriate.

Finally, and equally important, although this approach requires hard work, you will find it exciting, challenging, and rewarding, and administrators will remark on its efficiency and effectiveness.

Purposes and Audiences

Many excellent books have been written about teaching and learning. But that is not the focus of this book. This is a practical, descriptive handbook with you, the faculty member responsible for your course, and your peers (responsible with you for your curriculum project) as its primary audience. It provides you with one effective model for designing, implementing, and evaluating courses and curricula. It suggests design options that are available as you attempt to meet the diverse needs of your students. It provides guidelines to those you invite to help you in the design process. It helps to move the focus of course design from content coverage to student learning.

Although based on sound theory, the book is not a theoretical discourse. It is a practical guide for faculty and administrators, showing how to approach and implement the redesign of courses and curricula, the structures in which learning takes place.

The suggestions are derived from my own experience, the experience of many associates in various institutions in which I have worked on instructional development, and the experiences of creative faculty throughout the United States. Although many case studies are drawn from the records of Syracuse University's Center for Instructional Development, others are from large and small public and private colleges and universities that represent the broad spectrum of American higher education. The book shares the strategies that have worked well in making constructive, considered change of the sort higher education is presently challenged to initiate.

Getting the Most Out of the Book

As noted, this book has been designed to introduce you to an effective approach to course and curricular design. The process has been used successfully in institutions of all types, from community colleges to small liberal arts institutions and large research universities.

The case histories have been selected to show how faculty have addressed some of the common problems that we all face in attempting to improve our individual courses and entire curricula. An attempt is made throughout to include references to a wide range of excellent resources that can be useful to you as you move through the process.

In most chapters you will find specific case studies on either course or curriculum projects. Focus on those case studies directly related to your own project, keeping in mind that the examples have been selected for the type of problem they address rather than for the discipline involved.

Overview of the Book

In general the chapters of this book follow the model of course and curriculum design on which it is based. They are structured this way to "walk you through" the design and implementation process. Whenever possible, checklists are provided as a quick reference for answering questions and suggesting alternatives that should be explored. The sequence has also been designed to provide you with essential information when it will be most useful and to establish a frame of reference for what follows.

The sixteen chapters are ordered to provide you with a logical introduction to course and curriculum design and assessment. In Chapters One and Two the model is introduced; these chapters describe how your work in this area can be documented and recognized as the scholarly endeavor that it is.

The major portion of the book, Chapters Three through Twelve, describes the process itself. Starting with making the decision as to whether you should even begin (Chapter Three), the book moves on to getting the process under way (Chapter Four) and then discusses the crucial but often overlooked relationship between courses and the curriculum (Chapter Five). Chapters Six and Seven describe the design process in some detail, using case studies that illustrate the questions that should be asked, the data that need to be collected, and the options that should be explored.

Chapters Nine to Twelve focus on the elements of course design: clarifying instructional goals, developing an assessment approach that measures how well these goals are being met, deciding how your courses will be taught (your role and that of your students) and how you can best use the technological options available to you. These chapters pay particular attention to the research on teaching and learning and suggest excellent resources.

Chapters Thirteen and Fourteen are significantly different from those that precede them. Chapter Thirteen points out the importance of quality communications between you and your students and describes how an expanded syllabus can have a direct and positive affect on your students' learning and can reduce the pressures on you as their teacher. Chapter Fourteen discusses an issue that is creating an increasing amount of stress on campuses—diversity. The chapter looks at diversity within the classroom and as a campuswide instructional goal.

In Chapter Fifteen the focus is first on course and program evaluation and then on the use of assessment information to improve what we do. Chapter Sixteen outlines the characteristics of a quality education system, describes trends that are leading to attainment of the goal of quality education, and reviews some of the major lessons about course and curriculum design that I have learned over the past thirty years or so.

In the Resources section you will find, in addition to some excellent case studies, questionnaires, protocols, and a host of other materials that have been selected for their usefulness as you work through the course and curriculum design and assessment process.

Acknowledgments

First and foremost I would like to thank the many talented faculty whose work is represented on these pages and to extend my gratitude also to my present and former colleagues at the Center for Instructional Development at Syracuse University; they played an active role in the development and design of many of the courses, curricula, and evaluation instruments that are described here: Paul Eickmann, Edward Kelly, Joseph Durzo, Charles Spuches, Peter Gray, Barbara Yonai, Ruth Stein, to name but a few. Special thanks to Donald Ely, Philip Doughty, Jerry Kemp; to the reviewers Howard Altman and Sheryl Hruska for their suggestions; to the host of folks in the Professional and Educational Development Network in Higher Education, who have had a wonderful time critiquing my work over the years; to Martha Gaurdern, Julie Mills, and Stephanie Waterman for their graphic assistance; to June Mermigos for her clerical support; and to Bette Gaines, who, with her editorial assistance, brought a cohesiveness to the final manuscript.

Jamesville, New York   Robert M. Diamond
September 1997

THE AUTHOR

Robert M. Diamond is assistant vice chancellor, director of the Center for Instructional Development, and professor of instructional design, development, and evaluation, and of higher education at Syracuse University. He received his Ph.D. and M.A. degrees from New York University and his B.A. degree from Union College. He has held administrative and faculty positions at the State University of New York College at Fredonia; the University of Miami; and San Jose State University. A former Senior Fulbright Lecturer in India, he has also been president of the Division of Instructional Development, Association of Educational Communication and Technology.

He is codirector of the Syracuse University Focus on Teaching Project and director of the National Project on Institutional Priorities and Faculty Rewards, funded by the Lilly Endowment with additional support from the Fund for the Improvement of Postsecondary Education, the Pew Charitable Trusts, and the Carnegie Foundation for the Advancement of Teaching. He is a consultant to colleges and universities throughout the United States and overseas.

Diamond has authored numerous articles and books including *Designing and Improving Courses and Curricula in Higher Education: A Systematic Approach* (Jossey-Bass, 1989) and the article "Instructional Design: The Systems Approach" for the *International Encyclopedia of Education* (Pergamon, 1994). He is the coauthor of *Recognizing Faculty Work: Reward Systems for the Year 2000* (Jossey-Bass, 1993). He has also authored *Serving on Promotion and Tenure Committees: A Faculty Guide* (Anker, 1994), *Preparing for Promotion and Tenure Review: A Faculty Guide* (Anker, 1995), and "What It Takes to Lead a Department" (*Chronicle of Higher Education*, Jan. 1996). He coedited the New Directions for Higher Education volume *Reward Systems for the Year 2000* (Jossey-Bass, 1993, no. 81) and *The Disciplines Speak: Rewarding the*

Scholarly, Professional and Creative Work of Faculty (American Association for Higher Education, 1995).

Diamond coauthored the 1987 National Study of Teaching Assistants and the 1992 National Study of Research Universities on the Balance Between Research and Undergraduate Teaching, and he was responsible for the design and implementation of Syracuse University's award-winning high school/college transition program, Project Advance.

In 1989 Diamond received the Division of Instructional Development of the Association for Educational Communication and Technology award for outstanding practice in instructional development. The Center for Instructional Development was the recipient of the 1996 Theodore M. Hesburgh Award for Faculty Development to Enhance Undergraduate Learning.

Designing and Assessing Courses and Curricula

CHAPTER 1

A Learning-Centered Approach to Course and Curriculum Design

As a faculty member, you can undertake few activities that will have greater impact on your students than active involvement in the design of a curriculum or a course you teach. As a direct result of these efforts, learning can be facilitated, and your students' attitudes toward their own abilities can be significantly enhanced; they will be better prepared for the challenges they will face after graduation. Major course and curriculum design initiatives also tend to have an impact for many years after the project has been completed, and, as a result, the number of students these efforts affect is substantial.

As important as these activities are, we are seldom prepared to carry them out. Although you may have been fortunate enough to have participated in a strong, well-conceived program for teaching assistants, few faculty have had the opportunity to explore the process of course and curriculum design and to read the research that provides a solid base for these initiatives. This book is designed to help you go through the process. It will provide you with a practical, step-by-step approach supported by case studies, a review of the significant literature, and some associated materials that should prove useful and should save you time.

No Easy Task

Designing a strong course or curriculum is always difficult, time-consuming, and challenging. It requires thinking about what material you will cover, then about what your students will learn, and finally about how you as their teacher can facilitate this process. This demanding task forces you to face issues that you may have avoided in the past, to test assumptions with which you are comfortable and that are rarely challenged, and to investigate areas of research that are unfamiliar to you. You may become frustrated and wish to end the entire project. At times like this, keep in mind how important the activity is and press on. Most faculty who have used this model report that they found the process of design and implementation challenging, frequently exciting, and when completed, most rewarding.

Although curriculum development is always a team activity, course design is not. In both instances, however, the process can be facilitated and the end result improved if someone not directly involved with teaching the course or program serves as a facilitator. The facilitator may be a faculty member from another department or a staff member from the faculty development, instructional development, or learning center on your campus. The facilitator, who has no vested interest in the project, asks key questions, challenges assumptions, and helps you explore options, getting the big issues out in the open. The importance of the facilitator cannot be overstated. In a later chapter we discuss this role in detail.

Interrelationship of Course and Curriculum

One major problem we will highlight is the tendency to design courses that have little or no relationship to the curriculum that is in place or to the critical skills students need to acquire. Most observers and researchers agree that the sequence of courses our students take is more serendipitous than planned ("Learning Slope," 1991, p. 3A). These scholars frequently describe the educational experience of our students as disjointed, fractured, and totally unstructured (Boyer, 1987, p. 14). But if the curriculum, the courses, and the process of learning are not carefully integrated to produce clearly conceived learning outcomes, what else can we expect?

The research, too, suggests that in many cases college and university curricula do not produce the results we intend. Curricula that are not focused by clear statements of intended outcomes and that permit naive students broad choices among courses can result in markedly different outcomes from those originally imagined: by graduation most students have come to understand that their degrees have more to do with the successful accumulation of credits than with the purposeful pursuit of knowledge (Gardiner, 1996, p. 34).

After reviewing the research in this area, Lion Gardiner writes, "The curriculum has given way to a marketplace philosophy; it is a supermarket where students are shoppers and professors are merchants of learning. Fads and fashions, the demands of popularity and success, enter where wisdom and experience should prevail. Does it make sense for a college to offer a thousand courses to a student who will only take 36?" (1996, pp. 27–28). In its 1985 report *Integrity in the College Curriculum: A Report to the Academic Community,* the Association of American Colleges and Universities concluded: "As for what passes as a college curriculum, almost anything goes. We have reached a point at which we are more confident about the length of a college education than its content and purpose. Indeed, the major in most colleges is little more than a gathering of courses taken in one department, lacking structure and depth, as is often the case in the humanities and social sciences, or emphasizing content to the neglect of the essential style of inquiry on which the content is based, as is too frequently true in the natural and physical sciences" (p. 2).

Every institution should aim to ensure that by graduation all students will have reached those goals that the faculty agree are appropriate and will have the skills, attitudes, and competencies associated with their major and minor. Your challenge, as you design a curriculum or develop your course, is to ensure that these goals can be attained by those students who meet the requirements. As Rudolph Weingartner in his book *Undergraduate Education: Goals and Means* (1993) observes, "The educational payoff of a coherent curriculum is that students come to understand the connections in theme that convert a diversity of curriculum parts into a whole. It is the job of text and teachers to make such relationships visible, but they must be there to be pointed out in the first place" (p. 155).

In the chapters that follow I will discuss in detail the relationship of courses to curricula and show how you can ensure a direct and appropriate relationship between the two.

Course Design and the Delivery of Instruction

The best curriculum or course design in the world will be ineffective if in our classrooms we do not pay appropriate attention to how we teach and how students learn. Although faculty, employers, and governmental leaders agree that graduates need critical-thinking and complex problem-solving, communication, and interpersonal skills, research shows that the lecture is the predominant method of instruction in U.S. higher education (Gardiner, 1996, pp. 38–39).

To ensure that students develop the higher-level competencies that you determine to be essential will require thinking about how time is spent both inside and outside the classroom and perhaps rethinking what your role as a faculty member should be. The chapters on the design and delivery of instruction in this book describe the many options available to us and the relatively recent excellent research on teaching and learning that can inform our decisions.

A Basic Reference Library on Teaching, Learning, and Assessment

Although most of our personal libraries are extensive, they also tend to be rather narrow, focusing as they do on our discipline and our particular field of specialization within it. Few of us spend much time reviewing what is known about teaching and learning or exploring the various methods of student assessment available to us. Nevertheless, our working knowledge in these areas will help to determine our effectiveness as teachers and the quality of our courses and curricula.

Although I highlight a wide variety of resources throughout the book, several rather inexpensive basic volumes should be in your collection. Practical and down to earth, these books can serve as quick references for checking the effectiveness of different approaches to teaching, review for you the various ways of collecting data, and provide an up-to-date summary of related research. They will also lead you to other publications that can provide in-depth discussion of topics of interest to you. And you can have this collection on your bookshelf for approximately $100. Included in this listing (Exhibit 1.1) are two newsletters for faculty that regularly contain extremely helpful materials and updates of the latest research on teaching; these newsletters should be in every departmental library. Take a few hours early in the design process to review the contents of each of these references.

Accountability

A serious problem that institutions of higher education face is the perception by business leaders, governmental leaders, and the public at large that they have enthusiastically avoided stating clearly what competencies graduates should have and that as a result they have provided little evidence that they are successful at what they are expected to do. Unfortunately, these perceptions are not far from the truth. The public demands for assessment of programs have, for the most part, fallen on deaf ears, and as a result of this inattention and also of major budget problems, higher education in general receives increasingly less support from the public and private sectors. As governors and

Exhibit 1.1. A Faculty Member's $100 Starting Library on Teaching, Learning, and Assessment.

Classroom Assessment Techniques: A New Book for College Teachers (2nd ed.), by Thomas A. Angelo and K. Patricia Cross. San Francisco: Jossey-Bass, 1993 ($34.95).

The best basic reference on the various approaches to assessing students. Numerous case studies and examples.

Preparing for Promotion and Tenure Review: A Faculty Guide, by Robert M. Diamond. Bolton, Mass.: Anker, 1995 ($9.50).

An increasing number of institutions are recognizing teaching innovation and course and curriculum design as forms of scholarly and professional work. This booklet provides specific guidelines for documentation.

Redesigning Higher Education: Producing Dramatic Gains in Student Learning, Report 7, by Lion F. Gardiner. Washington, D.C.: Graduate School of Education and Human Development, George Washington University, 1996 ($18.00).

If you want a good and practical review of research on curriculum and course design, teaching, learning, and advising, this is the book.

The Course Syllabus: A Learning-Centered Approach, by Judith Grunert. Bolton, Mass.: Anker, 1997 ($14.95).

Provides you with practical suggestions on how you can improve student learning by providing them with quality information.

Tools for Teaching, by Barbara Gross Davis. San Francisco: Jossey-Bass, 1993 ($32.95).

A great place to start if you want to review your instructional options and get some sound advice on what to do and why. Contains forty-nine succinct and practical chapters on everything from lectures, discussions, and small-group activities to dealing with a diverse student body, using technology, making out-of-class assignments, grading, and improving student learning and motivation.

Newsletters for Departmental Libraries

The National Teaching and Learning Forum, edited by James Rhem. Phoenix: Oryx Press. ($39.00 annually)

Six issues during the academic year. Faculty write about innovations they have tried and lessons they have learned. Includes reviews of most recent publications and resources.

The Teaching Professor, edited by Mary Ellen Weiman. Madison, Wis.: Magna Publications. ($41.00 annually)

Published monthly except July and August, this newsletter contains excellent brief articles on teaching-related topics with up-to-date reports on the latest research.

Note: Quantity discounts are available on all items.

other public leaders have made extremely clear, this problem needs to be addressed if support is to increase.

Collecting and using essential information and then collecting data and reporting results are major elements in the process of course and curriculum design and implementation. One of the underlying assumptions in the work you will be doing is that the instructional goals you are developing and the assessment of your students' success in reaching them will be stated publicly. The better the information you have and use, the higher your probability of success. Only this type of information can answer higher education's severest critics. For this reason I will discuss in some detail the development and assessment of broad instructional goals and specific learning outcomes.

Faculty Rewards

Faculty members who take a major role in curriculum development or undertake the revision of an existing course or the design of a new one have often done so at their own risk. These time-consuming projects take faculty members away from those activities that have traditionally been most highly recognized in promotion, tenure, and merit-pay decisions: research and publication. As a result, nontenured faculty often avoid such activities. The message on many campuses is clear: if you wish to advance your career, this is not an activity on which you should spend your time.

Fortunately, the climate is changing. Building on the work of the late Ernest Boyer, president of the Carnegie Foundation for the Advancement of Teaching, and supported by grants from major foundations (the Lilly Endowment, the Fund for the Improvement of Post-Secondary Education, and the Pew Charitable Trusts), new initiatives at Syracuse University and at the American Association for Higher Education have focused on increasing the importance of teaching and curriculum-related activities in the faculty reward system.

As a direct result of these efforts and the willingness of many faculty and administrators to support them, the tenure and promotion systems on many campuses are being revised to include within the definition of acceptable and recognized scholarly and professional work such activities as course and curriculum design and instructional innovation.

As the American Historical Association asserts, limiting scholarship to research and publication has been a disservice not only to the institution, students, and individual faculty members, but to the disciplines as well: "The debate over priorities is not discipline-specific but extends across the higher education communities. Nevertheless, each discipline has specific concerns and problems. For history, the privilege given to the monograph in promotion and tenure has led to the undervaluing of other activities central to the life of the discipline—writing textbooks, developing courses and curricula, documentary editing, museum exhibitions, and film projects to name but a few" (1994, pp. 1–2).

Such statements provide faculty added justification for submitting course, curriculum, and instructional innovations to promotion and tenure committees as scholarly work. Statements describing the work of faculty in their fields have been developed by a number of professional associations, including the American Academy of Religion, American Assembly of Collegiate Schools of Business, American Chemical Society, American Historical Association, American Sociological Association, Association for Education in Journalism and Mass Communication, Association of American Geographers, Council of Administrators of Family and Consumer Sciences, Geological Society of America, Joint Policy Board for Mathematics, Modern Language Association, and National Office for Arts Accreditation in Higher Education (which includes the fields of landscape architecture, architecture, art and design, dance, music, and theater). These statements can be obtained from the associations directly, and many can also be found in Diamond and Adam (1995). Other associations are completing their own statements on faculty work for their fields.

As a faculty member engaged in course or curriculum design, you face a number of specific challenges in having your work accepted as scholarly or professional by the committees on your campus. Because promotion and tenure committees usually are made up of faculty from other disciplines with different vocabularies and different sets of priorities, they will need to understand that work of this type is indeed scholarly and professional. For this purpose you can use the promotion and tenure statements from your campus (if they have been revised) and from your department, but you will need also to refer to the work that has been done nationally to describe what scholarly and professional work is in your discipline. Although the developers of the disciplinary statement mentioned above were unable to agree on a single definition of scholarship, they were able to agree that if the following six conditions exist, an activity is indeed scholarly and professional (Diamond and Adam, 1993, p. 12):

1. The activity requires a high level of discipline-related expertise.
2. The activity breaks new ground, is innovative.
3. The activity can be replicated or elaborated on.
4. The work and its results can be documented.
5. The work and its results can be peer-reviewed.
6. The activity has significance or impact.

Your second challenge will be to document how your work meets these criteria. Here again, resources are available to help you. Designed specifically for this purpose, *Preparing for Promotion and Tenure Review: A Faculty Guide* (Diamond, 1995) provides specific guidelines for data collection and documentation. The book describes how the design of new courses can be documented for promotion and tenure review (Exhibit 1.2). Remember before you begin a course or curriculum project to collect any data (student learning, enrollment, retention, attitudes toward the field, job placement, and so on) that you can later use as base data to show improvement and impact.

If you are a nontenured faculty member or are coming up for promotion and you are appointed to or are asked to serve on a curriculum committee or to develop a new course, remember that this effort will be extremely time-consuming and demanding. For this reason, get the assignment in writing, and prior to accepting it, negotiate the tenure or promotion ramifications. Get a formal statement that this work will be considered scholarly at the time of your review or that your tenure clock will be stopped during the period of this assignment. Such tenure and promotion issues need to be addressed before you begin, and you need to plan accordingly.

A Brief Introduction to the Model

This book focuses on an approach that has been used successfully at institutions with very different profiles: private and public, large and small, and with varying budgets. The book offers an in-depth approach to systemic change. It shows how to move from concept to actualization, from theory to practice. Case studies illustrate the adaptability of the model; it can be used with equal success for broad curricular change and for course and program design.

Several factors make this model particularly relevant. As the case studies illustrate, programs that have been developed using the model meet the goals identified in major reports on educational change. Faculty who have used the model have a sense of ownership of the projects and programs developed, ensuring that these programs and projects will become part of the existing system and thus survive. Compared with other approaches, the model recommended here is cost-effective and provides visible results in the shortest possible time.

Since the model was first used in the mid-1960s, changes incorporated as a result of experience working with it and comments from faculty and staff have simplified the model and made it easier to use, reducing the time needed for implementation. Program assessment is

Exhibit 1.2. Documenting and Assessing the Design of a New Course for Tenure and Promotion Review.

Rationale

- Requires a high level of disciplinary expertise
- Can have major impact on student motivation, learning, retention, and attitudes toward the field of study; can also increase interest of high-quality students to major in field
- By improving learning, meets the stated goals of department, school, college, and institution

Evidence

- Descriptive essay—includes statement of needs and rationale for design
- Syllabi or student manuals
- Newly created course materials
- Video of class presentation (of innovative teaching strategies)
- Student ratings
- Student performance data (tests and test results); focus, if appropriate, on specific population
- Comments regarding student preparation from faculty teaching high-level courses in the discipline
- Review of course and materials by experts in field (faculty and/or other professionals)
- Results of field tests and revisions based on these data
- Comparative data on retention, class attendance, number of students selecting further study in the field

Criteria

- Shows high level of disciplinary expertise
- Represents an innovation or new approach in design, delivery, or content that can be replicated
- Learning outcomes are clearly stated and match the course objectives
- Meets needs of student population being served and stated instructional goals
- Is approved by department and curriculum committee

Source: Diamond, 1995, pp. 61–62.

a part of the process and places outcome measures of a course or curriculum within the context of national, state, and regional goals.

This approach has several additional characteristics that significantly affect its success. By using a person who is not a content expert to facilitate the design process, this model allows you and other faculty to focus on content and structure while ensuring that assumptions are questioned and alternatives are explored. The model also allows you to focus first on what an ideal program would look like, eliminating perceived limitations—many of which turn out to be more imagined than real. Furthermore, the model is data-driven, using information from a wide range of sources to help determine scope, content, effectiveness, and efficiency. This systems model places technology in perspective, using it where and when it is appropriate. Finally, and equally important, although this approach requires hard work, faculty find it exciting, challenging, and rewarding, and administrators remark on its efficiency and effectiveness.

The model follows a specific sequence that begins with an assessment of need and a statement of goals (moving from the general to the specific), which is followed by the design, implementation, assessment, and revision of your course or curriculum (Figure 1.1). This sequence assures a mesh of goals, instruction, and assessment.

As departments, schools, colleges, and universities under an external mandate to assess the quality of their academic programs are finding out, no matter where you begin in the process, you will need to go back to the statement of need before you can develop a statement of goals on which assessment must be based (Figure 1.2). For example, to assess your program you will need to know, first, where you are trying to go; and then based on this information, you will need to develop an assessment program that can help determine whether you are successful.

Those responsible for these assessment initiatives are reporting a number of common problems.

Figure 1.1. Basic Design Sequence.

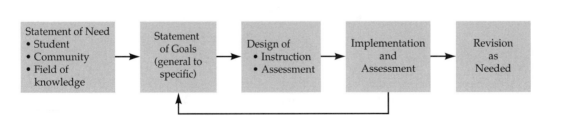

Figure 1.2. Assessment Sequence.

- Statements of outcomes do not exist for many curricula and many courses.
- When outcome statements do exist, there is often a gap between stated performance goals and assessment (assessment tends to focus on recall and recognition).
- When outcome statements do exist, there is often a gap between stated goals and what is taught.
- When outcome statements do exist, they often focus on content and not on critical thinking and learning skills.

In other words, in course and curriculum design it is best to resist the pressure that many of us feel to discuss assessment before we have agreed on the goals for the program or course we will be reviewing. Obviously, we will need to identify goals before we can have a meaningful conversation about assessment or about content and structure. Furthermore, when the focus is on assessment, we often feel threatened, which can undermine the sense of common purpose that any effort needs. Starting with a consideration of how to facilitate effective learning will establish a rapport among everyone involved that makes for a successful team effort. This process reduces stress because it facilitates getting where we want to go in far less time and with much less frustration.

In the next chapter we will discuss how a systematic approach ensures the most efficient use of your time and effort and that of your colleagues as you work together to improve your program.

CHAPTER 2

Systematic Design: Model and Benefits

National studies may call for change; states and national accrediting agencies may require institutions to redefine their goals and to determine whether they achieve them; and students, faculty, and staff may proclaim that improvements are needed. What happens in the classroom will, however, determine whether these improvements actually take place. Ernest Boyer, in *College: The Undergraduate Experience in America* (1987), pointed out that the changes that are necessary are not inconsequential. "The undergraduate college, the very heart of higher learning, is a troubled institution. In a society that makes different and contrary demands upon higher education, many of the nation's colleges are more successful in credentialing than in providing a quality education for their students. . . . We found divisions on the campus, conflicting priorities and competing interests that diminish the intellectual and social quality of the undergraduate experience and restrict the capacity of the college effectively to serve its students" (p. 2).

Traditionally, course improvement has been the responsibility of the faculty, and efforts to redesign curricula have usually been assigned to departmental committees established specifically for this purpose. In many instances the faculty involved have devoted a great deal of time and energy to these activities. Despite this effort they have received little recognition for their efforts, no matter how successful they have been in designing exciting new courses or revising curricula. Among such successful innovations in teaching were self-paced science laboratories, new courses in science for the nonmajor, and numerous applications of computer-assisted instruction. Other projects, often with outstanding merit, that have received little departmental, administrative, or collegial support have withered on the vine. For this reason, we must concern ourselves not only with the design of new or improved programs but with their acceptance and implementation as well. For significant academic improvements to occur and be retained, several conditions are essential.

- We as faculty must have ownership in the process, retaining responsibility for teaching and academic content.
- The academic administration of the institution must support these activities and provide the resources necessary for success.
- Priorities must be established, projects selected, and resources allocated accordingly.
- Assessment must be an integral part of the process, and the success of all instructionally related projects must be measured on the basis of changes in student performance.
- As needed, others should be available to assist us in the production of instructional materials and in assessment.
- The procedures that we follow must allow us to provide the most effective program we can with the time and resources we have available to us.

Although the focus here is on courses and curriculum, we should also keep in mind that what goes on in the classroom is only a part of the total instructional experience of our students. No matter how effective we are as teachers and how well designed our courses and curricula are, we will not be successful if our libraries and residence halls are not conducive to studying, if student advisers and counselors provide our students with little personal support, if few opportunities for recreation exist, and if we, as faculty, are rarely available to meet with students outside of the classroom, laboratory, or studio. Some of the most crucial goals of our educational system can be accomplished only by having students participate in activities that take place outside of the formal classroom, such as internships, practicums, and community projects. Optimum learning requires a rich social, cultural, and physical environment. A total educational program must be nurtured and planned by involving the staff from the offices of student affairs and residential life, among others.

Need for an Effective Approach

The needs for instructional improvement are too great and resources are too limited to allow us to be inefficient or ineffective in the way we address our curricular problems. We cannot afford to leave things to chance, hoping that the right question will be asked, the key people will be involved, and all the appropriate options will be explored. For this reason I provide in this book a model for course and curriculum design that will give you, the faculty involved, the requisite "ownership" in the design process and the results.

Following a specific effective model for course or curriculum design provides several important advantages.

- It identifies the key factors that you should consider in a sequential order.

- It serves as a procedural guide.

- It allows you to understand where you are in the process and, if others are involved, their role in it.

- It improves your efficiency by reducing duplication of effort and ensuring that critical questions are asked and alternative solutions explored.

Hannun and Briggs (1980), in their analysis of instructional system designs, found seven common elements:

- Planning, development, delivery, and evaluation of instruction were based on systems theory.

- Goals were based on an analysis of the environment of the system. For example, a two-year college must have goals different from those of a university.

- Instructional objectives were stated in terms of student performance.

- The design of the program was sensitive to the entering competencies of the students and to their short- and long-term academic goals.

- Considerable attention was paid to planning instructional strategies and selecting media.

- Evaluation was part of the design and revision process.

- Students were measured and graded on their ability to achieve desired standards and criteria rather than by comparing one student with another.

Most of the basic work on the application of systems theory to education took place during the 1960s, 1970s, and early 1980s. Models designed by Briggs (1970), Gerlach and Ely (1980), Kemp (1985), and Russell and Johanningsmeir (1981) are representative approaches that include these common elements while focusing on course and lesson design.

Other models are more narrowly focused. The work of Kaufman and English (1979) on needs assessment and the work of Wittich and Schuller (1979) on the use of technology are examples of models that can be used as steps within broader models that focus on course, curriculum, or program design. Also included in this category are models designed to assist in lesson design, such as Merrill (1977) on learning hierarchies, Keller (1978) on using motivation in teaching, and Popham and Baker (1970) on selecting instructional activities.

Although these approaches are, for the most part, effective in doing what they claim to do, they have one or more of the following limitations.

- They tend not to question what is being taught but focus primarily on improving the delivery and effectiveness of instruction.

- They tend to be suitable for use in a single course rather than in curriculum projects or other efforts that are larger in scope.

- They tend to narrow, rather than broaden, the focus of those who use them.

- They rarely address the political concerns of project implementation and survival.

As you begin to consider your project, remember that the process of designing, implementing, and evaluating a course or curriculum is complex. It requires you to be sensitive to the academic setting of your project; to be aware of the capabilities, interests, and priorities of the students the program is designed to serve; to have knowledge and appreciation of the discipline; to understand the resources and options available to you; to articulate those instructional goals that all students must meet regardless of their majors and long-term personal goals; to have a working knowledge of the research on teaching, learning, and assessment. To be successful, the approach used must contain these elements and be easy to understand and to use.

The model we will use (Figure 2.1), which I first developed at the University of Miami in the early 1960s, has undergone a number of significant revisions, but its basic structure is unchanged. A large number of faculty and support staff have used it to design a broad

Figure 2.1. Process for the Development of Educational Programs.

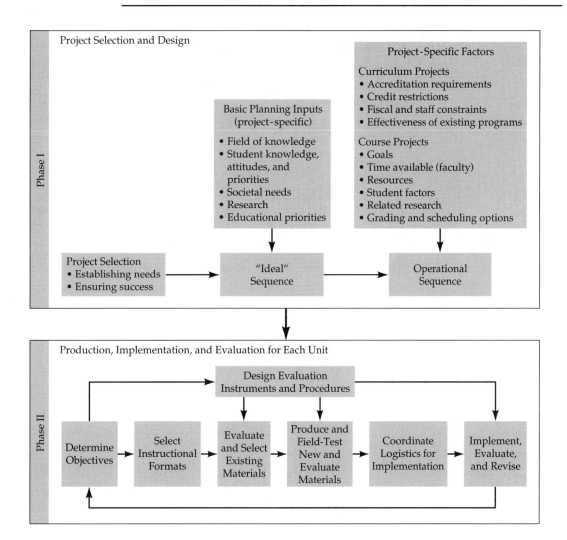

range of courses and curricula. Users report that it is easily understood, efficient, and effective. The model is less complicated than most of its type and requires less time between inception and implementation than others. The costs involved are also less. In addition, as will be shown through a number of examples, it can be used to design and implement courses, curricula, and other instructionally related projects such as workshops and seminars.

The model has two basic phases: (1) project selection and design and (2) production, implementation, and evaluation. Like most models, it is generally sequential, requiring that certain steps be completed before others begin. However, the linear nature of the process is somewhat deceptive. Ideally, some actions must precede others, and certain decisions should not be made until all relevant facts are known. But in practice all the data may not be available when an initial decision is required; information collected later may contradict earlier data, suggesting a different decision; or those involved may, for a number of reasons, wish to focus on an issue that is somewhat out of sequence. The model allows this flexibility. Although the overall flow of the model is generally followed, the steps in the model may overlap, as Figure 2.2 illustrates.

Characteristics of the Model

In addition to its simplicity the model has five other characteristics that when combined differentiate it from most others.

- It forces those using it to think in ideal terms.
- It encourages the use of diagrams to show structure and content.
- It relies heavily on the use of data.
- It encourages a team approach.
- It is politically sensitive.

Thinking in the Ideal

The initial goal of the design phase is to develop the "ideal" course or curriculum. When completed, the diagram that is developed represents the best possible instructional sequence for meeting the goals

Figure 2.2. Work Flow by Time.

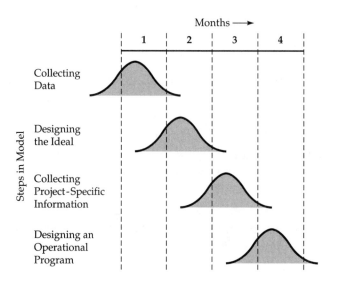

of the course or program. I have found it most efficient to start with the ideal and then modify it according to the specific administrative, material, and human constraints that exist. Limiting the original design to meet anticipated constraints unnecessarily limits the creativity and openness of the process and thus results in an inferior product. Another reason for trying to develop an optimum design is that anticipated limitations or constraints are often more perceived than real. How do you know you cannot do something until you try? The final design evolves slowly with many revisions as new data are provided and various viewpoints are discussed.

Even though working toward the ideal is an exciting part of the design process, it is not always easy. Many faculty find it extremely difficult to imagine abandoning the time frames, credit structures, course syllabi, and textbooks that they are accustomed to using. Comments from faculty who have been through the process of thinking in the ideal, however, have been generally positive:

> It forced us to "stretch" for the ultimate rather than starting out settling only for those things that we thought were possible.

> I was initially resistant to the "ideal" approach because I tend to be a pragmatic person who works and plans on the basis of resources available. However, once I got past the typical mentality, the freedom afforded by imaginative play in the ideal mode brought forth a number of surprising and positive ideas.

> Initially, the question was a challenge to abandon traditional assumptions about how the college classroom "should" look or work. That created the opportunity to consider faculty roles other than lecturer/demonstrator. I had great reservations about changing my role in the classroom. However, when I realized that in the ideal I could cover more materials in greater depth with adequate and better comprehension on the part of the students, I got very excited.

> There was no threat of failure in working with the ideal.

> Thinking in the ideal is an exciting and intellectually rewarding experience that allows the planners to test assumptions about content; about the students, their goals, abilities, and priorities; and about structure and methodology.

Use of Diagrams

Simple diagrams are an excellent method for visualizing an entire course or curriculum and for showing relationships and sequence. For these reasons, diagrams are used in this book to help illustrate the process of course and curriculum design. The diagrams used are for specific courses and curricula that have been developed using this model.

Boxes and arrows in such diagrams can sometimes be confusing when they are first used, but the technique of diagramming has, nevertheless, proven to be an extremely helpful communication device. A diagram showing the elements of a program in their proper sequence can clarify the scope of the project; help identify gaps, overlaps, and sequencing problems; facilitate modifications; and perhaps most important, clarify communication among those working on a project, and later, when the program is offered, between faculty and students. Experience has shown that using such terms as "in any order," "as required," or "as selected" to explain the connections in a flow chart can substantially reduce its complexity. Although at first you may not be comfortable with this technique, your feeling should change once its practicality becomes obvious.

> My first reaction was that all "those people" were addicted to rectangles and arrows, probably since the first grade. Over time, I appreciated the help of "visual" memory in rethinking and reconstructing course projects. It enables "time" to be visualized as well as relating subject matter and ideas to each other.

> I first thought it was too simplistic to capture the overlap built into a course, but with use I grew to see its merits rather than limitations.

> What a help; why didn't I think of it?

The early diagram for a course or curriculum will identify each of the major instructional components and the sequence in which they occur. During this stage the focus is on topics and elements of the program, not on how instruction will take place. Figure 2.3 is an example of this type of preliminary outline.

By the time the design phase is completed, the diagram will include (if appropriate to the specific course or curriculum) this information:

Figure 2.3. Preliminary Diagram: International Relations.

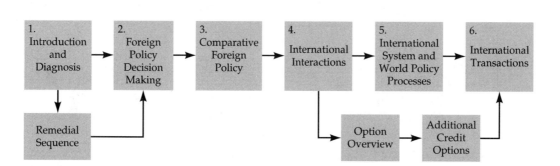

Credit: William Coplin, Michael O'Leary, and Paul Eickmann.

- The step-by-step flow chart of the course content or, in the case of curriculum design, the overall sequence of courses (Figure 2.3)
- When, in the total sequence, orientation and diagnostic testing sessions are scheduled
- The elements of the program that are essential and are required of all students—that is, the instructional "core" (particularly important in curriculum projects)
- The specific remedial units that must be available for the students and when they should be completed in relation to the other elements of the program
- Options and optional topics (and, if possible, which options may be used for additional credit)
- Whether seminars, faculty conferences, large-group sessions, in-class and out-of-class group activities, and independent study assignments are essential or recommended
- The separate tracks for specialization
- The instructional components with objectives that some students may already have reached; that is, where exemptions can be anticipated based on the data on entry levels of competence
- For courses, times for evaluation

The amount of detail in a particular diagram is directly related to how far along the design process is and to the scope of the program being developed: the farther along the project is and the broader the scope of the program, the more detailed the diagram will be.

Each of the larger elements in a diagram is broken down into a more detailed unit outline. For example, Figure 2.4 is a detailed description of one of the sections in the diagram for the course in international relations (Module 5, International Interactions). (Note that in the later version of the diagram the number of this unit has changed.) A single course usually consists of four, five, or even more of these unit outlines. Usually, for convenience and clarity, each of these outlines represents a self-contained unit of the course, covering several weeks of study, with its own set of objectives, options, and evaluation. In Figure 2.4, the unit outline identifies six segments of the course.

Although these diagrams should be as specific as possible, they should not be considered final or static. Diagrams may undergo constant and sometimes extensive modification as the preliminary (ideal) design is put into operation and is field-tested. However, the more specific and detailed the design, the clearer the goals will be and the easier and more rapid the transition from design to implementation will be.

Figure 2.4. Unit Outline for Module 5: International Interactions.

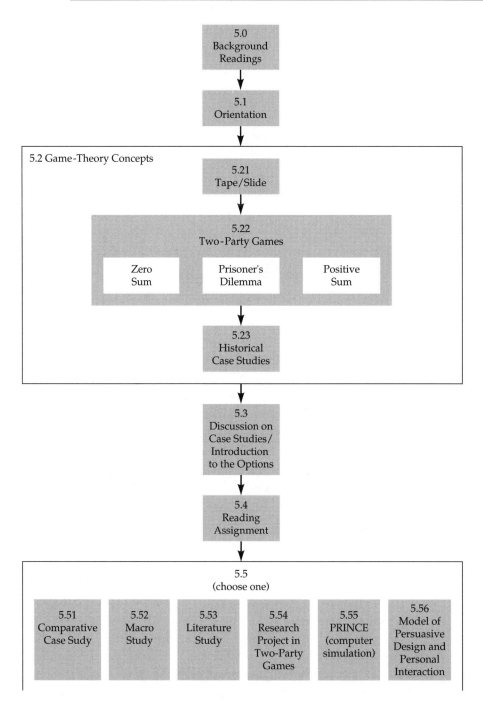

Credit: William Cohen, Michael O'Leary, and Paul Eickmann.

Although diagramming a course or curriculum is an effective way to show the relationship of content to sequence and structure, it can be a rather uncomfortable process until you are familiar with it. Exhibit 2.1 is an exercise designed to introduce you to the concept in a direct way. Figure 2.5, at the end of this chapter, is one response to this exercise.

Use of Data

Decision making in each of the phases of the model relies heavily on the collection and use of data. Whether data help clarify the problems that have been identified, provide information about the students or the professional field, or measure student performance, their accuracy is essential if the course or curriculum developed is to be successful. As different steps are discussed, you will see that data play a major role in both the design and implementation stages. In our model, data will be used to:

- Confirm and clarify the problem that is being addressed
- Provide information essential to the design of the program
- During the field-testing of the program, provide evidence that is essential for revision (data on learning, logistics, effectiveness, and so on)
- Provide information for the final evaluation of the program and for use in reporting the results of the project to external publics such as funding agencies and administrators

Team Approach

For a project to be successful, a number of talents are needed. Ideally, the design team will be composed of faculty who are responsible for the content of the program or course, a process person, and as needed, experts in assessment and technology.

Faculty.   The faculty are the key to any design project. Individually or as a group faculty members must have the necessary experience and content expertise and also be willing to devote the time and energy that will be required. In curriculum projects each major academic area must be represented. The selection of the participants is often crucial in determining a project's success. If you are working on your own course, particularly an introductory course, it is often wise to involve other faculty. Doing so will increase the content base and provide backup in case you or someone else leaves, is assigned to other courses, or is promoted to an administrative position. It

Exhibit 2.1. An Exercise in Diagramming: Exploratory Science 118.

The description below of an introductory science course includes a number of the structural options I will describe in case studies later in this book. Take a piece of paper and a pencil (with a good eraser—you will need it!) and diagram this course. Remember that there is no single answer; as long as your diagram shows all the important relationships and flow, it will be fine.

Three suggestions:

- Although for display purposes a flow diagram can go from top to bottom or from left to right, going from left to right is generally easier to begin with. Move to the vertical later in the process to get more information on a page.
- Keep it simple. Arrows crossing over arrows can be confusing.
- Have fun.

Exploratory Science 118

In this course the instructor faced several design problems. While some students were missing prerequisites in mathematics, others, having had advanced courses in high school, were able on the first day of class to pass the first of the six unit tests. To address these needs, the course that evolved was structured in a specific way. It began with an orientation session, which included a placement test. Depending on their test results, some of the students were assigned remedial work in mathematics, which had to be completed by the beginning of Unit 2; others were advised to drop the course and to take additional math courses before reenrolling; others were placed in Unit 1; and the students with the best knowledge of mathematics were exempted from Unit 1.

Units 1 and 2 were sequential; Units 3 through 5 could be taken in any order.

During Unit 5 students also had the option of selecting a special project for one additional credit. This project had to be turned in at the final exam, which followed the final unit. To meet the needs of the students, the final unit consisted of three sessions on science careers: the first session covered careers in business and industry; the second, careers in research; and the third, careers in the health professions. Students were required to select one of these sessions.

assures that all your hard work does not disappear if something unexpected happens.

Facilitators.   Surprising as it may seem at first, one of the most useful people on your project may be someone with teaching or professional experience outside the content area involved. At a growing number of institutions this person may be a staff member from the academic-support unit established to assist faculty in teaching; this person will have had experience in the design process, understands teaching and evaluation, understands the use of technology, and most important, can work well in a supportive role. Units called instructional or faculty-development centers or centers on teaching and learning now exist on hundreds of campuses in the United States and have staff who are trained to assist you in this way. If such a center does not exist, find a faculty member outside of your academic area who is willing to help, understands teaching and learning, has the process skills necessary to serve in this capacity, and is enjoyable to work with. Before you begin, this individual must clearly understand the role he or she is being asked to play and understand the approach you are going to use.

By coming to the project without the discipline's vocabulary and without the traditional viewpoints of your field, this person can test your assumptions. Without being a threat to you, he or she can question what is being done and why. For example, if the content or vocabulary of a project is unclear to this person, it may well be unclear to the students. In a sense, facilitators are surrogate students. They also might suggest new options and raise questions you may not have considered.

Individuals who can serve effectively in this role are not always easy to find. Not only do they need a range of human-relations skills and a firm knowledge of education and teaching; they also must be willing to work in support of a project that is not theirs but belongs to the faculty they are assisting. They are also people who are at home with new ideas and supportive of innovation. One experienced faculty member commented at the completion of a project where she served in this capacity, "While I understood that my role was to facilitate the design, I was, admittedly, skeptical that I could effectively do so with little to no knowledge of the subject matter. In the end, however, it was my objective perspective, background in education, and experience with undergraduates that proved most beneficial."

Ideally, the facilitator chairs meetings when several faculty are involved, brings other resource people to these meetings as appropriate, ensures that the model is followed, and equally important, keeps the project moving. Exhibit 2.2 offers some useful suggestions.

Exhibit 2.2. A Note to Facilitators.

As the process person on the project, your basic function is helping the faculty you are working with define and reach their goals for their courses or curriculum. Being from outside the discipline, you can raise issues that otherwise might go unaddressed, and you can question assumptions. The primary way you will do this is by asking key questions and exploring with your colleagues instructional options and various assessment techniques. At times you will find it helpful to put yourself in the role of the student. Is what is being said or written as clear as it can be so that all your questions are answered and so that you have the all the information necessary to do what is expected of you?

To assist you in this role we have included in the following chapters checklists of the questions that should be addressed and a number of additional references that may prove helpful. Many of these reference materials are in your library or in the faculty, instruction, or learning center on your campus. As you move through the process, list those questions that you feel will be most appropriate to address.

During the design phase you will find it helpful to talk through the sequence of the course or curriculum and, using the chalkboard, to develop the flow of instruction. After each design meeting copy the material from the board, edit it to make the sequence clearer, and then send it to the faculty so that they can review it and make changes prior to the next meeting. Just make sure before everyone leaves that the next meeting is scheduled and that all are clear about what they are to do prior to that time.

Always keep in mind that there will be surprises, some good and some frustrating, and that there will be times when ideal sequences will not be followed. I have found this role to be challenging, broadening (it is always an education learning about another field), rewarding, and enjoyable. It is worth the effort.

Faculty members have this to say about this "outsider's" role.

Not being from the same discipline removed the professional competition. The questions were marvelously facilitative and clarifying. We became aware of our assumptions. Elegant. Simple.

It was wonderful working with someone from another discipline because this person could give me an objective opinion of my work. It helped me to clarify what I was teaching.

It is hard for faculty to believe that someone who is not a subject-matter specialist can be of help in assessing or promoting the criticism and construction of a course. However, with quality personnel, the "fresh" eye and "naive" questions often open new insights.

Involving a person from outside my discipline prevented me from making assumptions. Kept me organized. The ability of this person to ask "dumb" questions constantly reminded me of a professorial tendency to assume students know things they do not—could not possibly—know.

Evaluators.   You may also need some assistance in designing survey instruments and assessment protocols. Although you or another faculty member can collect some data, sometimes specialized skills and objectivity are essential.

Evaluators must have a firm understanding of how different types of data can be collected, and they will be most helpful to you if they also can write and communicate effectively with those outside the field. Evaluation assistance can often be found in the instructional-support unit on your campus. If an evaluator is not available through this source, try the department of psychology, school of education, or research office. In case such a person is not available, I provide a wide range of sample instruments and techniques in the chapters that follow.

Support Staff.   You may also need secretarial assistance and the services of specialists in computer graphics and media production. Individuals with these skills are usually available through the instructional-media unit of most institutions.

Political Sensitivity

If there is one attribute that determines the success of a project, it is ownership. Many projects, often effective ones, die as the result of neglect or antagonism on the part of administrators, other faculty, or key academic committees. By involving these various groups from the beginning, the model helps generate the political support and ownership that you will need for implementation and approval. If faculty colleagues who feel they should be consulted are not, if administrators who will have to provide resources for implementation know little about the project, or if the steps that must be followed for formal approval are not taken, the new program, no matter how good it is, will probably not survive. This model will help you ensure that the appropriate faculty and administrators are involved and supportive and that a climate for success exists.

Where You Work: Options and Alternatives

All too often we begin a course redesign with a mental idea of what the program will look like—in effect picking the solution before we have defined our problem. In this model such decisions are delayed until all factors are considered. Throughout this book we will be discussing options you should explore as you develop a course or curriculum. We will identify questions you should ask and issues that you should consider. Although the questions are consistent, the answers to them will vary from project to project.

One of the factors that will help determine the options available to you is the institution in which you work. Although many design and instructional options are available to everyone, some may exist on one campus and not another. A large institution, for example, may have more specialists available to support you as you work, but a faculty member in a smaller institution may find that the support that does exist is more accessible and easier to find.

In later chapters I will discuss how such factors as class size, homogeneity of students, location of the campus, space available, and whether the campus is commuting or residential have a direct bearing on the ways learning can be facilitated. Although I explore many options, you will have to determine which is most appropriate for you and your students. Unless all options are explored, however, it is impossible for you to identify the best possible course or curriculum. Large or small, inner-city, urban or rural, each location has unique advantages, and each challenges you to make the most of what is available to you.

Summary

The systems model we will use in subsequent chapters is not a traditional one. More comprehensive than most, it forces us to think in the ideal and uses a facilitator from another discipline to direct us through the process. Relying on flow diagrams to show content and structure and using quality information throughout, the model is both effective and efficient. Although it may seem complex at first, faculty find this approach comfortable. In the chapters that follow, a number of case studies illustrate how to use each step of the model in developing courses and curricula.

Figure 2.5. Exercise Response: Exploratory Science 118.

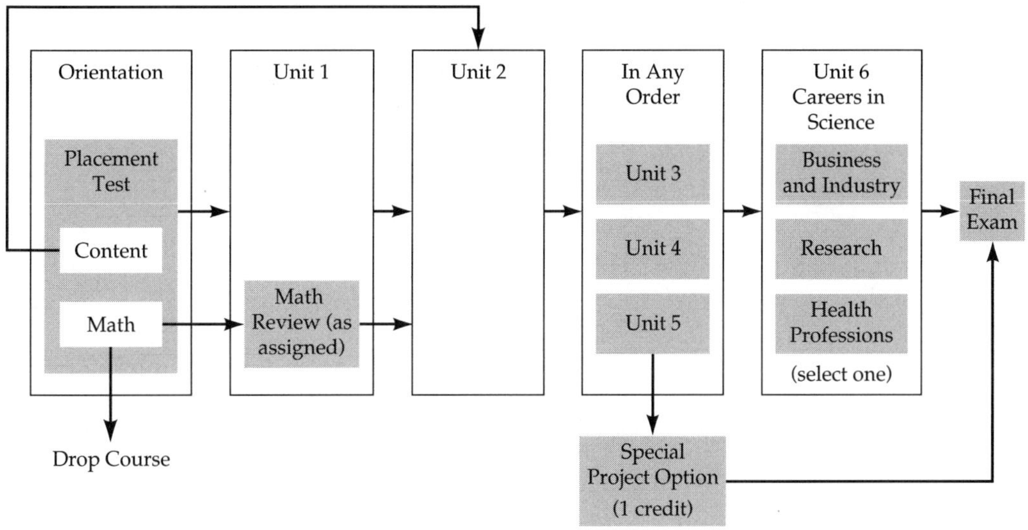

CHAPTER 3

Making the Decision to Go Ahead

Before you begin any course or curriculum design project, two major questions must be answered. Is there a need for the project? If there is, are the resources available to ensure the success of the project?

A decision to create or redesign a course or curriculum should not be taken lightly because it will require you and everyone else involved to commit a great deal of time and effort. In addition, entering into this activity can have a direct impact on your professional career and the careers of other faculty who are involved. If you are a nontenured faculty member at a research university, there may even be an element of risk, as noted earlier.

Projects begin after a person or group has concluded that a problem or need exists. After that conclusion has been reached, a systematic needs assessment can accomplish two purposes: it can specifically define the problem, and it can generate information that you will need later, in the design phase. Before you undertake such a formal needs assessment, however, be sure that the support necessary for success exists. Without this commitment, engaging in a course or curriculum development project is a waste of your time and your institution's resources. It can create frustration and anxiety for you if significant problems are identified and then nothing is done to correct them.

Why Projects Begin

Faculty members become involved with course or curriculum projects for a variety of reasons. For example, you may be convinced that the content of your course is outdated; you may be concerned with

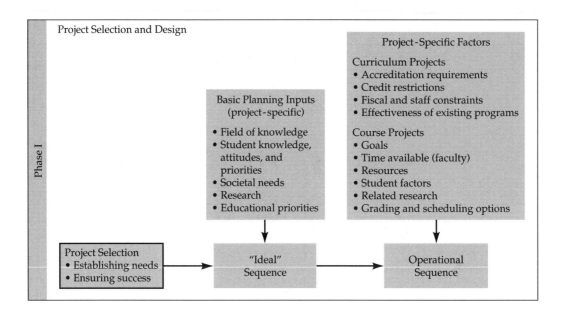

a high failure or dropout rate; or graduates may be telling you, informally or through formal assessment, that they left the institution unprepared for their career choices. You and others may have become increasingly concerned with your students' attitudes, a diminishing number of majors entering the field, or a perceived lowering in the quality of your students. You may have simply become bored with the course as you are presently teaching it—the academic seven-year itch. Some course or curricular projects begin when faculty find that they are no longer covering all they wish to and conclude that changes must be made. Other projects are undertaken as a direct reaction to concerns expressed by employers, the fiscal need for larger enrollments, or a strong desire on the part of an entire department to update or improve program quality. A project may begin when a faculty member becomes intrigued with a new instructional approach or technology and finds that to use it well he or she must first address some basic issues that have been ignored for years. Some projects begin because faculty views of their roles in the classroom change.

Questions to Consider

Whether the identification of a problem is based on hard data, hunches, vague feelings of frustration, or the desire to engage in a challenging and perhaps even enjoyable exercise, several questions should be asked before work begins. These questions constitute the evaluation component at the project-selection step of the design phase. Most often, these informal evaluation activities are performed by those most directly involved in deciding whether to begin a project.

How important is the project to the department, to you, to other faculty, to the chairperson, to the dean? If there is little support for what you are proposing, if few see the need or perceive the stated problem, if there are other problems that they feel are more important, beginning the project at this time may be a major mistake. There will be little support or assistance for your effort, and later on you may have difficulty getting needed approval from key committees and administrative offices. Although the lack of such support will not be a problem if you are revising an existing course, external approval is essential for curriculum revisions or new courses.

How will this effort be recognized in the faculty reward system? If you or other key faculty are coming up for tenure in the next several years, consider the impact a major project might have on the tenure decision. On some campuses a significant and successful commitment to course and program improvement is viewed positively. On others it may still be perceived by the tenure committee as detracting from what you should be doing: teaching, conducting research, and publishing. As noted earlier, this is the time to negotiate the weight this activity will have in decisions about promotion, tenure, and merit pay. For example, can your tenure clock be stopped during the period of this activity?

Are there others who can help and should be involved? Other faculty who teach the same course or who are directly responsible for the curriculum in which the course is offered should be involved or, at least, informed of what is being proposed. Are other faculty willing to assist: faculty who teach the follow-up course, faculty who send students to your course from other departments, faculty with special expertise that could be useful?

Do you and the others who will be involved have enough time? The answer to this question will determine not only whether you should begin but how long the project might take. Sometimes limitations in time and money have necessitated phasing in a new program rather than introducing it all at once. You can also negotiate released time or summer employment with your dean or department chair.

It is often best to use the academic year for design activities and summer for the production of materials (if salaries for summer work are available) for several reasons. First, the design phase can usually be completed during the academic year because it does not require an extensive number of hours each week. It takes time to collect, analyze, and interpret data, and others will want time to react to the draft designs, so scheduling meetings on a once-a-week or twice-a-month basis is fairly common. This schedule provides you with the necessary time to mull over what has been done and to make revisions between meetings with the facilitator and others involved. Second, released-time arrangements during the academic year rarely provide sufficient time to work on the project. If you are given released time, you will often be given additional committee and advisement assignments that take up the time set aside for the project. In institutions where summer employment is an option, you can schedule blocks of time for writing the new materials and preparing assignments and exams with no interruptions for other responsibilities. Third, during the summer, support and production people will usually be more accessible than they are during the school year.

Establishing Academic Priorities

One of the paradoxes of academic innovation is that often those projects most easily undertaken have little to do with the established goals or needs of the academic department, and support and investment are therefore highly questionable. While most significant in curriculum-related initiatives, priorities outside of your specific department or content area can affect the success of a course-focused project as well.

Realistic priorities are established from data collected from the community (alumni, employers, parents), students, the instructional staff, and the administration. Such data collection can answer important questions. What programs should be emphasized and improved? Where do problems exist? What changes are needed, and can they be made under the existing structure? Can and should fundamental restructuring be encouraged?

In establishing priorities, all those who are or should be concerned should be involved. Their participation is particularly important at the community level, where specific subgroups are often overlooked. The decision to revise a course that you teach can certainly be made by you alone. Determination of its importance, however, will often be made by others.

Although much has yet to be learned about how best to identify and describe an institution's academic needs and priorities, four groups need to be involved in this effort: students, society, faculty (individually and through their disciplines), and administration.

Students can provide accurate information about the value and effectiveness of academic programs. Unfortunately, structured attempts to gather these data are the exception. In many instances only the more politically active, highly capable student is heard. Nevertheless, you should seek input from all segments of the student population, including minority, international, and departing students. Often the students' immediate needs as they see them must be met before efforts to meet their long-term and more significant needs can be undertaken. Asking specific questions can help you identify problem areas: Are dropout or failure rates high in certain courses? Are the better students leaving certain programs?

The characteristics of your students can also make a significant difference. Different groups may require different objectives, procedures, and instructional elements. Designing the academic program for a highly transient student population poses a particular challenge. Junior colleges located near military establishments and in the inner city, for example, have a highly mobile student population. Such problems must be identified because they have a direct effect on the priorities of the program and on its design.

What are the needs of the society in which your educational program exists? These may be on a national or a local level or specific to the particular population a professional program is designed to serve. For example, a university serving a rural area and one in an urban center would probably have some priorities that are identical but others that reflect the unique characteristics of the community they serve.

Contacting your disciplinary or professional association can often provide useful information for determining society's priorities. For example, William Laidlaw of the American Assembly of Collegiate Schools of Business states (letter to the author):

> The customers of business schools, the companies who hire their graduates, tell [us] that business schools do a fine job providing a technical education, teaching analytical skills, and developing decision-making abilities. They criticize business schools for not teaching people management skills such as leadership, teamwork, and effective communication, and they feel business schools should do a better job of teaching ethics, technology management, and an international perspective. Without diminishing the knowledge currently imparted, companies want business schools to strengthen additional qualities and knowledge areas without lengthening the program or increasing the cost. Now the challenge is to figure how to meet customer demand.

You must also consider the future needs of society. For example, we must anticipate the skills that will be required by the time today's freshmen graduate and look for employment. All too often we have designed our institutions to meet immediate needs without giving enough attention to long-range requirements. A study by one professional group, which chose not to publish its findings for political reasons, concluded that the faculty in the field had "lost touch" with what was happening in the workplace. As a result, many graduates were unprepared for the jobs for which they were applying.

With sufficient effort relevant trends can be identified. The large number of teachers retiring in the 1990s and in the early years of the twenty-first century at all levels from elementary school to college will certainly have a direct effect on the job market. In addition, for the next several decades the need for graduates in all fields with competencies in technology, information systems, and computers can only be expected to increase. Increasingly, graduates have available to them job openings in a far wider range of fields than ever before as employers recognize the need for diversity in the competencies of their employees. It is imperative that we continue to monitor the occupational outcomes of our graduates. Significant changes in job opportunities are not the exception.

Some effort has been made on a few campuses to establish a close working relationship between the academic departments and those who hire their graduates. At Syracuse University, for example, boards of visitors have been established for each professional school to provide input and resources. The Center for Instructional Development at Syracuse University has found that advisory groups for design projects in the professional areas not only help to identify a need for the revision of existing programs but provide excellent suggestions for what should be included when programs are being designed. Those serving on these advisory groups are often willing to make student internships and other resources available to the programs.

When major content problems exist, the faculty are usually aware of them. Major discoveries, new theories, and discipline modifications have an impact on priorities. It is often helpful also to involve faculty in other schools or departments. Management specialists, for example, can provide insight on academic programs in school administration or political science, psychologists can be helpful in evaluating programs in mass communication, and some faculty from law schools can assess the usefulness of a course in advertising. In some instances faculty already have courses available that meet the needs of another department.

A central administration that is sensitive to the concerns of parents, alumni, students, and faculty and that is aware of both budget and resource limitations can also help to identify the specific academic programs that need the most attention. Administrators (as well as faculty) also have to keep the broad goals of higher education in mind. Because significant demographic changes are usually prominent and readily identified, they are likely to generate easily articulated goals. But there is a danger that new job-related objectives will displace the broader, less easily defined "liberal" goals of education. Administrators (among others) can prevent this from happening by ensuring that basic long-range needs are addressed; the need for these competencies will not change. Quality employees will always need communication, interpersonal, problem-solving, and critical-thinking competencies regardless of their fields and their roles within them. Those responsible for the curriculum must keep these basic goals in view as more discipline-related goals receive much greater attention.

Deciding to Begin Curriculum Projects

Two elements must exist before you begin a major curriculum revision. First, a solid base of instructional talent must be available in all the appropriate academic areas; every key department must be supportive and must be represented by faculty members who command the respect of their peers. (And because these talented faculty members often receive other job offers and leave, it is best to involve more than one faculty member from each academic area to ensure continuity.) Involving a quality teaching staff with classroom experience and expertise in their disciplines ensures that the project is academically respectable and that it will be durable. Outside expertise can be used, but consultants cannot provide the specific teaching skills, knowledge of content, and political base required.

Second, there must be institutional stability. Beginning a project is unwise if the school or department faces changes in administration—if the chair or dean is to be replaced shortly, for example. Under such circumstances any decision about curriculum redesign made today may be overruled tomorrow. A new department chairperson, interested in establishing his or her own program, can cancel a successful program by administrative fiat without extensive research into why it was undertaken and what effects it has had.

Exhibits 3.1 and 3.2 are checklists of the factors you should consider in deciding whether to undertake curriculum projects.

Realistically, curriculum projects take a year or more to complete. Everyone involved should plan accordingly, keeping in mind that the end result will usually be the need for new courses, the redesign of existing ones, and the development of a range of other programs and elements.

Deciding to Begin Course Projects

Although you will ask a number of the same questions for a course project as for a curriculum project, there are, as you might expect, major differences in beginning a large, often multidepartmental curriculum project and in beginning a course project over which the

Exhibit 3.1. Establishing the Need for Curriculum Design Projects.

External Factors	Yes	No	Need More Data
1. The existing program meets the present and long-term needs of your students.			
• Alumni feedback	☐	☐	☐
• Employer feedback	☐	☐	☐
• Recruiter feedback	☐	☐	☐
2. Graduates of your program are successful in finding a job or being accepted into graduate school.	☐	☐	☐
3. The curriculum meets accreditation standards. (if appropriate)	☐	☐	☐
4. The curriculum is up-to-date and sensitive to changing needs in the field.	☐	☐	☐
Internal Factors			
5. Attrition rate is acceptable.	☐	☐	☐
6. Enrollment is stable or increasing.	☐	☐	☐
7. Quality of students is stable or increasing.	☐	☐	☐
8. More students are transferring in than transferring out.	☐	☐	☐
9. Faculty like the existing program.	☐	☐	☐
10. Students are pleased with the existing program.	☐	☐	☐
11. Core learning outcomes are clearly stated for all students.	☐	☐	☐
12. Discipline-specific learning outcomes are clearly stated for majors and required courses.	☐	☐	☐
13. Students are assessed on their ability to meet these goals.	☐	☐	☐
14. Tests and other evaluation protocols emphasize higher-order competencies.	☐	☐	☐
15. Every student has the opportunity to receive the instruction and reinforcement necessary to meet these goals.	☐	☐	☐
16. There is a "capstone" or comprehensive assessment at the end of the program.	☐	☐	☐

Exhibit 3.2. Indicators of Potential Success for Curriculum Design Projects.

	Yes	No	Not Sure
1. There is top administrative support for the project.			
• Provost	☐	☐	☐
• Dean	☐	☐	☐
• Chair(s)	☐	☐	☐
2. The individuals in key positions will be in place for the duration of the project.	☐	☐	☐
3. Quality faculty representing each discipline/department that will be affected are willing to participate.	☐	☐	☐
4. Faculty who will be serving on the design team are willing to follow the model selected.	☐	☐	☐
5. Someone from the institution's academic-support center or a faculty member from another discipline is willing to serve as facilitator.	☐	☐	☐
6. The institution is willing to provide the resources needed for planning and implementation (travel, summer employment, released time).	☐	☐	☐
7. Necessary provisions have been made regarding promotion/tenure/merit pay for those faculty who will be donating extensive time to the project.	☐	☐	☐
8. These commitments are in writing.	☐	☐	☐

faculty member teaching the course has significant control. There will also be some modest but important differences between redesigning an existing course that is already being taught and designing a new one that must be approved not only at the departmental level but at the school/college and institutional level as well.

Designing New Courses

The primary justification for any new course is to fill a gap in the present list of offerings. However, before you begin to design a new course, make certain that your chair and dean are in total support of this initiative. It is also crucial that other faculty who may have an interest or competencies in the area either be involved in your design effort or be given the opportunity to participate. The least you should have is their approval to proceed. Although it may be frustrating at times, making changes is often a political activity. Without the support of other faculty and their agreement that there is a need for the new course, your getting approval will be difficult, no matter how good the course might be. In some instances you may find that faculty members will be offering a course much like yours in another school, college, or program. If there is a possibility of overlap, you will need to explain the differences between what you propose and what exists and communicate how your new course meets presently unmet needs.

Early in the process, you should also obtain all the information on the procedures that must be followed for the approval of new courses on your campus. Know which information you will need to provide to the various department, school, and curriculum committees.

In addition, many programs have "experimental" course numbers that can be assigned to a course while it is in the developmental or field-testing stage. Usually limited in their use to one or two semesters, such numbers allow you the freedom to try new approaches and give you the time to develop a comprehensive description of the course and to include some hard data in the documentation that will be needed by the review committees. The more detail you can provide the greater your chance of approval.

Redesigning Existing Courses

While new course initiatives focus on gaps in the present offerings, the justification for redesigning an existing course may be to address omissions or to improve the effectiveness or efficiency of the present offering. If an existing course is not going well, you know it, other faculty know it, your students certainly know it, as will your chair and dean. Your task is to determine exactly what the problems are. Resource A presents an approach you may want to consider for evaluating a course that you now teach. Focusing on the kinds of questions it includes can help you determine whether major problems exist and what they are, information essential to deciding whether to begin. Exhibits 3.3 and 3.4 are checklists of factors you should consider in making your final decision.

Summary

Before you begin you must clearly identify and understand the need for the course or curriculum effort you are proposing and be confident that all the elements are in place to ensure success. Not doing so will place the project at risk and result in wasted time. It can also have negative professional implications. In addition, the information you collect to show that a need exists will be invaluable to you later in the project as you develop the program itself. These base data can also be used to show the changes that have occurred as a result of your work. All too often this essential information is never collected, and as a result, claims of significant impact are difficult, if not impossible, to make. Finally, the more accurate the information you begin with, the greater chance you will have of developing a highly effective course or curriculum.

Exhibit 3.3. Establishing the Need for Course Design Projects.

	Yes	No	Need More Data
New Course			
• Meets need not met by existing courses.	☐	☐	☐
• Will permit the elimination of courses or will reduce duplication.	☐	☐	☐
• Will introduce a new area of content with a new or expanded set of learning goals.			
Existing Course			
• Is not successful.	☐	☐	☐
• Is outdated; new content must be added.	☐	☐	☐
• Has no clear statement of goals.	☐	☐	☐
• Does not measure student attainment of complex goals.	☐	☐	☐
• Has a high failure/dropout rate.	☐	☐	☐
• Does not prepare students for next course in sequence (if appropriate).	☐	☐	☐
• Depends primarily on lecture when other techniques may be more appropriate.	☐	☐	☐
• Elicits negative student/parent response.	☐	☐	☐
• Uses resources inefficiently.	☐	☐	☐

Exhibit 3.4. Indicators of Potential Success for Course Design Projects.

	Yes	No	Not Sure
1. There is top administrative support for the project (chair and dean).	☐	☐	☐
2. The administrators supporting the project will be in place for the next two years.	☐	☐	☐
3. If the course is to be taught by more than one faculty member, everyone involved is willing to participate in the project.	☐	☐	☐
4. Faculty working on the project will be given enough time (released time, summer employment).	☐	☐	☐
5. If extensive time will be required, adjustments will be made in the promotion and tenure criteria/timeline as appropriate, and agreement is in writing.	☐	☐	☐
6. Participants in the project are willing to follow the model selected.	☐	☐	☐
7. Someone from the institution's academic-support center or a faculty member from another discipline is willing to serve as facilitator.	☐	☐	☐
8. Administrators are willing to allow sufficient time for design, field-testing, and revision of the course that is developed.	☐	☐	☐
9. No major curriculum revisions are under way or planned that would affect the goals and content of the course.	☐	☐	☐
10. The course will be required, or the pool of students is sufficient.	☐	☐	☐
11. If resources are needed, they will be provided.	☐	☐	☐
12. Space for offering the course will be available.	☐	☐	☐

CHAPTER 4

Getting Started

This chapter focuses on getting your project under way and puts particular emphasis on the crucial first meeting of everyone involved. If your project is to redesign a course that you will be teaching, the meeting will be between you and the process person. If your project is a curricular one, the meeting might include several faculty besides yourself and your facilitator and also other individuals who may be essential to the success of the project.

Although a number of conversations must take place prior to the start of your work, the first formal meeting of those who will actively participate in the project is extremely important. At this meeting the overall goals of the project are discussed, and the basic instructional philosophy is articulated. The development procedures are described, the roles of all the participants are defined, and the fundamental groundwork for the project is laid. Basic institutional procedures and guidelines are also reviewed.

Who Should Be Involved

The initial design meeting should include the facilitator (serving as chair) and all the faculty who will be working directly on the project. A team of faculty, when possible, is always preferred because it provides a strong academic base. If a particular course is the focus of your project, make an effort to include all faculty who teach it. In curriculum projects the team should consist of carefully selected

43

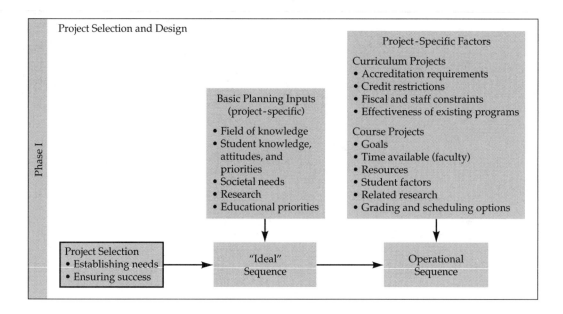

representatives from each of the major academic programs or departments involved.

For a curriculum project one faculty member should be identified as the key content expert and coordinator. This academic team leader should have the ability and the content expertise needed to coordinate the efforts of other faculty members. The team leader may be a department chair or a dean who wishes to be actively involved in the design process. In addition to directing activities that take place within the academic departments, the team leader acts as chair when the facilitator is not available.

If the group is large (over eight or so), appointing a small steering committee will increase efficiency. Everyone on the steering committee is expected to participate actively in the development process, and other members will not have such an active role. In some instances administrators (deans or department chairpersons) will wish to become members of the steering committee, and they should be encouraged to do so. This committee is absolutely essential for the success of large projects, and therefore the selection of its members should be given careful thought.

Graduate Students

Although graduate students may be members of a development team in order to provide support and the students' perspective, they should not play a major role. Delegating content decisions to graduate students is likely to elicit a negative response when the final design is presented to faculty for adoption. As noted earlier, influential, respected faculty must be involved whenever possible and must have ownership in the project from the beginning. In designing for the ideal you need the academic backgrounds and experience of such faculty.

Evaluation Specialist

Because data about the students and, when appropriate, the professional field are often presented at this initial meeting, including a person who can handle the collection and interpretation of this information is useful. Having an evaluation specialist (if one is available) attend this meeting provides an additional range of expertise and gives this evaluator a better understanding of your project as it gets under way. It also allows all who will work together later in the project to get to know one another.

Preproject Meetings

Before the first formal design meeting of the whole team, meetings must be held with key faculty and administrators. These meetings help you to establish priorities, determine the scope of your project, and identify others who should be involved, the resources available, and the procedures that will be followed. These preproject meetings can also help to develop the commitment that will be required from the department and other faculty. In some instances you may find that there is little support for what you have in mind, and as a result, you may decide not to begin. Also at this time any unresolved tenure and promotion considerations should be addressed, and participants should be told whether summer employment or released time will be made available.

Goals of First Formal Meeting

To be successful, the initial formal design meeting must achieve several important objectives:

- The goals and scope of the project and the anticipated time line should be reviewed and agreed on. Those participating must be comfortable with the plans for the process and project.
- There should be a clear understanding of what everyone will be responsible for.
- The role of the facilitator should be clearly defined. The facilitator is a process person who will help the participating faculty

by asking questions, playing devil's advocate, and offering suggestions.

- A commitment must be made to getting the development process under way so that everyone feels that progress has been made.
- An operational instructional philosophy for the course or program should be established.

It is also sometimes possible in the first meeting to begin to discuss what an ideal program might look like. At the end of this initial meeting the facilitator should review what has been accomplished and then send the summary to participants for comments and reaction. In addition, other basics should be covered such as meeting times and upcoming deadlines.

Developing an Instructional Philosophy

Throughout this book I will be describing what it means for a course or a curriculum to be learning- or student-centered. This shift from focusing on what we will cover to what our students will learn directly affects our role as faculty and the role of our students. It will determine the structure and nature of instruction, how goals are articulated, how students are assessed, and where and how learning takes place.

Lee Allen (1996), building on the work of Robert Barr and John Tagg, includes the following in a list of features that promote student-centered learning:

1. Students learn how to find knowledge, they do not wait for faculty to provide it.
2. Ongoing student and course assessments show faculty where teaching is effective and ineffective.
3. Students' performance on activities and assignments is assessed by more people than a single instructor.
4. Students construct the questions they need to ask, rather than expecting their teachers to choose the facts students ought to know.
5. Students become active and participatory learners; they are not just audiences for teacher lectures.
6. Students have opportunities to learn through teamwork and to be rewarded for group efforts, not just for their own actitivies.
7. Academic effort is measured by how much students learn, not how many hours faculty teach.

8. Faculty guide students, helping them formulate fruitful problems and questions and uncover effective ways to learn answers.

As Allen reports, those involved need to develop an understanding of assessment, learning styles, motivation, and various instructional methods and technologies—an understanding not often required in the past, when the focus was primarily on content and presentation.

Before you begin, everyone involved needs to agree about the instructional philosophy that will underlie the course or the curriculum. If indeed it is to be student- and learning-centered, every major decision made in the design process will need to be framed in that context.

Case Study: Getting the Right People Involved in Designing an Orientation Program for Teaching Assistants

In the summer of 1986, Syracuse University's vice president for undergraduate studies, Ronald Cavanagh, and the vice president for research and graduate affairs, Karen Hiiemae, decided to explore the possibility of implementing a required orientation program for all new teaching assistants. The first step was establishing a steering committee and appointing to this committee those individuals who would be essential for designing, implementing, and supporting any program that might be proposed. Because this project would involve faculty, administrators, and graduate students, the committee that was established had the following members (in addition to the two vice presidents, who served as co-chairs):

- The director of the graduate school.
- Two faculty representatives who were responsible for the training and supervision of teaching assistants in their departments. (Faculty from English and mathematics, the departments with the largest number of teaching assistants, were selected. These departments had already developed support programs for their teaching assistants, and it was imperative that this initiative not be perceived as a threat to the programs already in place.)
- Two graduate students, including the president of the Graduate Student Organization.
- A faculty representative from the graduate council, a universitywide body that supervised graduate education.
- The director of the Center for Instructional Development, who was to be responsible for the overall design of the program.

Once a decision was made to implement the proposed program, the steering committee was expanded to include a representative from the unit that provided support to international students and also the two individuals who would manage the program. Several additional support staff attended all meetings.

The planning that went into the selection of this key group was not wasted. Every committee member played an essential role in the successful design and implementation of the program. Two of the faculty members assumed responsibility for important elements of the program. In this project the graduate students played major roles in both the design and the implementation of training and social activities, and the graduate school developed administrative procedures that were essential for a smooth-running program. By selecting these key individuals to play an active role in the design of the program, ownership was ensured, the quality of the final program was enhanced, and a number of potential "turf" problems were eliminated.

Summary

Care must be taken in identifying individuals to be involved from the beginning of your project and, for curricular and other projects involving several courses, in establishing the committees and task forces that will carry out the project once a decision to move ahead is made. The following participants should be included (as appropriate):

- Faculty: for course projects—those with major teaching/administrative responsibilities (maximum, four to six); for curriculum projects—representatives of all major academic areas
- Administrator(s): dean or department chair (optional)
- Facilitator (chairs meetings, essential)
- Evaluator (optional)
- Graduate assistants (staff role only)

The initial design meeting should help all involved understand what they are being asked to do and how much time will most likely be required. The following topics should be covered:

- Need for and general goals of project (review)
- Instructional philosophy (for example, will the course or program be student- and learning-centered) and its implications
- Review of design model
- Roles of participants (including time commitment)
- Available resources (including stipends for faculty)
- Anticipated time lines
- Significant institutional policies and procedures
- Schedule for future meetings
- Initial work on design of program

CHAPTER 5

Linking Goals, Courses, and Curricula

As we teach our courses, we tend to lose sight of the fact that each course is but one element in a learning sequence defined as a curriculum. The closer the relationships are among courses, curriculum, and planned out-of-class activities, the more effective the learning experience will be for our students. So, whether you are working on the design of a single course or of a curriculum, it is imperative that you keep in mind the relationship between the two. A quality education does not happen by chance; it requires careful planning, skilled teaching, and an overall structure that ensures that every student has the opportunity to reach the goals of the program in which he or she is enrolled. A quality education requires a level of orchestration seldom found at colleges and universities and also the active involvement of a faculty that is paying a great deal of attention to structure, content, and process. It requires hard work.

Goals of a Curriculum

In general the goals of a curriculum evolve from the total of the instructional outcomes associated with three elements, which all students should reach by graduation (see Figure 5.1):

- All students should have basic competencies no matter what program they are enrolled in.

Figure 5.1. The Underpinnings of a Curriculum.

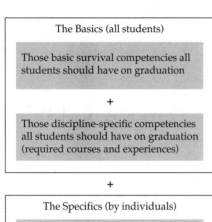

The Basics (all students)

Those basic survival competencies all students should have on graduation

+

Those discipline-specific competencies all students should have on graduation (required courses and experiences)

The goal: To ensure that each student on graduation will reach the identified level of proficiency in all areas

+

The Specifics (by individuals)

Course-specific instructional goals
  • Required
  • Elective

The challenge: How to ensure that the elements of the curriculum (courses and other student experiences) combine to make these goals attainable

- Students should have discipline-specific competencies related to the core requirements (usually the humanities, social sciences, and natural sciences).

- Students should also have discipline-specific competencies associated with major and minor concentrations and elective courses.

To ensure that every student reaches the required level of proficiency in each area that has been identified, several major tasks must be accomplished:

- The basic competencies for all students must be developed and approved by the institution. These competencies must be stated in terms that are measurable and demonstrable.

- A comprehensive plan must be developed to ensure that the basic competencies are learned and reinforced throughout the time a student is enrolled in the institution.

- Each disciplinary area responsible for a portion of the core curriculum must describe learning outcomes for the relevant courses that are congruent with the required competencies. For these courses a common set of assessment techniques and instruments must also be developed.

- Appropriate learning outcomes and assessment techniques and instruments must be developed for each required course in the major and for all electives.

Developing a Cohesive Curriculum _____

A curriculum must be developed sequentially, beginning with an institutional statement of goals and ending with the assessment of each student prior to graduation and after. As you move through the design process from defining general goals to developing course goals and then unit-by-unit objectives, statements of the goals become increasingly specific. The design of each course, the selection of instructional methods, and student assessment will be based on these statements.

In the process of moving from a statement of goals to deciding on and implementing a program, relating individual courses to the curriculum requires careful planning. If, for example, speaking skills are identified as a basic competency that every student must have by graduation, public speaking must be initially taught and then reinforced; and no student should be able to graduate without receiving appropriate instruction and practice in this skill. Courses must be analyzed to identify where this skill is or can be taught, and the curriculum must be structured so that every student has the opportunity to acquire speaking skills. In this case the relevant courses will most likely be smaller ones or the small discussion sessions within courses with large enrollments.

A curriculum committee might use a basic competency checklist (like Exhibit 5.1) to facilitate this task. The checklist assigns specific competencies to individual courses or other formal learning experiences and describes the level at which the competency will be taught, indicating in which courses the competency will be introduced, used, further developed, and assessed. Many competencies can be taught within regular, discipline-based courses. Those developing or designing a course must determine which of the basic competencies can be taught within it. As will be shown in Chapter Nine, developing these competencies can improve most courses; teaching students how to use computers, interpersonal skills (teamwork), problem solving, critical thinking, and basic statistics are widely listed competencies related to basic core objectives.

There is far more agreement about basic competencies than one might at first expect. When faculty are asked, "What basic competencies or skills should every college student have upon graduation?" I have found that responses are remarkably consistent. Typically included are communication skills (writing, speaking, reading, and listening), mathematics (including basic statistics), problem solving, critical thinking, interpersonal skills (both working in and leading groups), computer literacy, and interviewing skills. More recently the list has included understanding and respecting diverse cultures, resource utilization (the ability to find and use both human

Exhibit 5.1. The Underpinnings of a Curriculum.

Key
A: Introduced
B: Used
C: Further developed
D: Comprehensive assessment

Course Number

Competency (institution-specific)										
Communication										
Writing										
Speaking										
Listening										
Basic math										
Computer literacy										
Conflict resolution										
Critical thinking										
Ethics										
Interpersonal skills										
Interviewing skills										
Basic statistics										
Learning skills										
Problem solving										
Effective reading										
Resource utilization										
Respect for diverse cultures										
Scientific methods										

and material resources), self-understanding, "ethics," time management, conflict resolution, willingness to take risks, and the ability to adapt to innovation and change. Adding discipline-specific skills for the core and the major completes a set of learning outcomes for each graduate. Exhibit 5.2 lists those competencies that employers surveyed by the Conference Board of Canada (1992) regarded as essential. Although the list represents a business perspective, it can help you develop your own list of outcomes. (Brochure 1992 E/F, Ottawa: The Conference Board of Canada, 1992).

Although certain instructional goals are long-range and focused on performance well after graduation, it is possible within an undergraduate program to identify the skills, attitudes, and understandings that are the underpinnings of these long-range goals. However, it is a major mistake to take any published list of basic skills or competencies and accept it for use on another campus without revision. Not only will the specific items on such a list vary from institution to institution but the definition of each item will vary as well. The final list of competencies, their definitions, and how they should be assessed must evolve on each campus. Faculty ownership in the process is an essential element for success.

Examples of Curriculum Goal Setting

Resource B contains case studies showing how three institutions have decided on basic competencies and developed curricula. These institutions were selected for several reasons. First, they represent different types of institutions; second, the approaches taken vary considerably; and third, although each institution developed sets of basic competencies, the ways in which they structured and articulated their curricula are distinctly different.

Alverno College, a small Catholic liberal arts college, not only has developed extremely clear statements of learning outcomes but also has implemented assessment by portfolio, an approach that has been recognized nationally for its scope and sensitivity. Southeast Missouri State University was one of the first institutions in the country to develop a campuswide coherent core program focusing on a set of specific learning outcomes. Included in the case study is a description of its course-approval process, which ensures that courses approved for the core meet certain clearly articulated goals. The final case study, of Monmouth University, describes the articulation of learning goals for specific courses that are part of the general education requirement.

The remainder of this chapter presents a case study in the formulation of learning outcomes for a curriculum development project at Indiana University.

Exhibit 5.2. Employability Skills Profile: The Critical Skills Required of the Canadian Workforce.

Academic Skills

Those skills which provide the basic foundation to get, keep and progress on a job and to achieve the best results

Canadian employers need a person who can:

Communicate

- Understand and speak the languages in which business is conducted
- Listen to understand and learn
- Read, comprehend and use written materials, including graphs, charts and displays
- Write effectively in the languages in which business is conducted

Think

- Think critically and act logically to evaluate situations, solve problems and make decisions
- Understand and solve problems involving mathematics and use the results
- Use technology, instruments, tools and information systems effectively
- Access and apply specialized knowledge from various fields (e.g., skilled trades, technology, physical sciences, arts and social sciences)

Learn

- Continue to learn for life

Personal Management Skills

The combination of skills, attitudes and behaviours required to get, keep and progress on a job and to achieve the best results

Canadian employers need a person who can demonstrate:

Positive Attitudes and Behaviours

- Self-esteem and confidence
- Honesty, integrity and personal ethics
- A positive attitude toward learning, growth and personal health
- Initiative, energy and persistence to get the job done

Responsibility

- The ability to set goals and priorities in work and personal life
- The ability to plan and manage time, money and other resources to achieve goals
- Accountability for actions taken

Adaptability

- A positive attitude toward change
- Recognition of and respect for people's diversity and individual differences
- The ability to identify and suggest new ideas to get the job done—creativity

Teamwork Skills

Those skills needed to work with others on a job and to achieve the best results

Canadian employers need a person who can:

Work with Others

- Understand and contribute to the organization's goals
- Understand and work within the culture of the group
- Plan and make decisions with others and support the outcomes
- Respect the thoughts and opinions of others in the group
- Exercise "give and take" to achieve group results
- Seek a team approach as appropriate
- Lead when appropriate, mobilizing the group for high performance

This document was developed by the Corporate Council on Education, a program of the National Business and Education Centre, The Conference Board of Canada. This profile outlines foundation skills for employability. For individuals and for schools, preparing for work or employability is one of several goals, all of which are important for society.

Source: Employability Skills Profile: What Are Employers Looking For? Brochure 1992 E/F (Ottawa: The Conference Board of Canada, 1992).

Case Study: Developing a Statement of Learning Outcomes

The Bloomington campus of Indiana University, with its enrollment of over thirty-three thousand, is the flagship campus of the state system. At the time of the project described here, beginning with an emphasis on the goals and curriculum was a unique approach to curriculum or course revision. Those working on the project then moved on to learning outcomes and finally to course and curriculum development, including consideration of appropriate pedagogy. (This approach has since been adopted by other institutions, such as Monmouth University, as reported in Resource B.)

The Bloomington plan also had two features that were unique among major research universities and that were essential to its success. First, the institution's administration charged academic units with fiscal and academic planning and decision making, and second, the plan focused on general education. A major element of this initiative was the considerable time and resources devoted to developing a comprehensive performance measure of student learning.

Recognizing that until one has a clear statement of goals, assessment of success is impossible, the leaders of the initiative (faculty and administrators) developed learning objectives at both the undergraduate and graduate levels and then developed a set of principles to answer faculty questions about the goals, range, and consequences of student assessment. These seven Assessment Principles established that improvement in instruction and curriculum and improvement in student academic performance are the goals of assessment and that these goals should be formulated and assessed at the program level:

- Assessment will be conducted to *improve* the quality of academic programs and enhance student learning. Because assessment makes explicit processes and outcomes that are often implicit, it will also help us to provide more effective accounting of our value to public constituencies.
- The University will employ assessment in ways that most efficiently and effectively serve its central instructional mission.
- Assessment will focus on student attainment of academic standards. Although intellectual growth is an important indicator of a productive educational experience, we seek student outcomes that demonstrate proficiency in the abilities associated with general education, the major, and graduate studies. [Given the range of abilities and backgrounds students bring to IU Bloomington, this competency-based approach is more stringent than an approach simply showing positive change over time.]
- Each school will define for its academic units the goals of assessment, the general parameters for implementation, and oversee the quality of assessment efforts. All schools agree that: (1) faculty will participate in all phases of the assessment process; (2) student learning will be assessed using multiple measures; (3) assessment data will be used to enhance instruction and curriculum.
- Assessment results are primarily for IUB use, particularly in the development and enhancement of the teaching-learning environment. Data from assessment are an appropriate part of

program review and, as such, are to be given careful consideration by administrators and faculty. *The academic deans will act as stewards* for the assessment data generated by their units, providing access to data when it will contribute to the more general instructional enterprise.

- Assessment will be concerned with student learning in the broadest sense and include evaluation of student opportunities in research and creative activity, internships, and other extra curricular activities that are critical building blocks of the educational experience at a large research university.
- Productive engagement in assessment and effective use of assessment feedback will be recognized in annual budgetary reviews of departments.

This focus on improvement of instruction and student academic performance as the goal of assessment at Indiana University made student learning and retention at the program level the primary unit of analysis. Consequently, the initiative involved the entire academic community and moved the faculty into addressing the major issues of instructional goals, curriculum and course design, and teaching effectiveness.

The plan contained two levels of instructional goals: the general education outcomes for all students and the major-specific performance goals that were developed by the faculty in each discipline. The general education statement of goals for undergraduates was as follows:

Upon completion of their *undergraduate* degree, . . . students should be able to:

1. Read and listen effectively;
2. Write clearly and persuasively;
3. Think critically—be able to summarize information accurately, reduce information into meaningful components for analysis, perceive and create logical coherence and discernible themes and patterns across different bodies of information;
4. Gain intellectual flexibility and breadth of mind, be open to new ideas and information;
5. Formulate and understand their own values, become aware of others' values and discern the ethical dimensions underlying many of the decisions they must make;
6. Understand scientific methods that guide the formation, testing and validation of theories, and distinguish conclusions that rest on unverified assertion from those developed through the application of scientific reasoning;
7. Reason quantitatively, using mathematical and statistical methods in analysis and solution of problems;
8. Understand and be sensitive to the range of physical, geographic, economic, political, religious, and cultural realities pervading our society and world events.

All units of the university providing undergraduate education seek to achieve these learning outcomes, which encompass the cognitive skills that should be acquired in a general education. The leaders of this initiative concluded that because these objectives were developed from existing school statements, they had the substantial advantage of relating "new" assessment initiatives to academic skills and values that were widely recognized and endorsed by faculty, and therefore they gained ready approval from the faculty and administration.

As part of the assessment initiative, each undergraduate academic major added to this statement the learning outcomes for its own program. The statement for the business major included the following:

Students graduating in Business should:

1. Have a general knowledge and appreciation of human accomplishments in the physical sciences, arts, humanities, and social sciences;
2. Possess a broad-based knowledge of business and the business firm and the role each business plays in our society;
3. Understand the national, international, political, social, and economic environment that affects a firm's operation;
4. Be able to articulate thoughts orally and in writing and be computer literate;
5. Have a sensitivity to and appreciation of ethical issues;
6. Possess an appreciation of the opportunity and problems of managing complex organizations;
7. Have the skills and capability to work effectively with others in completion of joint tasks;
8. Possess the ability to find and formulate problems, think analytically and recommend solutions to problems.

Similar statements were developed at the master's and doctoral levels. For each of the objectives, student and unit assessment measures were developed based on these statements. (For additional information, write to Deborah Olsen, Office of Academic Affairs, Indiana University, Bloomington, IN 47405.)

Summary

In every institution the final determinant of the quality of the academic program is the performance of its graduates. The degree of success will depend on how well the curriculum is delivered through its courses and the other learning experiences provided to students. Every student must have the opportunity to reach and demonstrate every stated basic competency. Carefully articulated learning outcomes must be the basis on which instructional methods are chosen and the criteria by which competency is measured. The effectiveness of an institution or program and of individual faculty members is then determined by the ability of students to meet these goals. At the same time it must be recognized that all students will not reach these goals because their attitudes, willingness to work, and ability also play an important role in determining success. Our responsibility is to do all we can to facilitate the learning that is required.

In the past we have generally not tracked the total experience of our students, assessed their growth, and evaluated the success of individual academic programs. We have rarely been willing to describe our instructional goals or to determine our effectiveness in helping our students attain them. For some faculty members any approach that requires defining and measuring learning outcomes or structuring a curriculum is perceived as infringing on their rights. With active involvement on their part in the statement of goals and in course and curriculum design, these concerns can be overcome.

We really no longer have an option. Unless we relate our curriculum, our courses, and our teaching to clearly articulated goals, we will not have the effective educational system that parents, students, and our communities demand and that we ourselves desire. Fortunately, since the mid-1980s much has been done to assist us in this task. New instructional approaches have been identified that can help us develop the more advanced competencies that appear on most lists of intended outcomes, and the field of assessment can provide us with the tools and techniques necessary to evaluate how successful our students are. Both these areas will be described in detail in later chapters.

CHAPTER 6

Gathering and Analyzing Essential Data

This chapter presents a review of those questions that should be asked and the data that should be collected as work on the design of a course or curriculum begins.

Once the decision has been made to begin a specific project, basic data must be collected in five areas: the characteristics of the students—their backgrounds, abilities, and priorities; the desires and needs of society; the educational priorities of the institution, school, or department; the requirements of the appropriate field of knowledge including the academic requirements of accrediting agencies; and the results of related research. Surveys and achievement tests, as well as informal discussion sessions held to identify specific needs and outcomes, may be used at this point to gather information. The data collected in these five areas are extremely important because they help you to define the required and optional elements of your program, to determine whether remedial units or exemptions are appropriate, and to form the basis for selecting the basic content of instruction.

This information is also essential in developing the primary goals and learning outcomes for your course or curriculum. As you move through design, implementation, and evaluation, each of these goals will be fleshed out in detail (see Figure 6.1).

Student Inputs

An important source of data that is often overlooked is the student. If you are going to be successful, it is imperative that you have good information about your students.

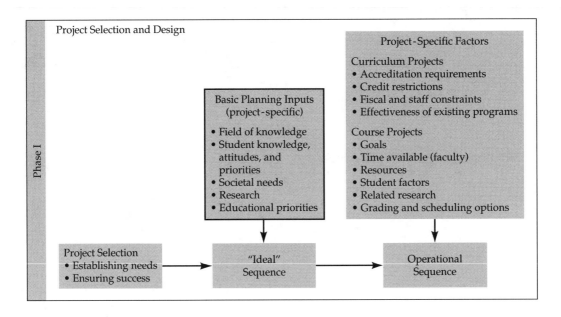

Entry-Level Knowledge of Subject

Surprising as it may seem, few faculty members are aware of what their entering students already know about the subject, and as a consequence they cannot be sure that the assumptions they make about their students are accurate. We more commonly overestimate skills, prior knowledge, and competencies than underestimate them. For example, studies by Pervin and Rubin (1967) and Dresser (1987) have suggested that insensitivity to students' backgrounds, interests, and needs is a primary reason many students feel dissatisfied with or leave their institutions. We tend to assume that our students have the prerequisites that our courses require. This gap between what we expect and what exists has proven especially critical in the areas of reading, writing, basic mathematics, and specialized science vocabularies. Some students fail science because they cannot handle simple mathematical problems. Others have difficulty in history and the social sciences because their vocabularies are not as advanced as the text presumes, and their writing, listening, and problem-solving skills are not up to the level anticipated by the instructor. The vocabulary level of many textbooks is, unfortunately, often inappropriate for many students. And in fact, the standard texts used in many introductory courses have become more difficult and complex with each new edition (Burstyn and Santa, 1977).

In studies undertaken at Syracuse University, for example, we have found that some students who can pass calculus tests have problems at the eighth-grade level with multiplication and division of fractions, decimals and percents, tables and charts, or word problems. An in-depth analysis of eight large-enrollment introductory

Figure 6.1. From Goals to Outcomes to Assessment.

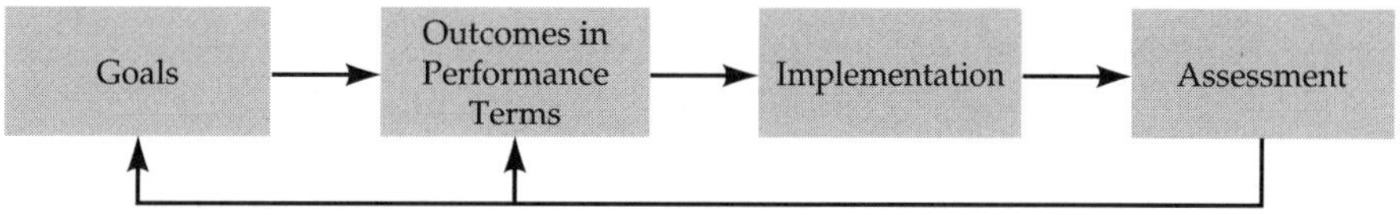

courses in the natural and social sciences revealed that all faculty members required and assumed competencies in performing operations with fractions, decimals, percents, ratios, and proportions (see Resource C). In addition, the textbooks in seven of the eight assumed that the students had a working knowledge of probability, basic statistics, graphs, and tables. A follow-up study in five of these courses showed a direct correlation between student success in the course and competency in the basic mathematics skills that were assumed in the texts (Hardin, 1992).

In other instances some of your students will know far more about a subject than you anticipate. Work experiences, familiarity and comfort with technology, taking college courses in high school, hobbies, and special interests all combine to make this a fairly common occurrence in almost every introductory course and in a growing number of advanced ones.

It is not unusual to find college-level courses taught in high school or high school materials taught in junior high school. One Syracuse University survey found that approximately 20 percent of the students in an introductory psychology course had had formal instruction in the subject while in high school. An additional 2 percent had been able to take college psychology courses at a nearby institution while still in the eleventh or twelfth grade.

The immediate problem created by such variance in the entering levels of students can be significant: we may underestimate the competencies of some students, while overestimating the abilities of others. Older students who have been away from the classroom for some time or students with specific learning disabilities add further dimensions to the mix.

The student who brings to your course advanced knowledge of the subject or relevant work experience can be an invaluable asset to your class when you use these competencies in small-group activities or when you have these students assist less qualified students.

Data describing students' academic levels are also useful for estimating the number of students who will need remedial and review assignments and the number who enter a program with some of the objectives already met and thus warrant exemptions or options or both, perhaps for additional credit.

Attitudes

The attitudes that students have toward a particular course or field of study can influence what they learn. If they are initially hostile to a subject, learning will suffer unless attitudes can be changed. As a result, it is vital that we take student attitudes into account when we design a course or modify a program by incorporating new materials or adding new options. Students who enroll in science courses for nonscience majors, for example, may dislike the science even before they begin the course. If this attitude is taken into account when the course is designed and steps are taken to change attitudes, a positive view of science can be developed in many students. Our enthusiasm for the subject can also lead students to develop positive attitudes toward it.

Unfortunately, in some instances, entering students may see little value in the knowledge and skills taught in a course. To produce the attitude necessary to improve student performance, we can relate the content of our course to their interests or take the time to explain why the course is important to them or provide them with work experiences that can show them the importance of specific competencies in a direct way.

A study at one institution, which shall remain anonymous for obvious reasons, showed that before its redesign, one physics course had been having a definite effect on the attitudes of the students. Students usually entered the course with a somewhat neutral attitude toward the discipline, but by the time they completed the course, their attitude had become completely hostile! In this instance the faculty had assumed the students were highly motivated science majors, but in fact they were liberal arts students who wanted a science course that met Mondays, Wednesdays, and Fridays at 10 A.M., and this was the only one available when they registered.

Priorities and Expectations

What do the students expect from your course, and what are their priorities as they relate to the area of study? If the students' expectations and priorities do not agree with initial content, new units added early in the program can modify their expectations, or new content can be built into the program that meets or modifies their priorities and expectations. Data on student expectations can often be enlightening to a teacher. For example, a Syracuse University survey in an American history course showed that the students were far more interested in the American Revolution and in the American Indian than had been anticipated. Assignments in these areas were easily expanded without changing the overall goals of the course.

The survey identified excellent topics for optional assignments and required papers.

Long-Range Goals

An analysis of the long-range goals of your students and their major fields of interest helps to identify special seminars, options, and projects that might be included in a course. Such an analysis also can help you to relate the course content to areas and topics that particularly interest students. The interrelationship of separate disciplines can have a direct and positive effect on the attitudes of students toward a course that might otherwise be perceived as unrelated and uninteresting.

A general mathematics course, for example, can have seminars or special projects relating to history (the role of mathematics in history), modern music (new mathematics-based notation techniques), and business (use of statistics). The opera portion of a general music course with a large enrollment of history and political science majors could include a discussion of the role of opera in history and politics, and the more general areas of art, history, music, religion, and literature can often be interrelated. For example, what determines the form and content of the music, art, or literature of a given period? This question cannot be answered without studying the politics, religion, and history of the period and the place.

Older Students

As previously noted, the increasing numbers of older students in our classrooms bring with them a wide variety of experiences, which often are an invaluable asset. At the same time these students present a number of challenges. Often having distinctly different goals from those of the more traditional students, they may also have been away from the classroom for some time. Rusty in some of the basic skills we may expect our students to have (using the library, understanding the format of a research paper, being computer literate), they may need time to adjust and additional assistance, particularly when they first return to the classroom. One element of a survey filled out by students on the first day of class can be questions about whether they are returning students and, if so, what experiences they have had since leaving school.

Gathering the Information

Surveys that you design for the purpose, studies conducted by other faculty or professional or disciplinary groups, publications in the field, and interviews that you conduct on your own can all help you to collect important information about students as you explore the design of your course or program.

Case Study: Introductory Course in Religion

In this project a survey instrument was prepared and distributed to a sample of students enrolled in an introductory religion course the semester before classes were scheduled to begin (see Exhibit 6.1). The instrument was intended to identify levels of interest in various topics that could be included in the course. The instrument was developed jointly by evaluation specialists and faculty from the Department of Religion.

When responses had been collected and tabulated, the students' interests were viewed in the context of the faculty's expectations. The data generated by this instrument (see Exhibit 6.2) were quite different from faculty's expectations and resulted in significant changes in the intended course design. In addition, the faculty could anticipate fairly accurately the number of students who would later choose different options within the course.

The value of this instrument to the project is best described by the faculty member who served as the course coordinator for the department:

> The test instrument employed in the development of experimental Religion 105 was designed to indicate what patterns, if any, of student interest, disinterest, expectation, recognition, or dislike would be likely to characterize a typical population involved in this course. The results of the application of this instrument at first appeared so ambiguous as to be useless. Under continuing consideration, however, they proved most helpful.
>
> Although initial analysis showed no clear pattern of interest for any particular subject matter, or issue, or method in the study of religion, it did reveal a wide variety of levels of recognition as well as diverse preferences for formats of presentation. What we came to see was that the concern for diversity, for flexibility, for variety of instructional formats was specifically the pattern that was common to the sample population. The test instrument clearly suggested modular construction and a flexible selection procedure. It also became apparent that a common base of meaning and of definitions had to be developed before the course could be effectively taught.

Case Study: Introductory Microeconomics Course

Data collected from students at the end of an existing microeconomics course helped to shape the objectives of the revised course and the materials that were developed for it. Data were collected regarding students' prior knowledge of the subject, attitudes toward course content and pacing, and the role of the course in their overall programs. The students were given an opportunity to respond to open-ended questions regarding the textbook, materials, and lectures and the extent to which these items complemented one another.

Exhibit 6.1. Survey of Student Interest in Various Topics in Religion.

The following list contains topics that could be included in this course. Rate each topic according to your level of interest in it. Use the following scale.

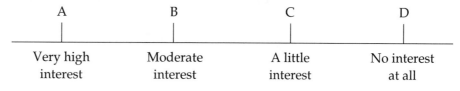

A	B	C	D
Very high interest	Moderate interest	A little interest	No interest at all

1. Women's lib and mythologies of creation
2. Ecology and creation stories
3. Psychotherapy and mystical experience
4. The problem of a good God and the existence of evil in the world
5. Science and religion
6. Abortion and the church
7. Pacifism and the holy wars of Judaism, Christianity, and Islam
8. Sex and an absolutist ethic
9. Number symbolism in the problem of the Trinity
10. Technology as a new religion
11. Apocalypticism and progress
12. Modern mythologies of the creative hero
13. The death of God in ancient religions
14. The religious history of the future
15. Should churches be taxed?
16. The artist as the religious hero of our time
17. God as relative rather than absolute
18. Is Zen possible in the West?
19. Yoga and drugs
20. Traditional religions and the occult
21. The religion of the American Indian and paleface Christianity
22. The end of religion
23. Polytheism in our time
24. Modern pantheons
25. Dreams and religion
26. The poetry of the Bible
27. Ballad and rock music as scripture
28. Job and psychology
29. "Jesus freaks"—then and now
30. Witchcraft
31. Capitalism in church and synagogue
32. Communes and religion
33. The birth and death of religious institutions
34. Are there other topics in religion of interest to you that are not listed here? Please list them on the back of your answer sheet.

Exhibit 6.2. Ratings for Levels of Interest in Possible Religion Course Topics.

High Interest
Percentage of students who judged their interest in the topic to be "moderate" or "very high"

Psychotherapy and mystical experience	63%
Abortion and the church	58%
Sex and an absolutist ethic	60%
Is Zen possible in the West?	57%
Yoga and drugs	53%
Traditional religions and the occult	56%
The end of religion	65%
Dreams and religion	60%
Witchcraft	70%

Low Interest
Percentage of students who judged their interest in the topic to be "little" or "no interest at all"

Number symbolism in the problem of the Trinity	62%
Apocalypticism and progress	71%
Should churches be taxed?	62%
Modern pantheons	82%
The poetry of the Bible	61%
Capitalism in church and synagogue	57%

The faculty member who taught the course recalled:

Several student concerns were clearly expressed in the data we collected for our survey. Two in particular were to have a major impact on my thinking as I worked through the redesign of the course: first, the lack of coordination the students found between the textbook and the lectures, and second, the lack of competency among some of the teaching assistants with respect to course content. The student manuals we developed were, in fact, specifically designed to resolve these problems. By setting forth objectives for each unit of the course, the manual establishes a common foundation of course content across all sections of the course. The inclusion of questions on the textbook readings that highlight the issues specified by these objectives provides my students with a clear correlation between the text and the lectures.

Societal Needs

The second major area of data collection is outside the institution: alumni, employers, recruiters, and published reports and research. Although most data of this type are related to and collected for specific programs, the information can be more generalized and have a direct bearing on several programs. An example is an effort to identify the knowledge, skills, and understanding that all students should have prior to graduation.

Quite often the perceptions of those on and off campus will be very different. The weight given to each basic competency and the perception of the effectiveness of higher education in helping students to reach these goals can vary considerably. Business and community leaders tend to be more pragmatic and focused than those within the academy (see Exhibit 6.3). Although the various populations within an external community will tend to agree, when there is disagreement, you, as the faculty responsible for developing the program, will have to make the final decision.

In addition to the material you can collect yourself from external communities, a host of other useful resources address the issues of goals and student outcomes. For example, in his book *Liberal Education and the Corporation*, Michael Useem (1989) provides an extremely useful framework for faculty in both business schools and the liberal arts as he focuses on those common competencies that each group of students will be required to have after graduation.

Although some of the data collected from community sources are general, some can be quite discipline-specific. For example, in a project that redesigned a music-education program at Syracuse University, most of the graduates said that at some time in their careers they were required to design an auditorium or a classroom for teaching and playing music—a task for which they felt they were totally unprepared. As a result, a unit on facilities design and equipment selection was added to the curriculum. In another survey major retailers identified specific math skills as a major problem and indicated a demand for computer skills in the field. These data had a direct effect on the retailing curriculum that was developed.

Such career-specific information will be essential as you develop the goals of your course or curriculum in order to keep the program focused on the needs of the community you serve. For example, although not quite as dramatic as the findings in Exhibit 6.3, differences in internal and external perceptions of a program appeared in a study reported in *Future Trends in Broadcast Journalism* (1984). In the study, conducted by the Radio-Television News Directors Association, radio and television news directors and faculty in related professional programs were asked to identify the skills that on-air people needed and then to evaluate recent graduates on the skills that were considered important.

For on-air people in television, four qualities were identified by 112 news directors as being particularly important: writing skills, the

Exhibit 6.3. Desirable Student Outcomes: Different Roles, Different Perspectives.

	Business/Government Leaders	Academic Leaders
1. Higher-order; applied problem-solving abilities	Possess and use these skills in complex real-world settings; creativity and resourcefulness.	Emphasis on technical skills or knowledge in discipline.
2. Enthusiasm for continuous learning	Flexibility and adaptability to change on the job and in one's life. Abilities to access new information and learn how to do new things.	Few agreed that preparing for continuous learning is an outcome that college can and should provide.
3. Interpersonal skills, communication, and collaboration	Oral communication a premium, needed for teamwork and communication with nonspecialists. Listening.	Valued but assume that these outcomes result from presumed "collegial" environment.
4. Strong sense of responsibility for personal and community action.	Personal integrity, and ethical and civil behavior, honesty.	Although shared as values, not often articulated as necessary college outcomes.
5. Ability to bridge cultural and linguistic barriers.	An awareness of and respect for ethnic and national differences— foreign/second languages skills for inter-cultural communication. Practice oriented. Actual experience.	
Sense of "professionalism"	High level of emphasis—include self-discipline and ability to work through an organizational structure and get thing done. "Civility."	Not a high priority.

Source: Based on a series of focused conversations conducted by the Education Commission of the States in 1994 with support from the Johnson Foundation and the Pew Charitable Trusts and in cooperation with the National Policy Board for Higher Education Institutional Accreditation, the National Governors' Association, and the National Conference of State Legislators. Reported in Romer, 1995, pp. 17–19 (reprinted in *AAHE Bulletin*, Apr. 1996, pp. 5–8).

Table 6.1. News Directors' Ratings of the Importance of Various Skills for On-Air Television People.

	Very Important (%)	Somewhat Important (%)	Not Very Important (%)	Don't Know/ No Answer (%)
Writing skills	96.4	2.7	0.0	0.9
Ability to communicate well on the air	96.4	3.6	0.0	0.0
Ability to think clearly	96.4	3.6	0.0	0.0
Ability to work under tight deadlines	92.0	7.1	0.9	0.0
Interviewing skills	83.9	14.3	0.9	0.9
Creativity and ability to approach stories from unusual angles	67.0	28.6	4.5	0.0
Knowledge of how government operates	66.1	29.5	2.7	1.8
Understanding of human behavior	55.4	44.6	0.0	0.0
Understanding of history	50.0	47.3	2.7	0.0
Editing skills	28.6	50.0	19.6	1.8
Ability to handle broadcasting equipment	21.4	50.0	28.6	0.0
Understanding of art and culture	18.8	61.6	18.8	0.9

Source: Future Trends in Broadcast Journalism, 1984, p. 39.

ability to communicate well on the air, the ability to think clearly, and the ability to work under tight deadlines (Table 6.1). More than 80 percent also identified interviewing skills (the ability to effectively interview others) as very important.

When the study compared the competencies needed with the qualities of those who were applying for positions, serious problems emerged. Recent graduates were rated low on each of the twelve categories, including the four qualities considered most important (Table 6.2).

University professors tended to be far more generous in the assessment of their graduates than were the professionals in the field. The majority of faculty, for example, stated that entry-level people could write very well and had the ability to work under tight deadlines.

The findings of this report are not unique. Recruiters and employers have consistently reported that although the college graduates they

Table 6.2. News Directors' Evaluation of Recent Graduates on Skills Considered Important for On-Air Television People.

	Rate Very Well (%)	Somewhat (%)	Not Very (%)	Don't Know/ No Answer (%)
Ability to handle broadcasting equipment (73)	8.2	61.6	27.4	2.7
Editing skills (77)	5.2	46.8	46.8	1.3
Writing skills (99)	2.0	29.3	68.7	0.0
Ability to work under tight deadlines (99)	3.0	40.4	53.5	3.0
Ability to think clearly (100)	5.0	67.0	26.0	2.0
Creativity and ability to approach stories from unusual angles (97)	4.1	51.5	42.3	2.1
Understanding of human behavior (100)	5.0	53.0	41.0	1.0
Knowledge of how government operates (95)	3.2	41.1	54.7	1.1
Understanding of history (98)	3.1	43.9	50.0	3.1
Interviewing skills (98)	2.0	50.0	46.9	1.0
Understanding of art and culture (80)	3.8	53.7	36.2	6.3
Ability to communicate well on the air (100)	1.0	46.0	52.0	1.0

Note: Each figure in parentheses is the number of those who said the skill is at least somewhat important; total number of respondents was 112.

Source: Future Trends in Broadcast Journalism, 1984, p. 39.

interview or hire know the content of their respective disciplines, few can write or speak effectively. It became obvious from these data that programs preparing students for this field must pay increased attention to the basic competencies of writing and speaking.

At times, the information and suggestions you receive from external communities will run counter to your own conclusions and be quite eye-opening. Not only can community sources identify competencies required for success in a field, but they can also provide insight into whether your instructional goals are being met. For example, as mentioned earlier, one professional group commissioned an external agency to review the discipline, the curriculum, and the needs of the field as described by employers and professionals. The final report, which created such discomfort within the board of directors that it was never distributed to the field, stated that the faculty had become isolated from the profession and that as a result the curriculum and the content of many courses within it were outdated and its graduates were unprepared. Usually, as was noted in Exhibit 6.3, the differences between the perceptions of faculty and those outside the academy are more subtle.

Questionnaires are extremely effective tools for collecting career-specific information. In one project, staff of the Center for Instructional Development assisted the faculty and dean of Syracuse University's College for Human Development in reviewing the four major undergraduate programs. The instruments that were developed for distribution to students, faculty, and alumni were somewhat unusual in that they were designed to serve two distinct purposes: to provide general information and to provide career-specific data focusing on particular programs and majors. Although the general questions were developed jointly with a steering committee, the career-specific sections were the product of extensive conversations with the faculty of each of the four major divisions of the college, they elicited the information faculty felt would be most useful in helping them evaluate and improve their programs.

The questionnaire sent to alumni (Resource D) had the following sections:

1. Professional skills and personal traits
2. For each field, specific topics and practical experiences that should be included in an undergraduate program and criteria for entry-level job candidates
3. View of the future
4. Individual background information

The information gleaned from these questionnaires is now being used in course and curriculum projects.

As mentioned earlier, establishing an employer and alumni advisory committee for projects in professional schools has proved extremely beneficial in both the quality of committee members' participation and the resources they can bring to the project.

The final curriculum or course objectives must include both general societal goals and the goals of the specific community the institution or program serves. Notice how the curriculum goal and specific objectives of the College of Agriculture at the University of Minnesota (Exhibit 6.4) combine and interrelate the basic competencies for all students and the goals unique to the agricultural community.

Exhibit 6.4. Mission Statement for the Curriculum of the College of Agriculture, University of Minnesota.

Goal

The mission of the College of Agriculture is to provide students with the educational experiences and environment that promote discipline competence, the capacity to attain career success in agriculture, food, or related professions, and a sense of civic responsibility.

Specific Objectives

Upon completion of a degree in the College of Agriculture students will be able to:

- Demonstrate fundamental knowledge of the biological and physical sciences
- Demonstrate specialized expertise in at least one agricultural discipline
- Develop specialized expertise in other disciplines as needed
- Apply their knowledge to solve problems in their chosen profession
- Appreciate and interpret works of art, literature, and the humanities
- Retrieve, analyze, and manage information
- Work in a team and manage human resources
- Communicate effectively (speak, write, listen, telecommunicate)
- Critically evaluate and integrate diverse viewpoints or data
- Make sound, responsible judgments on the ethical policy issues involved in the production of food and fiber
- Apply an historical perspective to the role of science and technology in agriculture
- Apply an international perspective to agriculture issues and decisions
- Act as responsible stewards of the land, natural resources and environment.

Source: Lunde and others, 1995, pp. 70–71. Reprinted with permission of the publisher.

Educational Priorities of the Institution _____

In collecting data it is important to identify the specific community your program serves. In some instances it is the local area or a particular section of the state; in others, as in the survey of the Radio-Television News Directors Association, it may be a national or international body of professionals or the specific accrediting agency for the profession. In other cases the unique characteristics of the institution influence or determine many of the goals of a curriculum. For example, metropolitan institutions such as the University of Memphis and Portland State University have revised their missions and many of their programs to focus on their community and to build close relationships between the goals of academic programs and the needs of their constituents. New courses have been added that actively involve students in the community as a formal part of their educational experience.

On both the curriculum and course levels, however, don't overlook the portion of the college community that is closest and thus easiest to ignore—the faculty in related departments and in yours. If the course is a prerequisite for other courses, find out what the faculty teaching these courses expect. Quite often we find a major gap, never discussed, between what faculty in an upper-level course expect from students and what faculty teaching a prerequisite course believe is possible.

Problems may also occur for political reasons. Projects have failed when a group of faculty opposed the effort for reasons that could have been avoided, such as not being consulted when they would have assisted had they been asked early in the design process. Overlooking these groups can be a particular problem in larger institutions in which departments within a single school or college may work independently or compete with one another for both students and financial support.

Institutional priorities provide useful information and should be identified because these priorities may directly affect the design of a curriculum and courses. Such priorities are often shaped by financial and material constraints and by specific campuswide initiatives (ranging from an urban emphasis to a commitment to commuter or distance education) that encourage focusing on one particular area or type of program and discourage focusing on another. They may determine the source and type of your students. Enrollment and financial considerations combined with the history of a given institution influence the programs that the institution offers. For example, church-supported institutions may have unique objectives, as the case of Alverno College in Chapter Five and Resource B showed. Likewise, we should not necessarily expect an institution located in a metropolitan area to have the same priorities or programs as one located in a rural setting. As needs differ, priorities also differ, and so should the characteristics and content of our academic programs.

It is important to state the existing priorities clearly. For example, if a principal aim of a lower-division course is to generate majors, this goal should be stated and understood. Unfortunately, this important objective is rarely acknowledged or discussed. There is nothing improper about trying to attract students to a discipline, unless, of course, there is no need for specialists in the discipline and recruitment is done solely to retain faculty positions. If this objective (attracting more students) is stated, emphasis can be placed on educating students about the discipline, the faculty, the department, the profession, the potential for jobs, and the program and on building a positive attitude toward them.

Field of Knowledge

The field of knowledge has often been the chief, and sometimes only, consideration in curriculum and course change. Changes in knowledge do in time reach the classroom. However, these changes have been most obvious in disciplines in which governmental support has been available. Unfortunately, most significant modifications of course content have been "crash" adjustments to resolve discrepancies that became obvious enough to raise a national clamor for improvement.

But content modification should be a continual process. As discoveries are made, as theories are modified, and as new areas evolve, the adjustment of the educational content should begin immediately. Therefore, you need to ensure that the content of any program you are designing is as contemporary and academically sound as possible, and that the instructional staff includes a continual process for updating in the overall design. Major journals and a review of the topics covered in national conferences along with conversations with professionals in the field are all excellent sources for identifying trends and content changes in the discipline. For example, to study the field of music education, the faculty involved with the redesign of the curriculum at Syracuse undertook these activities (among others) (Eickmann and Lee, 1976):

- Reading and studying music and music-education books, especially the most current ones

- Reading and analyzing articles, advertisements, and other information in the major professional journals in the discipline for the last ten years to identify general trends in music education

- Reviewing the research literature for the past fifteen years related to the teaching of music
- Reviewing and evaluating graduate research related to the teaching of music and reported in *Dissertation Abstracts* during the last fifteen years
- Examining curriculum guidelines published by major professional groups
- Surveying and studying the undergraduate music-education programs of all colleges and universities in New York State
- Examining and analyzing the competency-based certification guidelines and recommendations made by the New York State Education Department
- Reading and studying the literature about competency-based teacher education, a national trend affecting teacher-education programs in many states

It is also crucial, if you are working in a professional field requiring formal accreditation, to make sure your program meets the specific criteria for accreditation. Unfortunately, for many years these associations focused more on what was to be covered than on what was to be learned, often severely restricting the design options of faculty in these fields. Fortunately, accreditation standards are focusing increasingly on outcomes, providing the faculty with much more freedom to select the content and structure of the program. The American Assembly of Collegiate Schools of Business, for example, leaves the development of goals up to the individual department or program, focusing instead on how successful students are in achieving the goals that are agreed on as essential indicators of competence.

Research

Specific studies may be relevant to the project. These studies generally fall into three areas: the content of the discipline, the future direction of the profession, and pedagogy.

Content of the Discipline

In most professions formal studies are being conducted to determine what content is appropriate for the field. In some instances, such as industrial design, these studies may be sponsored by the national professional organization. In other instances they may be undertaken by a few faculty working independently on a course or curriculum project. Journals in the discipline that include articles on teaching and curriculum can often be an excellent source of information on recent studies related to course and program content.

An additional reference is the *Journal of Higher Education,* published by the Ohio State University Press and the American Association for Higher Education. For example, the July-August 1995 issue reported research by Paula Rayman and Belle Bratt on women science majors and their success after graduation, and the March-April 1996 issue contained a report on students' openness to diversity. Whatever the source, reviewing these studies can save time and effort or open up new paths of exploration.

Future Directions of the Discipline

The future direction of the profession or of the content and research component of the discipline should not be overlooked. Not only does reviewing the direction these areas may be taking ensure up-to-date content, but it also provides a basis for decisions regarding new content and objectives. Any new program, if it is to be successful, must be future oriented and based on the thinking of the outstanding practitioners and researchers in the field. As will be obvious from the number of references to it in this book, a fine source for information on future trends in education is *Change* magazine, published by the Helen Dwight Reid Educational Foundation under the leadership of the American Association for Higher Education.

Pedagogy

Ongoing research examines how students think, how they learn, and how they can effectively be taught. Although the findings about teaching and learning are most useful during the production and implementation stage, this information can affect the overall structure of the program. For example, a decision to implement mastery learning or to use the Perry (1970) research on how the thinking of students changes with maturity could determine the structure of the course and the sequence in which content is presented.

An excellent source of basic research in pedagogy as it applies to higher education is the federally sponsored National Center for Research to Improve Postsecondary Teaching and Learning at Stanford University. A most useful publication that should be in every faculty research library is Lion F. Gardiner's *Redesigning Higher Education: Producing Dramatic Gains in Student Learning* (1996). In it you will find an excellent review of the research on student development, the curriculum, teaching, and assessment. Concise, with excellent citations, it can save you a great deal of time and energy.

Time and Space

Two factors about which you need to gather information from administration and other faculty are time (the structure of your academic calendar, whether you have the option of using weekends, out-of-class hours, and time outside the semester) and space (on- and off-campus locations and their spatial options). For an excellent review of the research on these two topics, see Book 1, *Time*, and Book 2, *Space*, of William Bergquist and Diana Sharpe's *An Educational Feast* (1996).

You will also find *An Educational Feast* helpful as you consider the curricular structures and degree programs you are designing. They may be structured about disciplines, themes, problems, issues, or processes, for example. Gathering this information at the beginning of your project will enable you to keep in view the compelling educational ideal, vision, and mission that underlie your effort. Laurie Schultz Hayes (1995a), in a review of a successful curriculum project at the University of Minnesota, emphasizes the crucial need of involving as many faculty as possible in the design process. Otherwise, there will be little ownership or potential for implementation.

Summary

This chapter has covered the various questions that should be asked and the data that should be collected for use in the initial design phase. Remember that the quality of the data helps determine the success or failure of your project. To ensure that sufficient information is available for sound decision making, data should be collected in the following areas:

1. Students

   Entering level of competence

   Ability to meet assumed prerequisites

   Goals, priorities, and major

   Reasons for enrolling and background

   Attitudes about discipline, area, and so on

   Assumptions about course or program

2. Society (employers, recruiters, alumni, community leaders)

   Basic competencies all students should have by graduation

   Career-specific requirements

Existing gaps between required competencies and abilities of graduates

3. Educational priorities

Mission of institution, program, department
General goals of the program (course)

4. Field of knowledge

Required/essential content

Future trends in discipline/area of focus

Accreditation requirements (professional programs, state)

New content areas

5. Research

Discipline-related

Pedagogy (teaching and learning)

CHAPTER 7

Developing a Design for an Ideal Course or Curriculum

As actual designing begins on a course or curriculum, those involved use all the data that have been collected, their experiences, and their creativity to decide what an "ideal" program would look like. Because not all the data will be available immediately, this is a period of revision and a time for contemplation and discussion. Formal meetings are usually held no more than once a week, and semimonthly meetings are not uncommon.

Different faculty teaching in different disciplines often address the same general problems in significantly different ways. In this chapter I use several case studies to describe the initial design phase. These and the additional case studies in Resource E have been selected from a number of disciplines and address a wide range of academic problems. Because I use the same approach to discuss both course and curriculum design here, this chapter contains examples and case studies from both areas.

As you begin this most exciting and challenging phase of your project, it is crucial that you keep an open mind: brainstorm new ideas, explore all options, listen carefully to everyone else who is involved in the project with you. Now is the time to reflect on what has worked in the past and what has not, what you have heard from students and employers. Keep the discussion open and ensure that all ideas are heard.

Although fine tuning continues throughout the design and implementation process, few significant changes in sequence or content occur between the ideal conceptualization and the actual course.

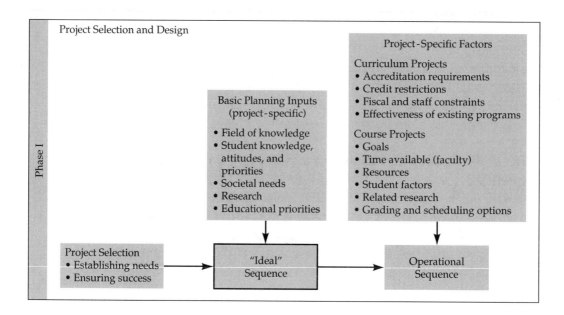

However, during the effort to reach for the ideal, the changes that take place in the design of a course or curriculum from one meeting to the next can be substantial. For example, Figures 7.1 and 7.2 are the first and third drafts of the design for the first semester of a two-semester course in communications design. Notice how the original idea of focusing on black and white line art in the first semester and color in the second was changed by the faculty member to an entirely different approach, with the color options available to the designer now serving as the theme for each unit. In addition, the laboratory portion of the course has begun, by the third draft, to take shape in both content and sequence. Major changes of this type often evolve as the faculty member continues to think about the course and answers questions posed by the instructional developer or other faculty. At other times changes result directly from comments of other faculty or professionals in the field or may be based on additional data that have been collected. During this stage, modification is both facilitated and encouraged.

Focusing on Structure and Sequence

Previous chapters focused on the development and articulation of the primary goals of a curriculum or a course. Chapter Nine focuses on stating these outcomes more specifically so that you, as a faculty member, will be able to judge how successful you and your students

Figure 7.1. Draft 1: Communications Design, First Semester.

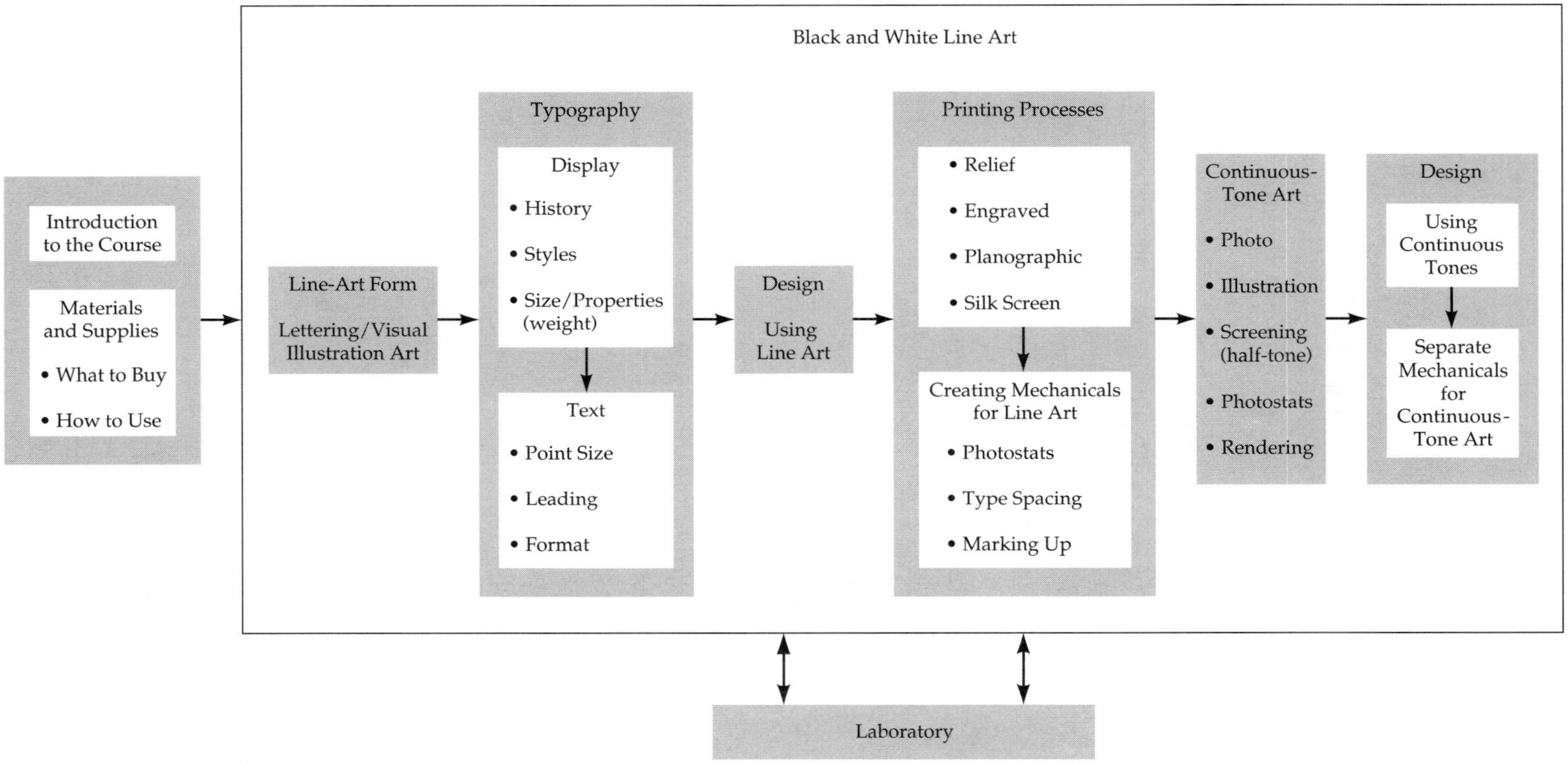

Black and White Line Art

Introduction to the Course

Materials and Supplies
- What to Buy
- How to Use

Line-Art Form
Lettering/Visual Illustration Art

Typography

Display
- History
- Styles
- Size/Properties (weight)

Text
- Point Size
- Leading
- Format

Design Using Line Art

Printing Processes
- Relief
- Engraved
- Planographic
- Silk Screen

Creating Mechanicals for Line Art
- Photostats
- Type Spacing
- Marking Up

Continuous-Tone Art
- Photo
- Illustration
- Screening (half-tone)
- Photostats
- Rendering

Design

Using Continuous Tones

Separate Mechanicals for Continuous-Tone Art

Laboratory

Credit: Toni Toland.

Figure 7.2. Draft 3: Communications Design, First Semester.

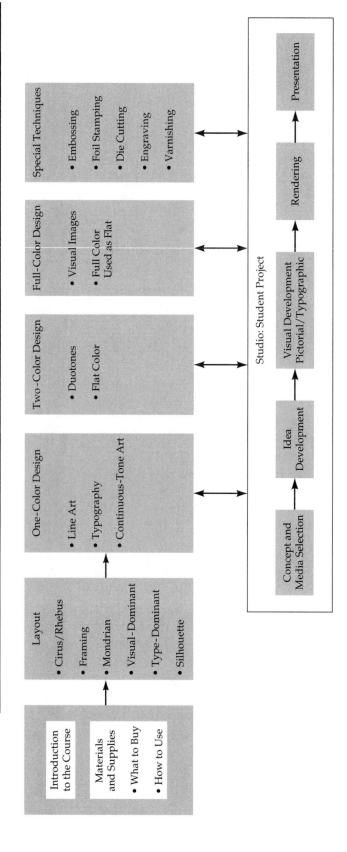

Credit: Toni Toland.

are in reaching them. We will also discuss how to select the most effective instructional strategy from the wide and expanding range of options now available to you.

At this point in the process our focus is on the major elements in your instructional program and how they should be sequenced to facilitate the learning you desire. This, as you might expect, is a rather complex process. You not only will have to take into account your general goals but will have to consider how they interrelate and how they can be reached within your discipline.

A number of studies and summary reports on teaching and learning can be of help as you address these issues. Exhibit 7.1 lists twelve elements of good teaching practice. Notice the number of items that focus on how the sequence of instruction should reinforce what students are learning and on the way in which we deliver instruction.

Reviewing the research on curriculum design (Exhibit 7.2) and on how to help students meet high expectations (Exhibit 7.3) is essential as you think through the design of your course or curriculum. The research summarized in Exhibits 7.1, 7.2, and 7.3 provides a base on which you can make a number of your design decisions. This is the time not only to apply what we know about teaching and learning but to test some of your long-held beliefs in those areas.

As you structure your program, keep in mind the specific population of students that will be enrolling. Adult students are significantly different from those who enter directly out of high school. If you have commuting students in your class, how can you provide them with the same range of crucial interactions available to students living on campus?

Patrick Terenzini and Ernest Pascarella, coauthors of one of the most comprehensive volumes on higher education, *How College Affects Students* (1991), stress the importance of thinking about the entire learning experience of your students and not just about what goes on within the classroom. Consider how you might build in community activities or internships or how you might combine what you are doing with the residential life of the on-campus students in a living-learning center or a campus activity. Considering such possibilities can only improve the quality of the students' educational experience. "*Real* college impact is likely to come not from pulling any grand, specific (and probably expensive) policy or programmatic lever, but rather from pulling a number of smaller, *interrelated* academic and social levers more often. If a college's effects are varied and cumulative, then its approaches to enhancing those effects must be varied and coordinated" (Terenzini and Pascarella, 1994, p. 32).

Exhibit 7.1. Research Findings on Good Teaching Practice.

Quality begins with an organizational culture that values:

1. High expectations. Students learn more effectively when expectations for learning are placed on high but attainable levels and when these expectations are communicated clearly from the outset.

2. Respect diverse talents and learning styles. Good practice demands carefully designing curricula and instructional efforts to meet diverse backgrounds and learning styles.

3. Emphasis on the early years of study. The first years of undergraduate study—particularly the freshman year—are critical for student success.

A quality undergraduate curriculum requires:

4. Coherence. Students succeed best in developing higher-order skills (critical thinking, written and oral communication, problem solving) when such skills are reinforced throughout their educational program.

5. Synthesizing experiences. Students also learn best when they are required to synthesize knowledge and skills learned in different places in the context of a single problem or setting.

6. Ongoing practice of learned skills. Unpracticed skills atrophy quickly, particularly core skills such as computation and writing.

7. Integration of education and experience. Classroom learning is both augmented and reinforced by multiple opportunities to apply what is learned.

Quality undergraduate instruction builds in:

8. Active learning. At all levels students learn best when they are given multiple opportunities to actively exercise and demonstrate skills.

9. Assessment and prompt feedback. Frequent feedback to students on their performance also is a major contributor to learning.

10. Collaboration. Students learn better when engaged in a team effort rather than working on their own.

11. Adequate time on task. Research also confirms that the more time devoted to learning, the greater the payoffs in terms of what and how much is learned.

12. Out-of-class contact with faculty. Frequency of academic, out-of-class contact between faculty members and students is a strong determinant of both program completion and learning.

Adapted from Romer, 1995, pp. 17–19 (reprinted in *AAHE Bulletin*, Apr. 1996, pp. 5–8).

Exhibit 7.2. Research Findings on Curriculum Design.

- Most curricula are unfocused, do not include clear statements of intended outcomes, and do not produce the intended results. There's a notable absence of structure and coherence.

- A number of conditions foster the development of college-level competences, including challenging courses, a supportive environment, active involvement in learning, high expectations, clearly defined and attainable goals with frequent assessment and prompt feedback. The goals must be challenging and communicated to the student.

- Providing a wide range of options in a general education requirement tends to be counterproductive. The most effective curricula tend to have a carefully structured core program with few electives.

- An effective curriculum provides multiple opportunities to apply and practice what is learned.

Source: Primarily from Gardiner, 1996.

Dealing with a Lack of Prerequisites

One of the most prevalent problems in course and curriculum design is the tendency of faculty to make false assumptions about the knowledge and skills that students bring to their courses. These incorrect assumptions lead to failure for the students who are ill prepared, boredom for their classmates who are often more than adequately prepared, and frustration for the faculty. The case study that follows describes a program designed to accommodate a wide range of entry levels for students in a required first-year course.

In Resource E you will find two additional case studies dealing with prerequisites; they illustrate different approaches for addressing this most significant problem in many introductory courses.

Case Study: Freshman English

Few courses generate as much emotion on any campus as the introductory course in writing. Disliked by most students and dealing with a subject that most faculty feel should have been taught (but was not) in the high schools, the freshman English (composition) course also presents a series of major design problems to anyone attempting to develop an effective offering:

- The course usually enrolls large numbers of students and to be effective must be taught in relatively small sections.
- Most English faculty look down on the teaching of expository writing, and in addition, as specialists in literature or creative writing, they often do not have the willingness, skills, or experience necessary to teach the subject. Consequently, on many large campuses the

Exhibit 7.3. Research Findings on Helping Students Meet High Expectations.

- The higher the quality of instruction, the less relevant to achievement are a student's entering abilities.
- Although some faculty believe many students simply lack the intellectual equipment required to learn, understanding the background and developmental and contextual reasons why students behave as they do can greatly enhance our ability to help them develop.
- Intelligence is made up of learnable skills.
- Most students can learn higher mental processes if these processes are made central to instruction.
- Cooperative learning with high standards and goals can significantly improve the success rate of high-risk students.

Source: Adapted from Gardiner, 1996.

freshman English course is delegated to graduate students with little background or interest in teaching writing or grammar.
- Students enter the program with an extremely wide range of writing skills. Although a small number have an excellent background in writing, most do not.

The problem facing the English faculty at Syracuse University was therefore not unique: how, with the resources available, to structure an introductory course that would develop the necessary writing skills in all students and also be sensitive to the extreme range of entering competencies.

The design team decided to totally rethink not only what was taught but how it was taught. In the process a number of major issues were addressed.

Content

In the past the course used literature and poetry as the basis for the writing. The faculty concluded that a major problem with this approach was that it forced students who were having basic writing problems to write about subjects that not only were new to them but were at times hard to understand. As a result, the faculty often found it difficult to separate confusion about the subject from problems with the technical aspects of writing. The faculty therefore concluded that they would focus on the writing by providing students with the opportunity to write about subjects that were familiar to them until they developed basic skills in structuring and organizing their essays.

Structure and Time

Recognizing that students entered the course with a wide range of writing skills, the faculty explored a number of structural options for dealing with this diversity. Two questions raised by the instructional developer helped the faculty develop solutions. First, because students entered the course with such a wide range of writing skills, did they have to begin at the same place? Second, because students learn at different rates, was it necessary for all to take the same amount of time to reach an acceptable level of writing performance? When the decision was made that both the beginning point and time could indeed be flexible, an entirely new approach to the design of the course became possible. Not only could students begin at different levels based on their entering competencies but they also could move through the course at their own pace.

Standardization Between Sections

Because the course relied heavily on teaching assistants, many of whom had little previous experience teaching composition, it became obvious early in the design process that the final structure would have to facilitate standardization in grading. The criteria used for evaluating writing would have to be taught to and understood by each of the teaching assistants and by the students, and grading standards would have to be consistent across all sections. To address this issue all new teaching assistants were required to take a formal course in pedagogy; in this course the grading protocol developed for the course would be taught.

Evaluation and Placement

If students were to begin at different levels according to entry writing skills, the problem of assessment also had to be addressed. The faculty felt that existing tests could be used for this purpose and proposed a combination of a commercially produced diagnostic test and a written essay. After several years the commercial test was replaced by one developed locally that was more suited to the specific needs of the course.

Remediation

One of the most difficult problems the faculty had to address was remediation—how to deal with those students who entered the course with writing problems at the basic level—problems with punctuation, usage, agreement, and so on. Although many faculty claim that teaching these skills is the responsibility of the primary and secondary schools, students nevertheless enter college without these skills, and they must be taught. The problem was even more complex because most of the teaching assistants had little training or interest in teaching basic grammar and usage. The decision was made, therefore, to combine independent study using programmed texts with tutoring. Furthermore, this tutoring would be done not by the teaching assistants but by part-time instructors experienced in teaching basic writing and hired specifically for this purpose.

The selection of the specific programmed texts that were to be used turned out to be far more difficult than was at first imagined. After identifying the specific skills they wished to have taught (approximately twenty), the faculty began a review of every programmed text on the market to identify those pages or frames that dealt effectively with specific topics. Although over thirty texts were available, the majority were found to be poorly written and to contain unacceptable treatments of some topics. In addition, one of the most effective publications was no longer available. After several years a number of texts with logical sequences were identified and used effectively. (At that time there were no computer units that could be used for this purpose.)

Results

The course that evolved differed markedly in structure from the existing course and from most traditional programs (Figure 7.3). Students are placed based on diagnostic tests in one of three instructional levels. Level I students are assigned to specific remedial areas according to need and may move up to Level II as soon as they can pass the criterion tests. In Level II students must write two passing papers before moving to Level III. In Level III students are required to take two four-week segments on fiction and poetry and may select from a series of minicourses or write a paper in an area of interest. The required segments are repeated throughout the semester for the convenience of students moving into Level III during the year. The writing topics are subjects familiar to the student until Level III, when literature is first introduced. Class size varies by level with individual tutoring in Level I, small groups in Level II, and larger sections in Level III. (Later, all levels limited class size to fifteen for teaching assistants and twenty for more experienced faculty and instructors.)

Recognizing that students would move through the course at different speeds, the project team contacted the registrar's office early on. Out of this discussion evolved a continuous-registration system, which permits students to move at various paces through the program—some taking as long as two years to complete the required six credits. The flexible credit system also allows students to earn from one to six credits in a single semester, permitting better-prepared students to complete the course in less than two semesters.

This design addresses remediation in Level I, the noncredit portion of the course. Research by Stern (1970) has shown that building remedial work into the regular program eliminates much of the stigma associated with "bonehead" English courses. In addition, the approach also eliminates the problem of awarding college credit for non-college-level work.

Case Study: Introductory Economics

Entry-level deficiencies in mathematics may be due to students' avoidance of the subject rather than to neglect of math skills (multiplication, division, fractions, decimals, percents, word problems, and graphing) in the final three or four years of precollege education. Whatever the reason, however, these deficiencies need to be remediated before students can take many courses.

Economics, for example, like many of the social sciences, relies heavily on mathematics for the presentation and interpretation of data. It was therefore not surprising to find that the lack of mathematics preparation would have to be addressed in a project that included the redesign of two existing introductory courses, microeconomics and macroeconomics, and the design of a new course specifically for noneconomics majors.

Figure 7.3. Instructional Sequence for Freshman English.

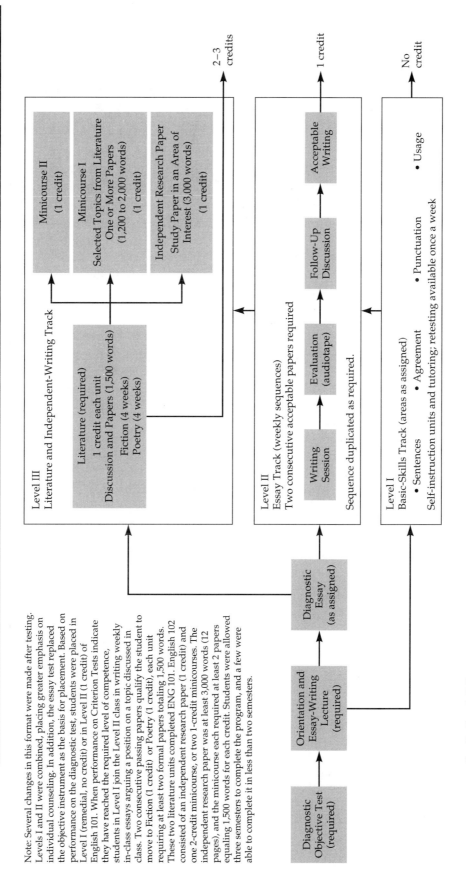

Note: Several changes in this format were made after testing. Levels I and II were combined, placing greater emphasis on individual counseling. In addition, the essay test replaced the objective instrument as the basis for placement. Based on performance on the diagnostic test, students were placed in Level I (remedial, no credit) or in Level II (1 credit) of English 101. When performance on Criterion Tests indicate they have reached the required level of competence, students in Level I join the Level II class in writing weekly in-class essays arguing a position on a topic discussed in class. Two consecutive passing papers qualify the student to move to Fiction (1 credit) or Poetry (1 credit), each unit requiring at least two formal papers totaling 1,500 words. These two literature units completed ENG 101. English 102 consisted of an independent research paper (1 credit) and one 2-credit minicourse, or two 1-credit minicourses. The independent research paper was at least 3,000 words (12 pages), and the minicourse each required at least 2 papers equaling 1,500 words for each credit. Students were allowed three semesters to complete the program, and a few were able to complete it in less than two semesters.

Credit: Randall Brune.

As a first step, a review was made of the text that would be used and of past examinations to identify the specific mathematics competencies required of the students. Identified competencies were basic operations with fractions, decimals, and percents, and the use of tables and graphs to represent the relationships between economic variables.

Before major design work began, a basic mathematics test was constructed to assess these prerequisite competencies; it was administered on the second day of class to a group of students enrolled in the basic microeconomics course that was then being offered. This testing not only provided data on the mathematics skills of the students enrolled in the course but permitted items on the test itself to be evaluated. Data collected showed that nearly 70 percent of the students had inadequate mathematics skills in at least one area. As a result, a diagnostic and remedial sequence (see Figure 7.4) was built into the three introductory courses for all first-time economics students.

A decision was made to use a diagnostic test followed by remedial programmed units assigned on the basis of test results. Although students are actively encouraged to complete the sequence, the programmed units are not required. Students are, however, provided with their test results and an analysis of the relationship of test results to performance in the course. An exhaustive search of available programmed and computer materials failed to locate appropriate materials for use in economics. For this reason, new programmed units were designed.

In addressing problems of this type, it is possible to build the remediation into the regular instructional sequence and exempt those students who have the competency from the class session. This option was not taken in this instance because faculty agreed that using in-class time for this purpose would be wasteful; the problem could be effectively eliminated for most students by two to three hours of out-of-class study.

It has now become possible to advise some students, on the basis of extensive data, either to complete these units or, in severe cases, to take additional mathematics courses prior to enrolling in the economics course.

Figure 7.4. Beginning Sequence for Introductory Economics Courses.

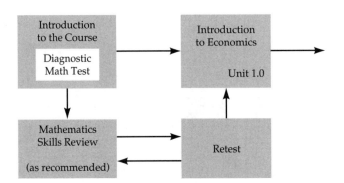

Credit: Jerry Evensky.

At the present time work is under way to develop and field-test a self-contained, computer-based, multimedia module (test, remediation, retest). Under a grant from the Fund for the Improvement of Post-Secondary Education the two delivery systems (programmed text and multimedia) will be compared with regard to impact and cost-effectiveness. This project will also test the same approach in three other introductory courses: chemistry, political science, and psychology. Field testing and evaluation will be conducted at Syracuse University and six other institutions that serve a wide range of students. Reports on this project should begin to be available in summer 1998 from the Center for Instructional Development, Syracuse University.

Case Study: Graduate Course in Education

A graduate course in cost-effectiveness in instruction and training, offered by the School of Education, forced the faculty member teaching it to answer three important questions:

- How could the course meet the needs of an extremely diverse student population—majors in higher education, management, and instructional technology, many from different countries?
- How could the course deal with entering students who do not have all the prerequisites?
- How could the course meet the needs of entering students with very different backgrounds, different expectations, and very different situations in which they would be expected to achieve cost-effectiveness in instruction and training.

Those who lacked prerequisites and who had an inadequate background for the course were assigned additional readings and other assignments, and the course design was modified to relate course content to individual professional goals. As part of the enrollment procedure that was developed, students are asked to complete a brief questionnaire that provides the instructor with information about why they are enrolling, related courses and work experiences they have had, and their professional goals. This information is then used by the instructor to prepare assignments and identify student teams for projects later in the course (see Figure 7.5). This design is unusual in that students are allowed to focus on their own areas of interest as they apply the general model that is being taught. This flexibility occurs in two areas: Unit 4.0, in which the students apply the model to case studies, and Unit 5.0, team projects.

This is an excellent example of how the basic content of a course can be left unchanged while the course itself is restructured to meet the specific needs of the students who are enrolled. A somewhat different approach to redesigning a course to account for different student interests and backgrounds is described in Resource E.

Figure 7.5. Course Description for Second Part of Cost-Effectiveness in Instruction and Training.

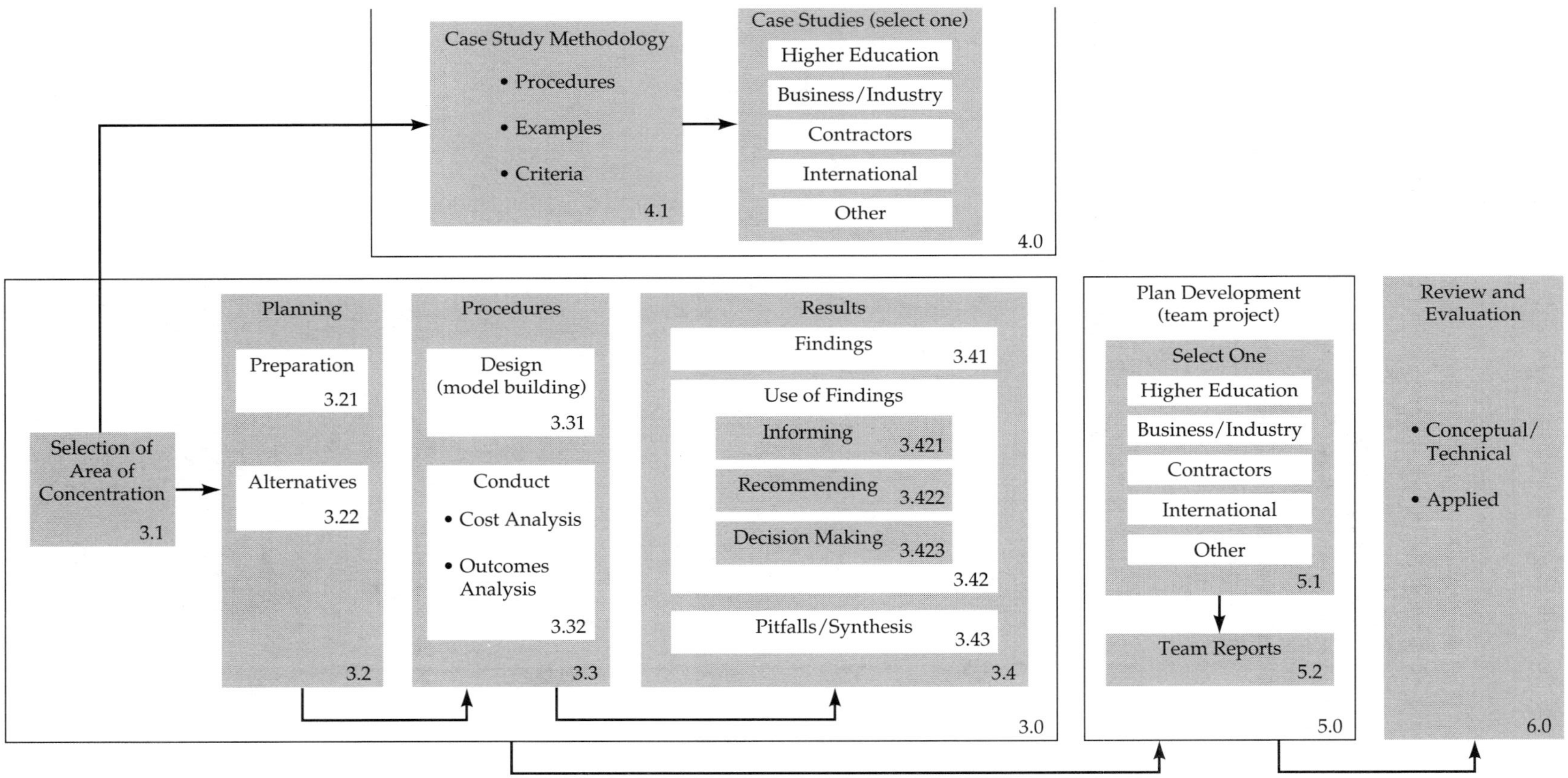

Credit: Philip Doughty.

Ensuring the Acquisition of Basic Core Competencies in an Introductory Course

Previous chapters described in some detail those core competencies that faculty and business and governmental leaders tend to agree should be required of every college graduate—communication skills, basic math skills, interpersonal skills, critical thinking, problem solving, the ability to work with culturally diverse populations, and so on. The challenge you will face is how to meet these requirements in a cost-effective way within your course or curriculum.

Case Study: Introduction to Business and Management

Before the fall semester of 1992 the School of Management at Syracuse University did not offer a freshman management course. Students began their formal discipline-related coursework in their sophomore year. They spent the first year meeting core requirements in the College of Arts and Sciences. The School of Management found that the delay in direct instructional contact with students led to a lack of community and caused a great deal of student frustration. The faculty had also come to believe that if their students were available to them during the freshman year, they could begin to teach a number of skills that students needed for success in their programs and later as professionals.

As a result, the faculty decided to develop an introductory first-semester course to be required of all first-year students in the School of Management. A team of faculty representing each of the departments in the School of Management was established. The Center for Instructional Development was asked to facilitate the design, implementation, and assessment process.

The team established three overarching objectives for this new course: to build a community of the students, faculty, and administration within the School of Management; to introduce the students to the field of business and to the professional options or areas of specialization that would be open to them; and to begin to develop in these students the skills needed for both immediate and long-term success. These goals became an integral part of the structure and delivery of the course. They were communicated to the students in the objectives section of the course manual, which included the following statements:

> SOM 200 focuses on the prevailing management thrust towards skills required for effective conduct in the business world. You will see that attention is given to teamwork, oral presentation, writing, computer skills, and social skills that are connected with being part of a large institution. SOM 200 has the following learning objectives.

> When you have completed this course, you should be able to:

> 1. Identify the skills that are necessary for success in business.
> 2. Understand how the skills necessary for success in business are applied in the "real world."

3. Create a plan for developing business skills while at Syracuse University.
4. Understand fundamental issues that arise when working in small teams.
5. Plan and carry out a project with a team.
6. Develop skills of analyzing an audience and tailoring written and oral reports to their interest and needs.
7. Use the S.U. on-line catalog to access library collections, services, and resources.
8. Research career information and become acquainted with relevant books, academic journals, and trade journals.
9. Cite sources in a written report, construct a bibliography, and discuss and evaluate the views of other authors.
10. Understand the concept of "computer system" as a means to an end in learning and in business.
11. Locate the essential computer facilities available to students on campus.
12. Use the two basic software application packages in the S.U. PC cluster: word processing and RiceMail.
13. Accomplish a smooth transition to college.
14. Build a strong identity with the School of Management and a solid direction for your future studies and career plans.

SOM 200 was designed to reach these objectives using a number of approaches (see Figure 7.6):

- The text selected, *Who Is Going to Run General Motors?* by Green Seymour, focuses directly on the essential competencies needed for success in business. The chapters of the book serve as the focus for the lecture portion of the course.
- Instead of faculty lectures, alumni and other business leaders describe their positions and explain why the specific competency under discussion is essential to them. Ample time is provided for discussion.
- Participation in course-related activities begins prior to the beginning of scheduled classes. At Syracuse over 90 percent of entering students have their complete schedules when they arrive on campus. During the time between final registration and the first class meeting, students are required to attend a brief orientation to the course. At this orientation they are shown the computer clusters that they will be using. Students not familiar with the computer system are required to complete an independent-learning sequence programmed to introduce them to word processing. This unit requires no additional faculty time.
- The laboratory portion of the course focuses on team building, introduces the students to e-mail (which is used throughout the course for communication among students and between students and faculty), spreadsheets, and the use of the library.
- A focused project requires all students to work in teams, to utilize computers, and to make an oral presentation.

Figure 7.6. Structure of Introductory School of Management Course.

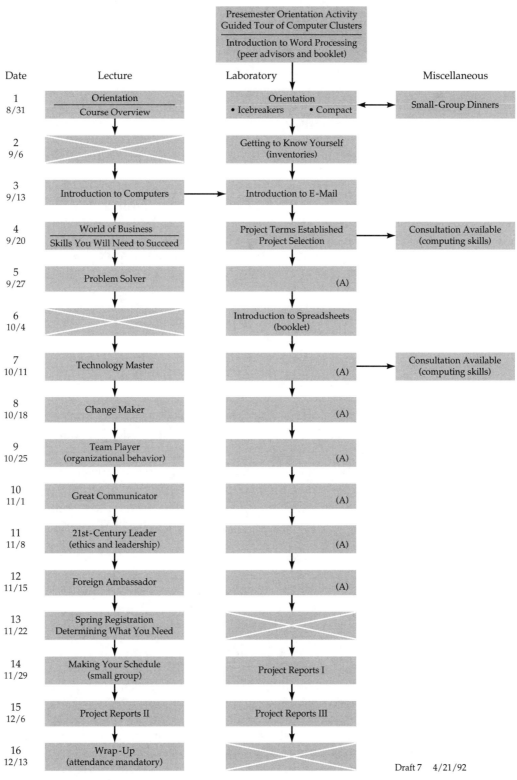

(A) One-page computer-generated assignment or two-minute
    presentation relating to lecture or other aspects of course due.

- Faculty, graduate assistants, and upper-division students all assist in the delivery of the course. Faculty teaching the laboratory portion of the course are assigned as advisers to the freshmen students in their section(s).
- To improve long-term planning and course selection, formal advising for second-semester courses is built into the course.

As a result of this course, students' attitudes toward the school and the university have improved, as has their academic performance. Faculty teaching subsequent courses report that the skills and attitudes of students have improved. Although a number of changes have taken place in the course since its first offering—new text, new units on library research and on being part of a team—the basic concepts of the program have been maintained.

From the first time the course was offered, there has been a strong desire on the part of the students to have the formal relationship with the school continue in the second semester. Although credit restrictions and accreditation requirements precluded having the course be a two-semester sequence, the school was able to initiate a successful second-semester internship program in which students have the opportunity to link with business and industries in the area. Offered through the university's Community Internship Program, the internship is a one-credit elective for those students who are interested in participating.

Designing an Ideal Curriculum

Up to this point the major focus in this chapter has been at the course level, but the same general process is followed when dealing with an entire curriculum. Here, however, the main task is to develop the relationships among the major instructional elements of a program. In time, these elements become individual courses or sequences of courses. Unless the curriculum is entirely new, some existing courses usually remain as they are, others are modified (changes in content, sequences, or credit hours), and still others are eliminated as new courses are introduced.

Case Study: Music/Music Industry

Figure 7.7 presents the lower-division structure of a new curriculum, Music/Music Industry. Notice in particular the features that create sequential movement: (1) attention has been paid to general entrance requirements and then to the program itself; (2) in the first two years only one additional course is required—Music Industry; and (3) those students who enter with competency in two instruments have the option of taking a special three-course sequence in the School of Management. Discussions with professionals in the field, an extensive review of the literature, and numerous

Figure 7.7. Structure of Bachelor's Degree Program in Music/Music Industry.

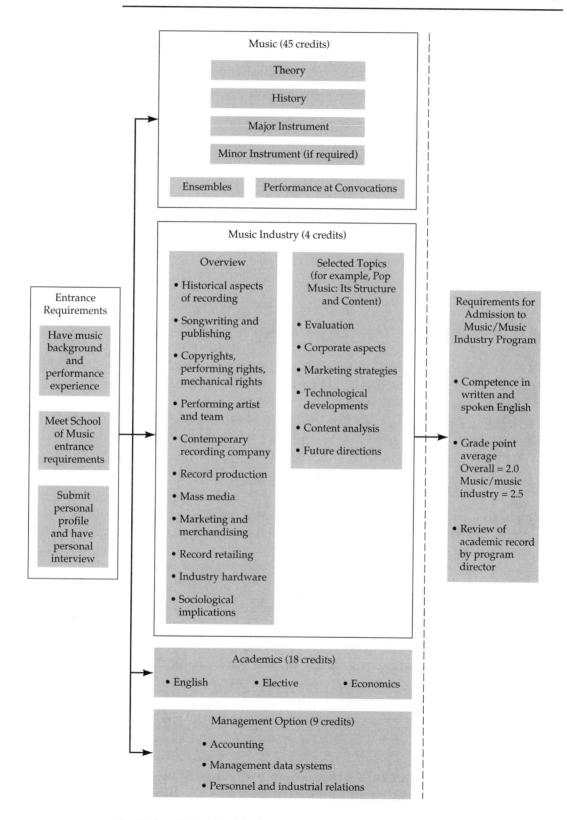

Credit: Ronald Lee, Paul Eickmann.

surveys were used to provide the data on which both the curriculum and course designs were based.

The faculty thought that adding the overview course on the music industry was essential not only for introducing the students to the field but also for providing them with an understanding of the profession before they were required, at the end of their sophomore year, to select a major field of specialization and to apply for formal admission into the program.

Case Study: Master's Program in Management

Figures 7.8 and 7.9 are the beginning parts of two drafts of the curriculum for a proposed master's degree in business administration program (MBA) in management. Designing this complex curriculum, which involved several departments, took many months. Notice that while some elements in the sixth draft appear to have undergone little change by the fourteenth version, the overall structure has changed and has become far more specific. Major emphasis was on two issues: what topics should be required of all students and in what order. In addition, the fact that many MBA students enter with work experience had to be addressed.

This project did not begin until all departments in the school agreed to actively participate—a process that took nearly one year. By the time the project was completed eighteen months later, the design included a general description of the total curriculum with a list of student performance outcomes for each course or unit within it.

The design that evolved had several significant structural elements. Notice how sensitive this structure was to the entry level of the students. Although some students enroll directly from an undergraduate program, which may or may not be in the field, others are older students entering after several years of work experience. Individual counseling and formal evaluation permit assigning prerequisite courses as they are needed. The Managerial Team Dynamics and Leadership Development sequence was added specifically to develop the "survival skills" (speaking, interpersonal, and writing skills, and so on) that were mentioned repeatedly by employers and recruiters as being essential for success in the field. In the Instructional Core (3.0), although some units (or courses) are required of all students, others are assigned according to the student's specific major on the basis of decisions made in each academic area. Also note that career counseling and placement are not left to chance but are proposed as an integral part of the total curriculum. (Notice also how the use of the phrases "as required" in Unit 1.5 and "as assigned" in Unit 3.4 simplify the diagramming process.)

Case Study: Master's Program in Instructional Design, Development, and Evaluation

The Graduate Department of Instructional Design, Development, and Evaluation (IDD&E) within the School of Education at Syracuse University serves an extremely diverse student population that includes international

Figure 7.8. Part of Draft 6: Proposed Master's Degree in Business Administration Program in Management.

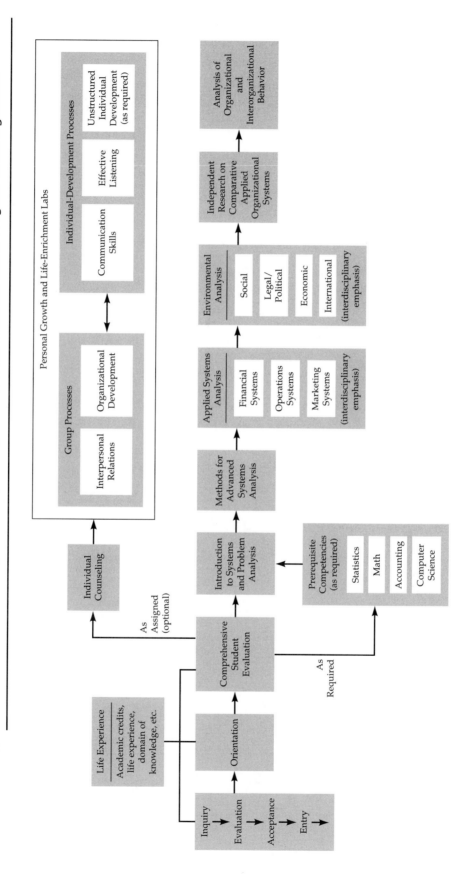

Figure 7.9. Part of Draft 14: Proposed Master's Degree in Business
Administration Program in Management.

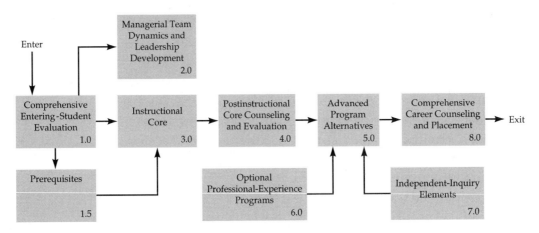

Part 1

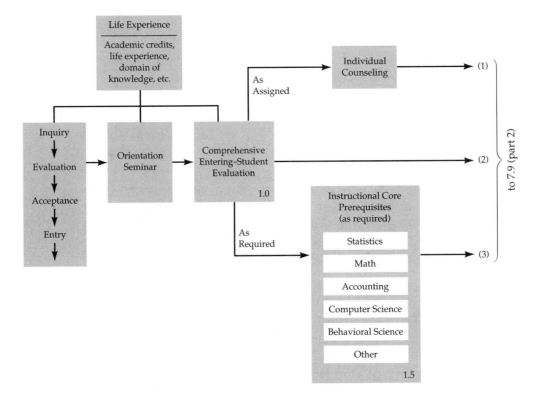

Credit: David Wilemon, Robert M. Diamond.

Figure 7.9. (continued).

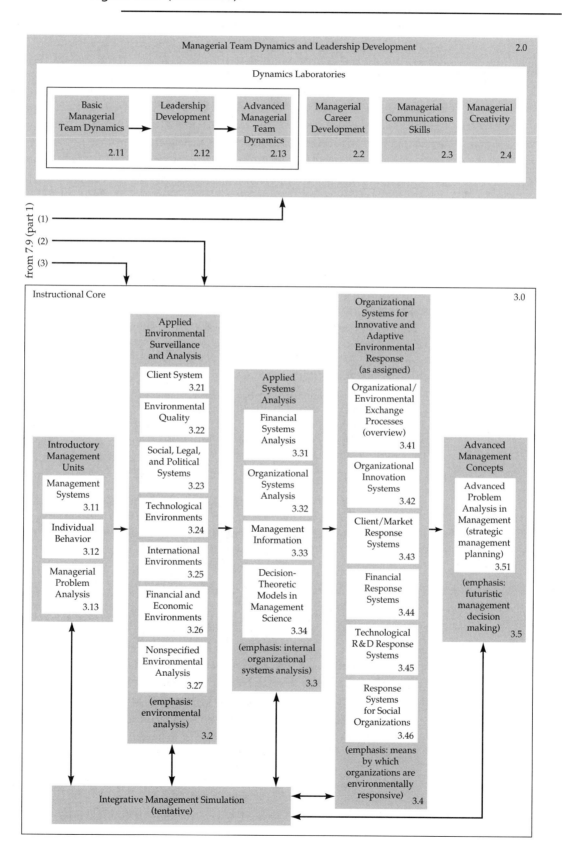

students; students who are returning to higher education after a number of years in business, industry, and education; and some who are entering the field directly after completing undergraduate degrees. In addition, the program has to serve the needs of both full- and part-time students.

Although the faculty wished to rethink both its master's and its doctoral programs, a decision was made to focus first on the master's degree because many of the elements of this program would become prerequisites for the more advanced degree. Because the small department of six faculty members decided not to begin work on the curriculum until everyone could participate, the project took place during the summer. By September the design was ready for presentation to students and other faculty in the school.

To assist in the design process, a survey was developed and administered to alumni. A special insert for recent graduates and present students focused on the current program (see Exhibit 7.4). Whereas the basic instrument included questions on the importance of major program areas, on practical experiences that had contributed to the education of the alumni, and on the importance of a number of professional and personal traits, the insert focused on advisement, admissions procedures, placement, and assessment.

As faculty reviewed the data and discussed their own concerns about the existing program, several important issues emerged. These ranged from the need to provide exemptions from certain elements of the program for those students who entered with related on-the-job experiences to the desire to provide all students with basic discipline-related competencies in a manner that was both sequential and logical. For these reasons, the major focus of the initial effort was on the design of the core program: content elements, order of presentation, and the relationship of the core program to the areas of specialization.

The sequence developed (Figure 7.10) has several noteworthy features:

- A weekend retreat is used to introduce the program, the major elements within it (development and evaluation), and the specific model on which both elements are based. It also provides an opportunity for the new students to meet the faculty and each other in a somewhat informal setting (A).
- One course, Learning Theory, is taken before all the others and serves as a base for what follow (B).
- A number of basic skills (C) are used within the core courses, and at the conclusion of the introductory program, students having deficiencies in these areas are required to take courses to improve these skills. In addition, the inclusion of these skills in the core courses is not left to chance. Specific skills are assigned to specific courses: for example, students are required to use computers in certain courses and to make formal presentations in others.
- The basic development model is reinforced throughout the program by the use of case studies, with the appropriate areas of learning theory and evaluation built into these same exercises (D).
- Running concurrently with the development core for full-time students and available sequentially for part-time students are courses providing an overview of the field (E) and of instructional evaluation (F).

Exhibit 7.4. Questionnaire Insert for Recent Graduates.

A. How would you rate the *advisement* you received during your IDD&E program? (Circle the appropriate response and comment; give examples of effective and ineffective procedures.)

(1–4)

	Very Poor	Poor	Fair	Good	Very Good	
1. Academic (courses, program)	1	2	3	4	5	(5)
comments and examples:						(6–8)
2. Career (internships, jobs)	1	2	3	4	5	(9)
comments and examples:						(10–12)
3. Dissertation	1	2	3	4	5	(13)
comments and examples:						(14–16)

B. 1. How would you rate the *admissions procedures* (including communications) at IDD&E? (Circle the appropriate response.)

Very Poor	Poor	Fair	Good	Very Good	
1	2	3	4	5	(17)
					(18–20)

  2. Suggestions for improvement:

C. 1. How would you rate the *orientation* you received upon entering the IDD&E program? (Circle the appropriate response.)

Very Poor	Poor	Fair	Good	Very Good	
1	2	3	4	5	(21)

  2. Suggestions for improvement:

D. 1. How would you rate the *placement assistance* offered by IDD&E? (Circle the appropriate response.)

Very Poor	Poor	Fair	Good	Very Good	
1	2	3	4	5	(25)

  2. Suggestions for improvement: (22–24)

E. 1. Please rate the effectiveness of the following *assessment and appraisal* methods used in IDD&E. (VI=Very Ineffective, N=Neutral, VE=Very Effective, NA=Not Applicable.) (Circle the appropriate response.)

	VI		N		VE	NA	
a. Master's comprehensives/intensives	1	2	3	4	5	NA	(29)
b. Portfolio (doctoral preliminary)	1	2	3	4	5	NA	
c. Doctoral qualifying exams	1	2	3	4	5	NA	
d. Dissertation-proposal defense	1	2	3	4	5	NA	
e. Dissertation defense	1	2	3	4	5	NA	(33)

  2. Please make any comments or suggestions on how we may improve assessment and appraisal methods at IDD&E. (34–37)

F. 1. How would you rate the general quality of the IDD&E program in terms of: (VP=Very Poor, P=Poor, G=Good, VG = Very Good.) (Circle the appropriate response.)

	VP	P	F	G	VG	
a. Intellectual stimulation	1	2	3	4	5	(38)
b. Academic/intellectual freedom	1	2	3	4	5	
c. Collegiality with faculty	1	2	3	4	5	
d. Friendliness of support staff	1	2	3	4	5	

Exhibit 7.4. (continued).

___

e. Camaraderie with other graduate students	1	2	3	4	5	
f. Opportunity to explore outside interests	1	2	3	4	5	(43)

2. Please make any comments or suggestions on how we may improve the general quality of the IDD&E program.   (44–47)

Thank you for your assistance!

Several other courses are offered later in the core but are not shown in Figure 7.10. In addition, tracks of specialization were developed, and credits were assigned.

Summary ___

This chapter has described the exciting and challenging process of designing an ideal program. The case studies have illustrated how each course or curriculum is unique. No single, all-purpose design fits all cases. As students, faculty, institutions, resources, and disciplines vary, so must the course or curriculum that is developed. Notice that although I have discussed content and structure, I have, for the most part, not explored instructional formats or instructional objectives. These activities take place much later in the process. The next chapter describes how, through analysis of resources and options, field tests, and so on, this idealized version is modified and eventually becomes the program that is offered.

Figure 7.10. Proposed Core Curriculum for Master's Program in Instructional Design, Development, and Evaluation.

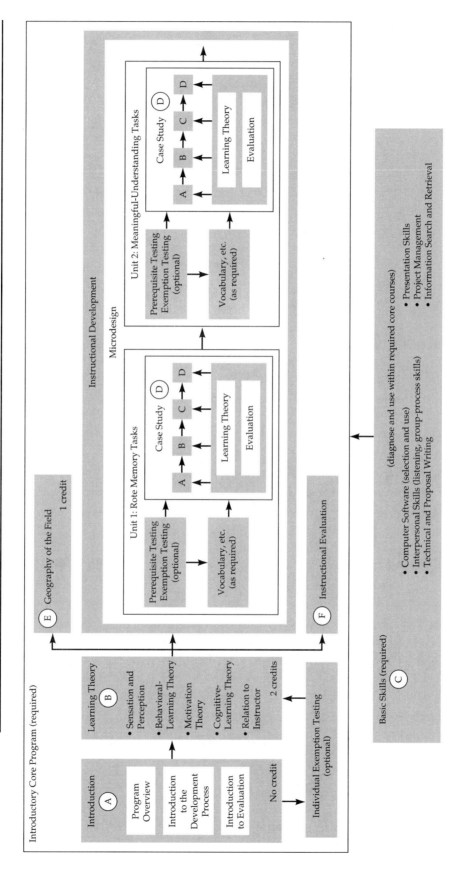

Credit: Donald Ely, Philip Doughty, Barbara Grabowski, Charles Reigeluth, Alexander Romiszowski, Nick Smith.

CHAPTER 8

Adjusting from the Ideal to the Possible

At some point in the development process the preliminary, or "ideal," design phase is completed, and modification begins in order to meet the practical limitations of the real world. This transition from the ideal to the possible is gradual. It is impossible to identify a specific point at which one stage ends and another begins. The separation is described here more to clarify the transition than to indicate a break in the process.

Throughout the process you will use information you have gathered from a number of sources, but you will rely on your own insights and experiences as you decide which modifications are necessary for your design to be implemented. This is in effect the time for a reality check, the point at which you decide, based on the resources and constraints you have, how close to the ideal your new course or curriculum will be. You will probably find that your final design is far closer to your ideal than you originally thought it would be.

There are fundamental differences from this point on between curriculum projects and those focusing on a single course. In a curriculum project you determine the courses that together will make up the total program. In designing a course you determine its specific elements, class meetings, projects, and activities. Obviously, these are differences in detail, in purpose, and in the factors that must be considered. In addition, although curriculum projects terminate at the completion of this phase, course-related projects move into the production, implementation, and evaluation activities of Phase II (see Figure 8.1).

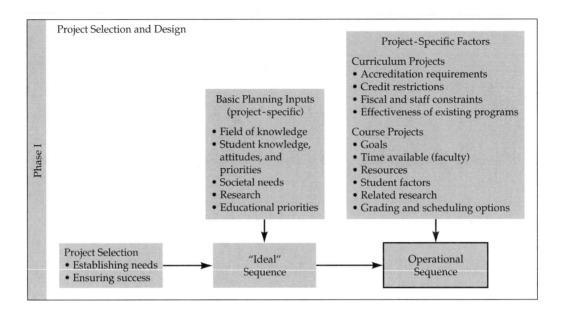

At the end of this phase in designing a new curriculum the focus shifts from the total curriculum to the courses within it. This change occurs once the operational diagram is complete and it becomes possible to identify which existing courses need major revision, which new courses must be developed, and which existing courses will continue much as they are. For the new and revised courses that have been identified, the design process will begin again if time and resources permit, with the focus on thinking in the ideal on a course-by-course basis. When the entire process is completed, each of these courses will become part of the new curriculum. One major advantage of this approach is that the materials produced by the completion of Phase I also serve as the supporting documentation required by school, college, and institutional curriculum committees responsible for approval of new programs or new courses.

Curriculum Projects: Factors to Consider

In moving from an ideal to a possible, or operational, curriculum, several major factors must be considered—factors that are, in some instances, outside your control. Among these factors are the following:

- Accreditation requirements. Does the proposed curriculum include those academic areas, credits, and courses required by the institution or by external professional agencies? These requirements may range from a basic liberal arts core to specialized technical or professional courses.

Figure 8.1. Development Process.

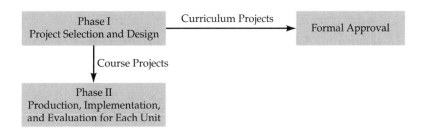

- Credit restrictions. Can the proposed program fit within the number of credit hours required for the major or minor? State departments of education, individual institutions and the schools and colleges within them, and often external certification agencies specify the minimum and the maximum number of credits a student is required to take within and outside a single academic area or discipline. Are these standards being met?

- Fiscal and staff constraints. Is the proposed curriculum financially feasible? Can it be staffed? If new positions and new facilities are required, can the needed fiscal resources be found? If class size is to be reduced to permit oral presentations or group projects, are there sufficient instructors?

- Effectiveness of existing courses and programs. If some elements of an existing curriculum are to be used, are they effective and do they meet the needs for which they have been selected?

To answer some of these questions you must involve the dean of the school or college and in some instances the academic vice-president as well. Even though they may not be active participants, involving these individuals with the project from the beginning ensures that they have early knowledge of what is being proposed and why.

Case Study: Retailing Major

Figure 8.2 is the third draft of the idealized version of an undergraduate curriculum in retailing. Figure 8.3 is the operational version of the same program.

Although the general content stayed the same over the ten-month period between these two versions, there were changes in the sequences. These modifications were made for three main reasons. First, an analysis of existing faculty resources and of the total number of credits that could be required during a single semester or over the total four years of the program showed that several of the original

Figure 8.2. Ideal Curriculum for Retailing Major.

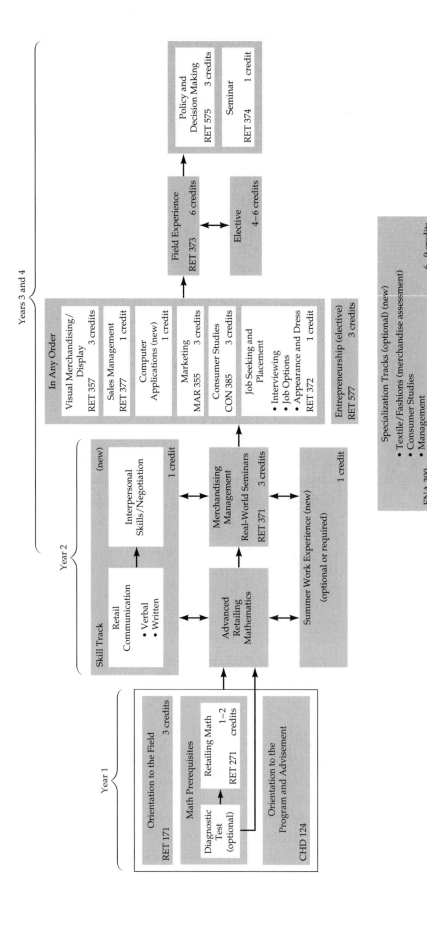

Figure 8.3. Operational Curriculum for Retailing Major.

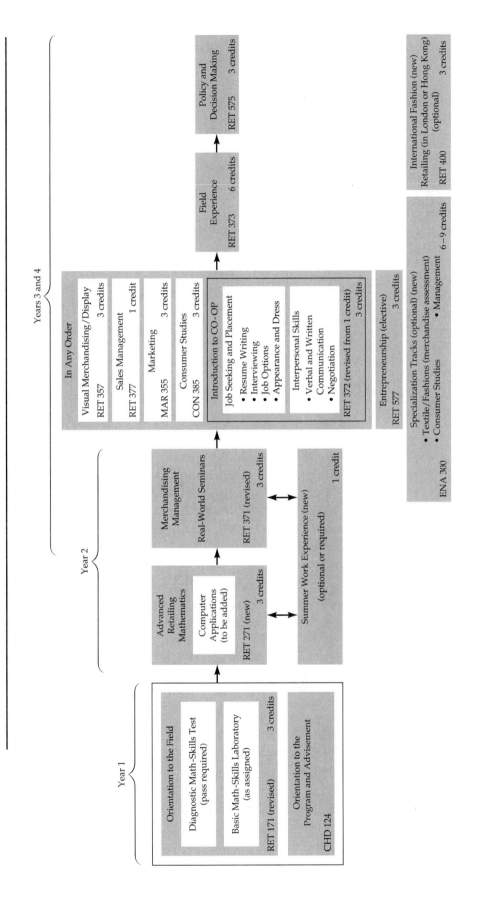

ideas could not be implemented as planned. As a result, the proposed one-credit skill track was combined with the existing one-credit Job Seeking and Placement course into a three-credit course that students are required to take prior to their field experience. The new computer-applications unit, rather than standing alone as an upper-division requirement, was moved into the three-credit Advanced Retailing Mathematics course.

The second major reason for modifications was the effectiveness of some of the courses. Data showed that the single Retailing Mathematics course was not successful, mostly because passing the diagnostic math test, while encouraged, was not required. Consequently, students who had avoided mathematics throughout their academic careers entered this important course inadequately prepared. In the revised program students are required to pass a diagnostic test of mathematics skills in order to continue in the retailing program. A Basic Mathematics-Skills Laboratory was added to support students identified by the test as needing additional help in meeting this requirement. As a result, student attitudes and achievement have improved.

The final reason for changes in the structure of the curriculum was the support found outside the department for cooperative programs. For example, with the support of the university's Division of International Programs Abroad, retailing-related course offerings were developed in both London and Hong Kong as part of the final-semester-abroad program.

In the modification effort information collected from recruiters, employers, and alumni had a direct impact on the computer-applications unit, the communications area, and the interpersonal skills area and strongly supported the increased emphasis on basic mathematics.

In the final version of this program only one of the required courses was new. However, three others, while retaining their course names and numbers, underwent major revision. In two of these, changes in credit were also made.

Course Projects: Factors to Consider

As noted earlier, the focus in curriculum projects now will shift to the beginning design steps for those courses that are either new or in need of major revision. In course projects, however, you will have enough detailed information at the end of this phase so that Phase II, which includes, production, implementation, evaluation, and revision can begin (Figure 8.1). Once a course project begins, as much time or more is spent on reaching the operational design (the last step in the design phase) as is required for the production, implementation, and evaluation phases that follow.

When the operational diagram is completed for a course, each instructional component or unit has been specified (options, remedial units, seminars, large-group meetings, term activities, and topics for independent study or special projects), and the overall sequence of these units has been determined. In addition, the entire program is placed in a realistic time frame. Although modification continues throughout the entire developmental process, the changes beyond this point are usually relatively minor, with little effect on the overall design. As a result, it should be possible at the completion of the operational diagram for you to assign the development of specific units to other faculty if more than one faculty member is involved and to schedule implementation or field testing. It is often a good idea to complete Phase I (design) by the end of the spring semester so that the summer can be used (if time and funding are available) to select and produce instructional materials, design syllabi, and construct tests to meet the goal of fall implementation.

The entire instructional program is based on the decisions that are now being made. The modification from ideal to operational design is based on several factors, each directly affecting the course that evolves. Attention at this time to all these factors, especially goals, time, and resources, is essential.

Goals

While individual lessons or class objectives are dealt with in the production phase of a project, the major instructional approach of a course must be decided here. If the major focus of the course is on information dissemination, lectures and independent study become the obvious instructional modes. If the major emphasis is on problem solving, critical thinking, and other more sophisticated goals, instruction will be built around laboratories, small-group activities, and practical experiences. If speaking skills are to be developed, the time necessary for presentations must be built into the instructional sequence. The development of interpersonal skills requires time for group meetings and planning. At this point the consequences of having instruction be content-focused or learning-centered become apparent. Each objective for the course suggests a variety of instructional approaches. Chapter Eleven describes how to select the appropriate instructional approach for the goals you have established.

Time

How many hours a week are students available for instruction, and when are they available? Is the schedule flexible? Can the period be extended? Is there time for independent study and teamwork?

At first, implementing individualized instruction and flexible scheduling may create havoc for a registrar, but administrative policies must serve the academic needs of the program. Flexible-credit and continuous-registration options can improve the quality of your course or program. Unfortunately, this flexibility is sometimes difficult to develop, especially in state systems where central-office controls may severely limit local administrative flexibility.

You must also take into consideration the time students have to complete assignments outside of class and the number of days students have between classes. Whether the institution is on a semester, trimester, or quarter system has a direct effect on the design of a course. In some scheduling systems the limited time between class sessions severely limits the amount of work students can be expected to do outside the classroom.

At this point you must also directly address the needs of adult and commuting students. In one project the faculty found that combining four three-credit courses into two six-credit courses meeting six hours a week produced more flexibility and more time for small-group work within the class. In this format classes could meet as a group for one hour or so and then break into teams for project work and special assignments, thus ensuring that commuting students could participate since these important activities were taking place during regular class time.

Resources

Several kinds of resources should also be considered as you design your course.

Human Resources.   As faculty we have a wide range of human resources available to us as we explore the best possible way of promoting learning; these resources are often overlooked and underutilized. At this point in the process you should explore the range of options available to you.

Within your institution faculty inside or outside your department may be willing to teach the course jointly with you or to assist in their area of specialization. The course you are developing may be far stronger if it is jointly offered by several departments. Or you may decide to develop a link between two courses that are interrelated. These ventures could range from combining students from several courses into project teams (where the specialization from each course is essential for success) to formal coordination between writing and speech courses and a disciplinary course. In this kind of coordination the paper is written or the speech is delivered in a content-focused course but is a formal assignment in both courses. Each paper or presentation is evaluated by both the content expert and the specialist in communication, with each focusing on his or her area of expertise. For the student the importance of speaking or writing within a discipline is reinforced, and the final result is far better than if the courses are not combined.

On many campuses highly talented teaching assistants can play a variety of roles from handling laboratory sections and assisting with logistics to being responsible for entire sections or areas of instruction. Increasingly, faculty are also using upper-division students as tutors, small-group discussion leaders, or project advisers in lower-division courses. These peer tutors not only improve the quality of the course but benefit from the learning experience. Although such students are often paid, others volunteer as part of an assignment in another course or for credit.

Other on-campus resources we tend to overlook are the many administrators who have been outstanding teachers. At Syracuse University the College of Arts and Sciences has used several top administrators, including the academic vice chancellor, vice presidents, deans, and directors, to help staff their Freshman Forums, a one-credit orientation to the university and to being an effective learner. Those involved have found the experience personally rewarding, stimulating, and enlightening. Most were thrilled at the opportunity to return to the classroom and spend time with students.

A host of human resources are also available to you off campus. Although there are budgetary implications, part-timers or faculty from other institutions in your area may fill a gap or meet a need. The wide range of experts in the community can be an invaluable resource. Business and government leaders and other practitioners, many of whom may be alumni, can bring to your classroom "real-world" expertise. Native speakers of other languages who are living in the community, often the wives and husbands of students or faculty, can contribute to foreign-language courses. How to best involve these people will be determined by your needs and their availability.

The involvement of others is, however, never easy. It takes time to locate them and requires careful coordination of schedules. For example, although team teaching can bring significant new dimensions into your program, it has disadvantages (Exhibit 8.1). You will have to decide when the results are worth the effort. Select the combination of talents that can provide for your students the most effective learning opportunity without creating an impossible logistical problem for you.

Do not assume that other people will not want to be involved. Individuals often provide their services because they enjoy doing so. Other departments may be willing to make resources available because it opens up for them a new group of students or with the

Exhibit 8.1. Team Teaching: Advantages and Disadvantages.

Advantages

- Enthusiastically supported by students, when it works well.
- Enthusiastically supported by faculty as a means of professional development and collegiality.
- Can be an inexpensive way for a faculty member to prepare to teach in a new subject area of discipline.
- Demonstrates commitment of institution to teaching and to lively interchange of ideas between faculty members; excellent marketing tool.
- Wonderful vehicle for interdisciplinary education (for both the students and participating faculty members).

Disadvantages

- Requires unique skills and attitudes among participating faculty members to be successful.
- Expensive for institution (if participating instructors receive full-credit for teaching the course) or faculty member (if participating faculty receive partial credit, but are expected to or want to attend all class sessions).
- Tendency for faculty not to attend all class sessions especially if they have heavy teaching loads; thus the course becomes sequentially taught rather than team taught.
- Often requires extensive preparation; faculty members generally are used to working alone and are unfamiliar with subject matter outside their specialty.
- Often produces fragmented presentations due to limited preparation time.
- The larger the team, the more often there tends to be discontinuity or lack of integration between individual faculty presentations.
- As team size increases, faculty attendance tends to drop off, sense of responsibility for the course decreases.
- Tendency of faculty to treat teammates' specialty areas as sacrosanct produces shared classroom rather than true team teaching situation.

understanding that you can provide services for them in return. A dean or provost may have funds specifically set aside to support innovation and academic improvements. If you need student help, you can often arrange compensatory credit for these students. Upper-classmen and graduate students often elect to earn experience credit through their academic unit if the project relates to their field of study. You will be surprised how easily you can involve others when you have solid justification for doing so and ask the right people.

Computers.　Several additional resources are extremely important as you determine the structure of your course. On the top of the list is computer availability. What percentage of your students have their own computers? On a growing number of campuses purchasing a computer is a requirement. But you must make sure that the computers the students own can handle the system and memory your assignments will require. Are appropriate computer clusters available on campus, and what is their availability? Will you need to request the use of specific classrooms? The answers to these questions will determine whether you can use e-mail for networking among students or between yourself and your students, whether you can build the resources of the World Wide Web into your planning, and the type of assignments you can give your students. See Chapter Twelve for further discussion of this topic.

Community Resources.　Other resources such as museums and art galleries in your community should be examined for possible use in your course. In such areas as music, art, literature, and history, related exhibits, concerts, and plays may be available in your community or from a national source. What resources do local libraries contain? How can you use them?

Instructional Materials.　Already-developed instructional materials should be examined before new materials are developed. Are there commercial series or packages of materials that you can use? Commercially available programmed or computer-based units if effective and if designed for the specific population involved are ideal for remedial work, for example.

Space.　Limitations of space may also force major changes in the design and content of your program. How large are the lecture halls, and can media be used effectively in them? It may be necessary to modify the course design substantially if there are not enough seminar rooms available for group work or if the rooms are not available at key times. Similarly, in a science course the availability of laboratory stations and equipment is an important consideration. Creative use of the space available, however, is also an option. Some faculty are finding that even in a fixed-seat auditorium their students can work together for five to ten minutes at a time simply by turning in their seats.

Funding.   How much money is available for development and implementation? Are there funds to support your work over the summer or to permit your release from other assignments? Does your college or university have a small grant program that can fund innovations in teaching or course design? A growing number of institutions have such a program, and the ways available funds can be used are often flexible. If disposable materials must be used or if students frequently use equipment that must be replaced or repaired regularly, can a course fee be instituted? Can some of the new materials be sold to the students, reducing the cost to the department? You are always operating with fiscal constraints, which may require you to design one course to handle more students for the same amount, a second course to cut costs, and a third to make better use than it now does of existing resources.

Your final course design will, moreover, be affected not only by the total funds available for development and implementation but also on occasion by restrictions on how money can be spent. Most funding sources, particularly the federal government, specifically limit how and where grant money can be spent. For example, certain grant dollars may be available only for staffing and personnel, whereas other funds must be used only for the purchase of equipment and materials. The ideal is to have maximum flexibility in developing the instructional design.

In addition you must keep in mind what resources will be available once your program becomes operational. If a grant supports development and pilot testing, make sure the course can continue after these funds are used up. All too many innovative programs developed with foundation or governmental support have died soon after their subsidies were withdrawn. Interdisciplinary courses, too, can be a particular problem if faculty are not rewarded for their participation. The excitement of being involved in an innovative project is brief.

Students

The data you collected earlier on the students now play a major role in the design of your course. How many students do you anticipate will enroll, and who are they? What learning experiences have they had? Will additional orientation be required to smooth course implementation? Are there students with identifiable attitudes, problems, backgrounds, or strengths who should be separated at certain times for specialized instruction? How many commuting students do you have? If you have an adult population, what experiences will they bring to your classroom? Should special units be included to build on students' interests? How many students can be expected to select certain options? How many will probably have to be assigned to remedial units? Do some students have related experiences that suggest they should be given exemptions or that they could be used as resource persons? Can more students be accommodated by identifying the most capable and exempting them from modules they have already mastered? If you have adult students, do they need some review? A brief survey given to your students on the first day of class can tell you a lot about their interests and backgrounds. By including review questions in this survey, you can also ascertain whether students have the necessary prerequisites.

The location of the students and the times they are available can also affect your plans. Full-time students allow design options that are not possible when a class has many part-time students who are available for only a few hours a week. A course that relies primarily on independent learning, team activities, internships, or off-campus assignments must be designed far differently than the standard class. This factor is becoming increasingly important as a growing number of institutions explore the potential of distance education.

Related Research

Which approaches and techniques work, and which do not? What instructional options do you have? What has been tried elsewhere, and what happened when it was? If an approach did not work, why didn't it? Are some of your projects the same as those being undertaken at other institutions, and how are they different? For example, research on the use of audiocassettes or e-mail for grading papers can have immediate significance for freshman composition courses and others that require a great deal of writing and for distance learning. Three excellent sources for research on instructional approaches and on the application of technology in teaching are Barbara Gross Davis's *Tools for Teaching* (1993), Wilbert McKeachie's *Teaching Tips* (1994), and the ERIC Clearinghouse on Information and Technology Resources at Syracuse University (315–443–3640; eric@ericir.syr.edu). Another resource you should check is the faculty-support unit on your campus. Many of these centers or offices have comprehensive libraries on teaching and learning and a retrieval system that will make your work even easier.

Unfortunately, approaches that are not successful are tried again and again by those who regard their efforts and skills as unique and who consider past results irrelevant. Use existing materials, and learn from the experience of others. Although many failures are not reported in detail, it is wise to study related projects at other institutions. A phone call or letter to those working on a similar project often proves extremely helpful, and if travel funds are available, a visit to such a project can also be useful. Unfortunately, national recognition does not necessarily correlate with either quality or replicability. In many instances the recognition a project receives may result more directly from the fact that particular external agencies or foundations supported the effort than from the quality and practicality of the project itself.

Can a successful project be replicated, or is success the result of a single outstanding faculty member or unique circumstances? Are there both positive and negative features of a particular technique, and what are they? What have been the experiences, for example, at Michigan State, MIT, Maricopa Technical Community College (Phoenix), Carnegie-Mellon, Brigham Young, San Jose State University, and Miami-Dade Community College, where courses have been developed to include major instructional-technology applications? Which applications have the faculty found most useful, and what suggestions do they have for implementation?

If you are exploring *service learning,* you will be interested in the experiences of Portland State University, Indiana University/Purdue University at Indianapolis, Drexel University, Bentley College, Evergreen State College, LaGuardia Community College, and the University of Colorado at Boulder, which have tried to interrelate the classroom and the community. If you are dealing with students who must travel long distances or who live in isolated areas, check the creative applications of technology that have been implemented at the University of Miami, the University of Hawaii, the University of Guelph, Empire State College in New York, University College at the University of Maryland, the British Open University, the University of South Africa, and Sydney Technical College in Australia. Each of these institutions serves large numbers of off-campus students by using various approaches to distance learning. These campuses can provide you with examples of successful efforts and warn you about unsuccessful ways to bring discussion and interaction into this nontraditional setting.

How useful and cost-effective are the interactive video units developed at University College (University of Maryland) and Utah State University? Is the evaluation approach that is used successfully at Alverno College transferable to larger campuses with a wider range of programs and more heterogeneous student populations? Whether it be the use of the case method in business courses at Harvard University or the use of journal assignments in the writing-across-the-curriculum program at Miami University, much useful information is available from other institutions.

Capitalize on the successes and failures of other institutions, and use existing materials whenever they meet your needs. Not to do so is a waste of your time, talent, and resources. You will also find useful information in the books and periodicals, many noted throughout this book, that focus on various instructional and assessment techniques. Time spent now in exploring options and what others have learned will significantly reduce the problems you face later on.

Grading and Scheduling Options

Your grading system may also have to be revised if new credit structures and time frames are introduced—an additional problem for the registrar and, if it is used, for the computer center. Minicourses and credit options require an administrative system that allows additional credits to be earned and easily recorded.One way to maximize schedule flexibility is to block-schedule a course, as was done in the introductory course in religion described in Resource E. A subject may traditionally be taught three hours a week, but scheduling it twice weekly for two hours greatly increases the options because every student can meet during any of those four hours. This schedule, for example, permits the use of two-hour classes or two one-hour sessions running back to back. When nontraditional scheduling is planned, it is important to explain to students that although the course may be scheduled four or five hours a week, they will not be required to attend all these sessions. The amount of time allocated to all the instructional units must equal the total time allotted for the semester. If a continuous-registration system, flexible credit, or the flexible use of space makes sense for the project, get the registrar involved early. When such decision makers have some ownership in the project, they can often be helpful.

As all these factors are explored, you will be able to outline the course as it will be implemented. At this stage expect most changes to be modest. During the preliminary design period, major additions and deletions and changes in content are common; as you move from the ideal to the possible fine tuning will be more usual.

Some minor modifications may occur in the design of a course or curriculum during the production stage that follows, but most of the remaining changes take place after field testing or initial implementation. These later adjustments are based on the data collected during the initial offering of the new or revised program.

Case Study: Introductory Philosophy Course

Figures 8.4 and 8.5 diagram an introductory philosophy course, Writing and Philosophical Analysis. This course was developed specifically to permit students to meet the writing requirement of the Syracuse University Arts and Sciences Core Curriculum. Notice how the writing emphasis has been built into the entire fabric of the course. The two drafts represent the changes that took place in a single design meeting. In units II, III, and IV the instructional sequence became more clearly defined, and one section in Unit III was eliminated to reduce the grading load on the instructor. In addition, although the number of papers increased, the length of many was reduced, and types of essays required was also determined.

Summary

This chapter discussed moving from the ideal to an operational program. You can use the topics discussed here as benchmarks when you develop the operational design of your curriculum or course. This and the preceding chapters have examined some courses and curricula that are traditional in design and others that are unusual in their concept and structure. Although these courses vary substantially in design and sequencing, each was produced using the same model for development.

After the operational sequence is complete, production, implementation, and evaluation can begin. A major advantage of this approach is that once the operational elements of the instructional sequence are identified, many of the specific units can be developed simultaneously (if more than one faculty member is involved) because each unit has general objectives, a time frame, and a clear relationship to the other components. The number of units that can be undertaken at one time and the time that can be saved are limited only by the availability of faculty. The following chapters discuss in detail the development of outcome statements and the instructional design and technology options available to you as you implement the course that you have designed.

Figure 8.4. Ideal Design for Introductory Philosophy Course.

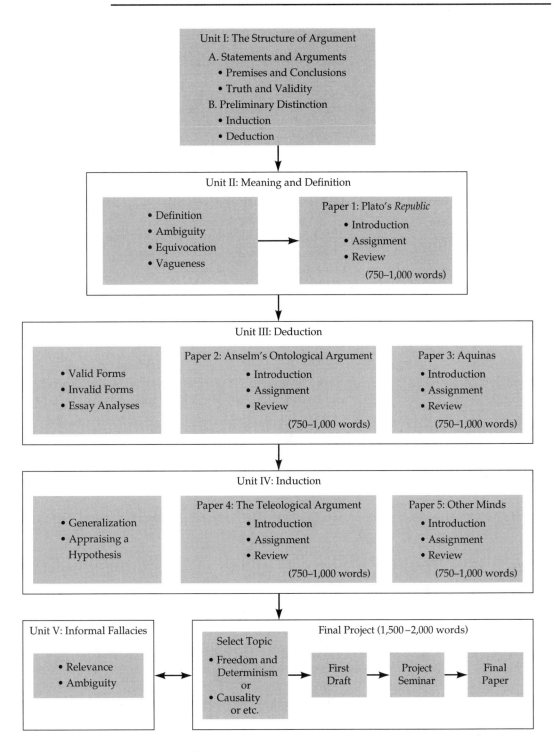

Credit: Stewart Thau.

Figure 8.5. Operational Design for Introductory Philosophy Course.

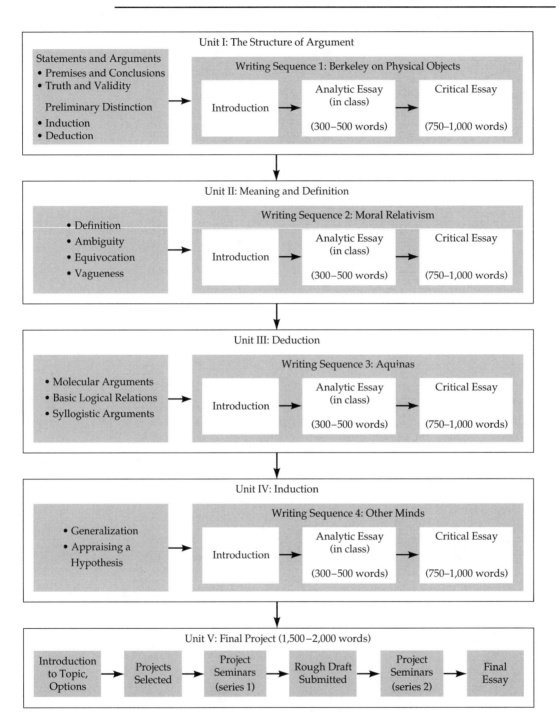

Credit: Stewart Thau.

CHAPTER 9

Clarifying Instructional Goals and Objectives

In previous chapters I described the importance of developing a clear statement of instructional goals for your course stated in terms of student performance. These statements will serve as your starting point as you consider how learning should occur and how students should be assessed. In this chapter I describe the qualities of well-written objectives and provide you with an approach to developing them that faculty have found to be efficient and effective. I will then, in the following chapter, discuss in detail the relationship between your instructional goals and your evaluation of students' performance and show how these data can be used to improve your course.

Once the outline of a course is complete (Phase I), the production, implementation, and evaluation activities begin (Phase II). During this phase several activities take place:

- Objectives are specified.
- Evaluation procedures and instruments are developed.
- Methods or strategies of instruction are chosen.
- Materials are selected or developed (or both).
- New units and materials are field-tested (when possible).
- The program is implemented, evaluated, and when needed, revised.

During this phase you should anticipate that you will make further changes in your design. Although these modifications are

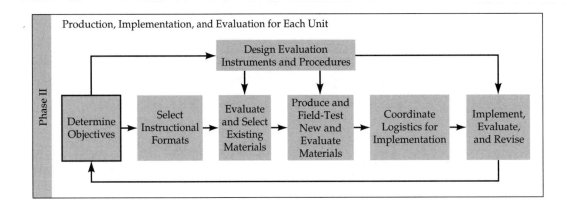

usually minor, they can determine the overall success of your project. Changes usually take place in two areas: time and content. If it becomes clear that the specified objectives cannot be reached in the time allotted, some objectives and content may be eliminated or modified or moved to other courses while other units are given more time. Even after implementation most courses undergo fine tuning as problems are identified and addressed, changes occur in the discipline, adjustments are made in the content, or other faculty with different strengths and backgrounds enter the program. This chapter focuses on the first step of this phase: determining objectives. Later chapters will cover the other steps in Phase II.

As you move through this first step, take care to build the broader, more general goals of the curriculum into the objectives of your course. As I have noted previously, these non-discipline-specific objectives exist for every course; they include those skills and competencies that every student needs after graduation—the abilities to write and speak effectively, to work well with others, to engage in critical thinking, and so on. One of your challenges will be to identify those basic goals that fit appropriately within your course.

Matching Assessment and Instructional Methods to Objectives

A report by the National Institute of Education, *Involvement in Learning* (1984), called for increased emphasis on undergraduate teaching and learning and concluded that "institutions should be accountable, not only for stating their expectations and standards, but for assessing the degree to which these ends have been met" (p. 21). This report and several other major publications in the mid-1980s began to focus the nation's attention on problems associated with the performance of the American system of higher education. These early reports and those that followed have led to a more direct legislative role in higher education.

State and national political leaders have championed the establishment of state and national standards in response to these reports, and institutions are being pressed to make appropriate changes in courses and curricula to implement assessment programs that will demonstrate whether outcomes are positive. The success of these initiatives depends on six factors: the quality of the goals that are developed, whether these broad operational goals are stated in performance terms, whether these broad goals are translated into course-specific goals, the match between the objectives and the assessment instruments (at all levels of instruction), the match between the objectives and the instructional methods selected, and the involvement and ownership that individual faculty and academic departments have in the overall effort. These factors must be considered by those involved in course and curriculum design if the assessment movement is to succeed in preparing students to meet the demands placed upon them by the society in which they will live and work. Otherwise the likely result will be friction among faculty, administrators, and state officials, weakening the institutions the movement set out to improve and failing to meet the needs of our students.

In Resource F you will find a description of how one institution, Truman State University, implemented a campuswide assessment initiative. In their introduction to the report on which this case study is based, the authors make the following observation (Magruder, McManis, and Young, 1996, p. 1):

> Assessment can have a profound transformation impact on an institution. For this result to occur, however, such core values as the improvement of student learning through the systematic collection of performance-related data and information must become integrated into the institution's culture. Successful assessment is much more than techniques, processes, or even outcomes; it is a cultural issue that affects how a community of scholars defines its work and its responsibilities to its students. Significantly, the culture of assessment is typically a somewhat unstable arrangement that requires continual nurture and support even at an institution with undergraduate education at the heart of its mission. A vigorous assessment program will require the faculty to step outside the security of their disciplines or departments, to view student learning from a holistic perspective, and to accept collective responsibility for the success of their institution's educational program. In the contemporary academy this level of commitment is neither easy to initiate nor easy to sustain. Yet, the rewards for success can be enormous for both faculty and students.

Assessment is only one important element in the academic program. The quality of the improvement in higher education is determined also by the instruction that takes place. As Theodore Marchese (1987, p. 8) writes in his review of the assessment movement, "Assessment *per se* guarantees nothing by way of improvement, no more than a thermometer cures a fever. Only when used in combination with good instruction (that evokes involvement in coherent curricula, etc.) in a program of improvement, can the device strengthen education." However, both instruction and assessment start with a statement of instructional goals. Without well-stated and appropriate objectives a good instructional program cannot be developed, and assessment lacks a basis on which to collect data or make decisions.

In this case study you will find a discussion of the process that was followed, the problems that were encountered, and the impact of the initiative.

Importance of Stating Objectives

Robert Mager (1975) tells the story of a sea horse who, with money in hand, swims off to seek his fortune. After purchasing flippers and a jet-propelled scooter to speed up his travels, he comes across a shark. The shark informs him that if the sea horse swims into the shark's mouth, he will find his fortune. The sea horse follows this advice and is never heard from again. The moral of this fable is that if you are not sure where you are going, you are likely to end up someplace you do not want to be.

If we are to determine whether academic programs are successful, we must initially determine the goals of courses and curricula. We must state in specific terms what we expect our students to be able to do and then design evaluation instruments and procedures that adequately assess whether students meet these criteria at the end of the instructional program.

In addition to forming the base on which assessment programs must be designed, clearly stated performance objectives offer important advantages at the course and program levels:

- Fairness in both testing and grading is facilitated.
- The goals of the course, its content, and the evaluation procedures are both consistent and interrelated.
- Objectives allow evaluators to determine which practices and materials are effective and which are not.
- The emphasis is changed from what faculty members must cover to what a student should be able to do as a consequence of instruction.

- A logical instructional structure is communicated by identifying a sequence of objectives and thus content—that is, the student must be able to do *a* before he or she can do *b*.

- Communication among faculty and between faculty and support staff is improved.

- Self-evaluation by the students is encouraged because they know what is expected of them.

- Efficient student learning is facilitated and anxiety is reduced because the students are provided with direction and they know what the instructional priorities are.

- Students understand how the course relates to other courses and to institutional goals.

Misconceptions About Objectives

A major obstacle for the assessment movement has been and continues to be the necessity of stating outcomes in performance terms. In their report on over eighty course and curriculum projects, Bergquist and Armstrong (1986) noted that stating goals in performance terms was the first major problem. "While viewed by the architects of Project QUE (Quality Undergraduate Education) as the foundation of academic planning, the outcomes approach was one of the more controversial elements of the project. The crux of the challenge was aptly described by one campus coordinator (who chose to remain anonymous): 'The major shift to describing program goals in terms of student outcomes required effort on the part of faculty, most of whom had conceptualized their teaching in terms of their content area rather than with reference to student outcomes'" (p. 82).

The authors concluded, however, that although focusing on the results of learning did not gain total acceptance among the several hundred faculty and administrators who were involved, at the end of the project the majority viewed the approach as both practical and essential.

Unfortunately, the use of the term *behavioral objectives* has been a second major hurdle to overcome. Behavioral objectives were defined in terms of minutia, leading to long lists of steps toward limited goals. The result was frustration on the part of the faculty who were most open to experimentation and change. In *On College Teaching* (Milton and Associates, 1978, p. 3), Ohmer Milton, in reviewing Robert M. Barry's early and excellent chapter on clarifying objectives in the same book, writes, "In my judgment the weakest area of classroom instruction is that of specifying course objectives. He [Barry] quite properly avoids the unwarranted simplicity of much that is written about college course objectives—a simplicity especially true of many treatises about 'behavioral objectives.' All too often, this concept has been carried to ridiculous extremes and has earned a resulting contempt among senior faculty who are now in leadership roles." No wonder that as it developed its statewide assessment program, New Jersey (State of New Jersey College Outcomes Evaluation Program Advisory Committee, 1987) diligently avoided using the term behavioral objectives, focusing instead on college *outcomes*, another name for behavioral objectives.

Learning outcomes need not be low-level cognitive skills. Many faculty have come to equate a behavioral objective with a multiple-choice, true-false, or similar selected-response format. This misconception is unfortunate as well as incorrect. Objectives legitimately can include changes in attitude and in performance skills. The students' abilities to relate philosophies to concepts and to defend their answers, to relate history to current events, to design a structure or write an article that meets prestated criteria, and to perform cooperatively within a small group are examples of valid higher-order instructional outcomes that can be measured.

The way the assessment approach was described to faculty deterred its acceptance. Because many of the early advocates of stating goals in performance terms focused on minutiae and on complex classification systems, they alienated the very people they were hoping to convert. Horror stories from these early efforts still abound.

From Broad Statements to Specifics

However important broad course and curricular goals may be, you need also to develop statements that are useful to you and to your students—objectives that are clear and concise and that can be measured within the framework of the instructional unit.

As discussed previously, however, before you develop your course-specific objectives, you should refer to other, more general statements created by the college, university, or state. Because individual courses are the vehicles for developing many of these general competencies, faculty are responsible for including within their statements course objectives that are content- and discipline-specific and appropriate objectives from the broader list. Goal statements must become increasingly specific as they move from the national and state levels to the college or university, to the school, to the department curriculum, and finally to the course. In most instances the more specific goals are also more easily measured.

In addition to the broad goals you may be addressing in your course that are not discipline-specific, there may be others that together constitute a complex goal that will be reached later in a student's academic program. For example, the Task Force on the Student Experience of the Faculty of Arts and Sciences, Rutgers University, Newark, New Jersey, compiled a list of the competencies they believe describe the "qualities of the liberally educated person" (Resource G). The qualities, characteristics, abilities, and competencies in this list are described in observable and measurable terms. However, as the following examples demonstrate, these characteristics still require additional specification before student performance can be assessed.

These are two of the competency statements in the category of "scientific reasoning":

1. [The student] demonstrates an understanding of the scientific method of inquiry, including accurate measurement based on observation and the use of controlled experiment.
2. [The student] identifies the assumptions and limitations of the scientific method of inquiry and distinguishes the extent to which this method is applicable in various situations and contexts in all disciplines and fields of inquiry.

The faculty would have to adapt these statements, rewriting them to apply to their specific courses. They would have to describe how the student will demonstrate "an understanding of the scientific method of inquiry" or how the student will identify "the assumptions and limitations of the scientific method" in an applied context.

This problem of moving from general program goals to operational goals at the course level is one that all faculty members face. For example, Exhibit 6.4 is a list of the thirteen basic learner outcomes as articulated by the College of Agriculture at the University of Minnesota. These include such statements as "make sound, responsible judgments on the ethical policy issues involved in the production of food and fiber" and "apply an historical perspective to the role of science and technology in agriculture." The challenge for faculty teaching within the program is how to move from these broad statements to specific learning outcomes—that is, what the students have to do to show that they can apply a "historical perspective" and "make sound, responsible judgments."

In the end then, you, as the faculty member responsible for the course, must write your own objectives. Although a course may fulfill the requirements of others (professional agencies, the board of trustees, the university, the department), the objectives must be developed to satisfy the individual responsible for instruction.

Writing Objectives

To be useful, objectives should contain three basic elements:

- A verb that describes an observable action
- A description of the conditions under which the action takes place: "when given x, you will be able to . . . "
- The acceptable performance level—that is, what percentage of correct answers will be considered acceptable, how many errors will be permitted, how many and which examples must be included, and so on

In addition, before you begin this task the student for whom the material is designed should be described, and the prerequisites should be identified. Problems often are the result of a mismatch between the students we have designed the course for and the abilities and experiences of those who have enrolled.

Use clear, concise words to describe student behavior in these objectives, words not open to misinterpretation. Mager (1975) provides the following suggestions for terms to avoid and terms to use.

Words Open to Many Interpretations	*Words Open to Fewer Interpretations*
To know	To write
To understand	To recite
To really understand	To identify
To appreciate	To sort
To fully appreciate	To solve
To grasp the significance of	To construct
To enjoy	To build
To believe	To compare
To have faith in	To contrast

Categorizing Objectives

Although there are almost as many ways of categorizing objectives as there are authors of textbooks on the subject, the use of such a system at the course level is questionable (although it may be helpful to categorize goals when you are reporting them outside your institution). Exhibit 9.1 provides one approach to considering the objectives appropriate for your courses. Although this detailed approach has been in use for thirty years, many consider it *the* way to categorize goals. It will be up to you to organize your objectives in the way you are most comfortable with. However, it is rarely cost-effective for you to spend a great deal of time analyzing the type or level of your objectives. Far more essential is ensuring that useful statements are

Exhibit 9.1. Taxonomies of Educational Objectives.

Cognitive Objectives

1. Knowledge—Recognizing or recalling facts, terminology, principles, theories, etc.

2. Comprehension—Simple understanding; ability to describe in one's own words, to paraphrase, to give examples, or to translate from one form to another (words to numbers).

3. Application—Using material in a new way; applying concepts, laws or theories in practical situations to solve problems.

4. Analysis—Understanding the organizational structure of material as well as content—breaking it down into component parts, drawing comparisons between elements, distinguishing cause and effect relationships.

5. Synthesis—Combining the parts into a *new* whole; creatively arranging or rearranging to get patterns and structures new to the learner.

6. Evaluation—Comparing material to known standards; judging or decision-making based on appropriate criteria—either internal criteria (e.g., organization) or external criteria (e.g., relevance to purpose).

Affective Objectives

1. Receiving—Being aware or willing to attend to something; learner is passive but attentive, listening with respect.

2. Responding—Complying to given expectations; learner participates actively by reacting as well as showing awareness.

3. Valuing—Accepting importance of the attitude; learner displays behavior consistent with a belief or attitude though not forced to comply.

4. Organization—Committing oneself to a set of values; bringing together different values and resolving conflicts between them; building an internally consistent value system.

5. Characterization—Behaving according to a characteristic "life style" or value system; maintaining a consistent philosophy regardless of surrounding conditions.

Source: For cognitive objectives: adapted from Bloom and others, 1956; for affective objectives: adapted from Krathwohl, Bloom, and Masia, 1964.

written, that they include all the elements that should be addressed, that they are measurable within your course, and that when students reach the end of the course, you can be confident that the goals you established have indeed been met.

In one project in the School of Management at Syracuse University, learning outcomes were grouped within the basic themes of a six-credit course on technology, allowing the faculty on the curriculum committee to see how the elements of the program were interrelated and were built on one another. Later on this same approach was used to communicate to the students the goals of the course and what they were expected to achieve.

Process Objectives

In some instances the overall objective focuses more on the process than on the students' ability to reach a specific outcome. Such an objective might, for example, be conceptualizing a value. In their discussion of how to test the conceptualization of a value, Krathwohl, Bloom, and Masia (1964, p. 157) write, "The process of conceptualization is largely cognitive, involving abstraction and generalization; . . . the emphasis is less on the *quality* of the cognitive process[es] than on the fact that they are being used."

In testing the conceptualization of a value you might use examples in which there are no right or wrong answers and ask the student to express a point of view. Here, you are more interested in the process the student used to reach the point of view than in the conclusion. For evaluation purposes, focus is then on the process used, the alternatives explored, and the student's justification for the conclusion. Or you might ask your students to list a number of alternative solutions to a problem and then to defend the solution selected.

An Almost Painless Way to Specify Objectives

When we faculty are asked point-blank to state our instructional (or behavioral) objectives, we have several reactions. First, we tend to resent the question; second, we often produce far more objectives than could ever be used; and third, most of these objectives are at a trivial level because they are the easiest to write. This process has a tendency to disenchant many faculty, as it is time-consuming, often boring, and usually frustrating.

As an alternative to writing objectives in the abstract, a facilitator can help us to develop strong, clear objectives by playing the role of the student and asking us, "If I'm your student, what do I have to do to convince you that I'm where you want me to be at the end of this lesson, unit, or course?" Out of this discussion will come performance objectives that are measurable and that tend to be far more important and at a higher level than would be produced otherwise. This process, while difficult at times, is generally comfortable and efficient, and produces the specific statements that are needed for the development of projects.

Specifying Grading Practices

As a final step for evaluation purposes you need to establish a standard of performance that will explain the basis for your grades. In some instances a grade may cover a number of objectives combined within a broad level of performance. You will also have to select among grading options—for example, pass/fail or the mastery approach, where performing at a high level is the only way to pass, or more traditional A, B, and so forth. Waiting until you see how well your students have done on a test before you determine grades is a disservice to you, your course, and your students.

Representative Samples of Objectives

A sampling of objectives from various courses follows. Note that each is written directly to the students, tells them what they must do to be successful, and identifies what they must be given before they are evaluated.

- *Government.* When given a major decision made by a governmental leader, you will be able to identify the major factors that the leader had to consider and discuss why the action was taken and what apparent trade-offs were made.
- *Economics.* Demonstrate graphically and explain how a change in expectations will affect the *loanable funds market.* (Begin with an appropriately labeled graph that represents the initial equilibrium.)
- *Management.* Identify (based on readings, case studies, and/or personal experiences) those activities that are most likely to distinguish effective, well-managed technology development programs from ineffective programs.
- *Statistics.* When given two events, you will be able to determine whether they are independent or whether there is a relationship between them (that is, one event affects the probability of the other). On the basis of this determination, you will be able to select and use the appropriate rules of conditional probability to determine the probability that a certain event will occur.
- *Religion.* When given a definition of the term *religion,* you will be able to identify which of the following characteristics is emphasized: feeling, ritual activity, belief, monotheism, the solitary individual, social valuation, illusion, ultimate reality, and value.

- *Music.* On hearing musical selections, you will be able to identify those that are examples of chamber music and be able to identify the form, texture, and makeup of the ensemble.
- *Art.* When shown a print, you will be able to identify whether it is a woodcut, an etching, or a lithograph, and you will be able to list the characteristics on which this identification was based.
- *Psychology.* When given a case study, you will be able to identify whether it describes a case of schizophrenia and, if it does, which of the following schizophrenic reactions are involved: hebephrenic, catatonic, or paranoid.

Although many objectives lend themselves to this format, for others you may find this approach awkward and confining. Such broad goals as critical thinking, effective speaking and writing, interpersonal skills, leadership, and the development of a positive attitude toward a particular subject need to be described to your students in somewhat different terms. For example, if you want your students to develop the ability to manage change, one of your goals for the students at the end of the sequence might be to "identify sources of conflict between yourself and others and take steps to eliminate this disharmony." In demonstrating competence in writing, one skill for which you might hold students responsible is to "be able to incorporate information from various sources to support the hypothesis that you are developing." In Chapter Fifteen you will find several examples of how others of these broad goals can be described in detail.

Limitations of Objectives

As you establish outcomes for your course, keep in mind the limitations of objectives. Some broad objectives or goals cannot be measured given time and program limitations. In art and music, for example, a secondary goal may be to develop in the student viewing and listening habits that will last throughout a lifetime. This goal cannot be measured after a single course or even after a four-year program. In these instances you need to select as objectives the skills, knowledge, and attitudes that you believe will result in the desired behavior. Evaluation must focus on the objectives that fit within the scope of the course.

When overused, behavioral objectives can limit creativity and reduce instructional excitement. As noted earlier, instructional outcome statements are a means for selecting your instructional methodology and evaluating student performance. The process of developing and testing for specific objectives is important, but it should not preclude flexibility and, as opportunities arise, adding new elements. In addition, the larger goals of a course must always be kept in view. For example, although it will never appear on a quiz or your final examination, the primary goal of a course may be to excite the students about a subject area or field of study. This is not to suggest that we should eliminate performance-based objectives but to emphasize that although they may be necessary, they have inherent limitations that must be recognized as one develops and uses them.

Summary

No matter what the specific form, statements of objectives should do the following:

- Describe in performance terms what your goals are.
- Communicate to your students your expectations and how the students will be assessed.
- Serve as the basis for selecting instructional methods.
- Serve as the basis for your assessment of student achievement.

Keep in mind that the clearer your statement of outcomes, the easier it will be for you to design your course and assess your students' success in reaching the goals established for your academic programs.

CHAPTER 10

Designing Assessment Instruments and Procedures

Many external pressures are brought to bear on higher education to address the issues of assessment. These pressures are not new. In the mid-1980s, *Transforming the State Role in Undergraduate Education* (Education Commission of the States, 1986) stressed the importance of undergraduate education for economic and international development and challenged the states to take a direct and active role in improving the assessment of students. More recently, in his 1995 report to the Education Commission of the States, Roy Romer, governor of Colorado and chairman of the commission, spoke for many when he observed (1995, p. 1):

> I continue to be amazed at the resistance I encounter to examining whether we can measure and report on effective learning at individual institutions and provide good information to inform consumers about their choices. I also continue to be amazed at the inability of policy makers and public leaders to create meaningful and useful accountability systems for higher education. . . . It is not sufficient to rest on the laurels of past success or the record of the present. For all its rich history, there are too many signs that higher education is not taking seriously its responsibility to maintain a strong commitment to undergraduate learning; to be accountable for products that are relevant, effective and of demonstrable quality; and to provide society with the full benefits from investments in research and public service.

Equally important, if we are to be successful as teachers, we must be sure that the goals we have developed are being reached

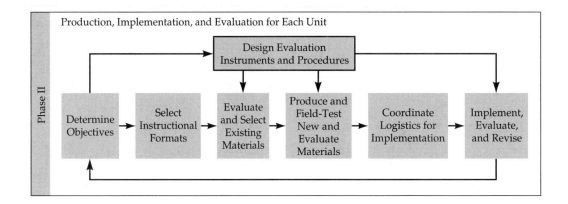

by our students and that the assumptions we are making about them are accurate; if there are problems, we need to know what they are and why they are occurring. Continual assessment is an activity that we as faculty should be engaging in even without external pressure.

In response to these concerns a major assessment movement is under way in higher education. Several states have passed legislation requiring assessment, with the regional accreditation associations finally addressing the issue as well.

Course-Related Assessment

By this point in the design process all major instructional objectives should be stated for your course and for each instructional unit. Work can now begin simultaneously in two areas: the selection and design of the evaluation procedures and instruments that are necessary both to implement the course and to determine the success of the students and the course (this chapter), and the design and production of the instructional units themselves (Chapter Eleven).

As you think through the design and implementation of your course, keep in mind that student assessment at the course level provides data both on individual student performance for grading purposes and on the overall effectiveness of instruction for identifying those areas that may require improvement. Another function, of course, is that it helps the student to assess his or her own progress in meeting course goals.

As you develop your approach to assessment, make sure it includes the more complex goals of your course and that you build it in throughout the semester. You will then have a good sense of what is and is not working and the opportunity to make adjustments immediately as problems occur.

Collecting Useful Information

Like most faculty members, you are not unfamiliar with the process of assessment. You do it all the time in assessing the quality of the work of your students and in using information to improve the quality of your courses. What most likely will be new is the care that you will be taking to ensure that data you collect measure how well your students reach the specific goals that you have established. Although evaluation specialists may help you develop certain assessment instruments and protocols, it is imperative that you play an active role in the process. As John Muffo (1996, p. 1) has observed, we as faculty will most readily accept the results of studies if we gather the data ourselves. Only when we can trust the data will we do what they imply is necessary to improve a course.

Based on the objectives that you have developed and the overall structure of the course, it is now possible to design procedures and instruments that serve four distinct purposes:

- Identifying students for remediation and exemption. Such identification requires specifying anticipated prerequisites and designing a diagnostic instrument or procedure that tests for the prerequisite abilities. Tests of this type must be very specific to permit remedial assignments to be made on the basis of individual need. Most tests used for course placement are too general for this purpose.

- Determining whether the objectives (of individual units and entire courses) are being met by measuring student performance. This includes the measurement of newly acquired skills, knowledge, and attitudes. There must be a perfect fit between the stated objectives, the content of the course, and the student evaluation instruments that will be used. All too often the objectives that are given to the students have little in common with either the content of the course or the questions that are asked on the tests and examinations. Unless all three elements are closely interrelated, significant problems will develop, and the students will become frustrated and antagonistic.

- Determining whether and how students' attitudes toward the course and the discipline or field have changed. Some courses have, as an unstated objective, the goal of improving the attitude of the student toward the field or profession. For comparison purposes, questions about attitudes can be built into course orientation activities or prerequisite tests and then into end-of-course evaluations.

- Determining whether the overall course design and the materials and procedures are efficient and effective. Survey instruments used at the end of a specific unit or entire course can collect useful data on pacing, interest, structure, and overall design.

Unfortunately our assessment of student performance is one of the areas where American education is most vulnerable. As the research indicates (Exhibit 10.1), assessment practices have generally focused on the low-level skills of recognition and recall. As a result, there are significant gaps between what we as faculty say our major goals are and the way we evaluate the competencies of our students. Research also indicates that the tests we use are often unreliable or of questionable validity, which should make us uncomfortable about the way in which grades are assigned and interpreted.

Although much is yet to be learned about student assessment and how we can document a student's overall performance, we can do a much better job than we have in the past of allowing our students to demonstrate what they have learned. A number of institutions and associations are leading the way in exploring how this can be done: Alverno College and Evergreen State College to name but two. As you move through the process of developing an assessment plan for your course, a review of the literature on this subject will reduce your work and result in a well-understood and fair assessment program for your students. You will also find that certain assessment techniques are particularly effective for specific types of learning objectives. A list of excellent references on this topic is at the end of this chapter.

Assessing Group Work

In some instances the assessment technique you use can also facilitate the learning you hope to accomplish. For example, one of the most common learning goals of core programs is the ability of the student to work effectively as a member of a team. As more and more of us integrate group work into our courses, we find that to do so successfully requires careful orchestration. The goals of the exercise have to be clear; students must understand their responsibilities; and assessment must be designed to accurately reflect the work of the group and the work of the individual.

Charles Walker (1995, pp. 4–5) has developed the Classroom Assessment Technique (CAT) to help faculty members monitor student groups and detect problems early on. He has identified the following essential steps for constructing team assignments:

(1) pick a task that is worthwhile, feasible, and best done by, or only done by, a group; (2) set task goals for the group that are specific and concrete and that allow unambiguous feedback on their accomplishment; (3) discuss and select strategies and procedures that will help

Exhibit 10.1. Research Findings on Testing and Grading.

- Most tests now in use ask for factual recognition or recall.

- Although faculty desire students to develop higher-order cognitive skills, the tests that are used rarely measure these competencies.

- When essays are used, faculty tend to emphasize knowledge of facts, and students write essays to meet this expectation.

- A small proportion of faculty (less than 20 percent) report using "problem-solving" items on essay tests.

- Grades are used primarily for external reporting and not to give feedback to students.

- The low level of classroom assessment and the lack of attention to validity and reliability call into question the results of most tests and the grades that are given.

- Publisher-provided test items tend to focus primarily on recall items.

- Nearly 50 percent of students report never or rarely having to write an essay examination or test.

Source: Primarily from Gardiner, 1996, pp. 66–68.

the group achieve its goals within the time limits that have been set; (4) define and assign roles and duties that are exclusively faithful to the goals and procedures of the group; and (5) acquire the resources (human effort and expertise, financial, informational, institutional, and time) that are necessary for the group to accomplish its goals.

As part of the model he has also developed a team response form that he finds not only helps students learn the social and organizational skills necessary but places on the group itself the responsibility for dealing with conflict and other interpersonal problems (Exhibit 10.2). Being task-focused, this approach also helps to steer faculty and students around sensitive personal and interpersonal matters that can often create major problems.

If you wish to evaluate students independently to assess their effectiveness within the group, other measures and reporting techniques will have to be used. Although you can usually assess the overall work of the group on the basis of its report and final presentation, it is more difficult to assess the level of individual contributions. Two approaches are available to resolve this problem. One method stresses from the beginning that a major goal of the activity is to improve each student's ability to work as part of a team, a competency that appears on most lists of skills a student should have achieved before graduation. In this approach students are advised that they will each receive two grades for the assignment: one for the final team report and one for their individual contribution to the

Exhibit 10.2. Group Assessment Form.

Course	_____	Section	_____
Instructor	_____	Date	_____
Name (optional)	_____	Group	_____

1. Is the work of your group worthwhile and challenging?

2. Does your group have specific goals and objectives? List the specific goals of your group on the back of this form.

3. Do the members of your group agree on the goals? Do you have consensus on the priority of these goals?

4. Has your group discussed strategies and procedures for attaining your goals? Have you identified any effective procedures?

5. Does each member of your group have a role, that is, unique responsibilities to help your group do its work? On the back, list the name of each group member and his or her specific responsibilities.

6. Does your group have the resources (member skills and knowledge, time, and other essentials) that it needs to achieve its goals?.

Source: Walker, 1995, pp. 4–5. Copyright 1995 Jossey-Bass Inc., Publishers.

team as assessed by others in their group. These assessments by team members are prepared in duplicate—one copy for the instructor and one for each team member. Stressing throughout that the goal is to help one another improve team skills prepares the students for a final one- or two-page paper reviewing the insights they have gained about their teamwork skills. But determining individual contributions in this way requires honest input from each member of the team, something that students are not comfortable doing, particularly if their evaluations are negative. An approach that does not depend on students' evaluations of their teammates is to have the groups give each member a specific responsibility for the final report or presentation, thus allowing you to evaluate the effort of the team and of its individual members.

Assessing Specific Goals

There are very focused approaches to assessment that you should explore if what they measure directly relates to the goals of your course. For example, Lloyd Bostian has identified seven general types of writing assignments that can serve as excellent tools for assessing the writing skills of students (Bostian and Lunde, 1995, p. 155, reprinted with permission of the publisher).

- 1–2 paragraph responses to questions posed in class about a reading, a lecture point just made, or an instructor's next topic. Such assignments define or explain, evaluate or criticize, propose or recommend
- 1–3 page papers synthesizing or analyzing readings, reviewing articles or book chapters, class notes, or other material
- 1–3 page benchmark papers showing knowledge students have about a course topic before instruction begins
- 2–5 page research papers, position papers, or laboratory reports
- Journals or logs containing the students' own observations and thinking about the course and material presented
- Term papers or final reports
- Essay examinations, in-class or take-home

The assessment of writing skills should be based on the answers to three basic questions: first, who will do the assessment (yourself, other faculty, graduate students, other students); second, what criteria will the reviewer use; and third, how will feedback be given to the students. Elizabeth Jones, under a grant from the U.S. Department of Education, has developed a useful Writing Goals Inventory (1994). By filling out the first three pages out of eight of this inventory you can ascertain which criteria you will emphasize in assessing writing assignments (Exhibit 10.3).

Even more specific is the National Center for Education Statistics publication *The National Assessment of College Student Learning* (Greenwood, 1994), in which several basic skills (writing, speaking, and critical thinking) are divided into their various components; each component is then defined, described, and followed by examples of how it can be assessed. For example, the following is the description of Verbal Reasoning Skills (p. 57):

Category description: The skills listed under this rubric include those that are needed to comprehend and defend against the persuasive techniques that are embedded in everyday language (also known as natural language).

Skill

Recognizing and defending against the inappropriate use of emotional and misleading language (e.g., labeling, name calling, ambiguity, vagueness, hedging, euphemism, bureaucratese, and arguments by etymology).

Examples of Use

Critical thinker (CT) recognizes the use of biased language in numerous contents such as the following examples: (1) accidental killing of US troops referred to as "friendly fire"; (2) use of labels such as "pro-choice" and "pro-life" to create favorable impressions; (3) report of research that "suggests" a finding instead of stating the results; (4) use of the term "disinformation" instead of "lies"; (5) calling an opponent

Exhibit 10.3. Writing Goals Inventory.

	Extreme Importance			Medium Importance			No Importance		
	1	2	3	4	5	6	7	8	9

(Please place an "X" in one box per item.)

Awareness and Knowledge
of Audience
Goals

College graduates should
be able to:

a. Address audiences whose
backgrounds in the topic
vary widely ☐ ☐ ☐ ☐ ☐ ☐ ☐ ☐ ☐

b. Address audiences whose
cultural and communication
norms may differ from those
of the writer ☐ ☐ ☐ ☐ ☐ ☐ ☐ ☐ ☐

c. Define their anticipated
multiple audiences ☐ ☐ ☐ ☐ ☐ ☐ ☐ ☐ ☐

d. Clearly understand their
audiences' values,
attitudes, goals, and
needs ☐ ☐ ☐ ☐ ☐ ☐ ☐ ☐ ☐

e. Consider how an audience
will use the document

f. Choose words that their
audience can understand ☐ ☐ ☐ ☐ ☐ ☐ ☐ ☐ ☐

g. Understand the relationship
between the audience and
themselves ☐ ☐ ☐ ☐ ☐ ☐ ☐ ☐ ☐

h. Understand the relationship
between the audience and
the subject material ☐ ☐ ☐ ☐ ☐ ☐ ☐ ☐ ☐

Purpose for Writing
Goals

College graduates should
be able to:

a. Be aware of the multiple
purposes and goals they are
acting on when they write ☐ ☐ ☐ ☐ ☐ ☐ ☐ ☐ ☐

b. State their purpose(s)
to their audiences ☐ ☐ ☐ ☐ ☐ ☐ ☐ ☐ ☐

Exhibit 10.3. (continued).

	Extreme Importance			Medium Importance			No Importance		
	1	2	3	4	5	6	7	8	9

(Please place an "X" in one box per item.)

c. Use vocabulary appropriate to their subject and purpose(s)

| ☐ | ☐ | ☐ | ☐ | ☐ | ☐ | ☐ | ☐ | ☐ |

d. Arrange words within sentences to fit the intended purpose(s) and audience(s)

| ☐ | ☐ | ☐ | ☐ | ☐ | ☐ | ☐ | ☐ | ☐ |

e. Use appropriate tone of voice

| ☐ | ☐ | ☐ | ☐ | ☐ | ☐ | ☐ | ☐ | ☐ |

f. Make appropriate use of creative techniques of humor and eloquence when approaching a writing task

| ☐ | ☐ | ☐ | ☐ | ☐ | ☐ | ☐ | ☐ | ☐ |

g. Draw on their individual creativity and imagination to engage their audience (e.g., using narrative, description, metaphor, and/or similar means of expression).

| ☐ | ☐ | ☐ | ☐ | ☐ | ☐ | ☐ | ☐ | ☐ |

Pre-Writing Activities
Goals

College graduates should be able to:

a. Analyze their own experience to provide ideas for writing

| ☐ | ☐ | ☐ | ☐ | ☐ | ☐ | ☐ | ☐ | ☐ |

b. Create ideas for their writing

| ☐ | ☐ | ☐ | ☐ | ☐ | ☐ | ☐ | ☐ | ☐ |

c. Retrieve material from their memories to write

| ☐ | ☐ | ☐ | ☐ | ☐ | ☐ | ☐ | ☐ | ☐ |

d. Plan the writing process, using effective writing strategies and techniques

| ☐ | ☐ | ☐ | ☐ | ☐ | ☐ | ☐ | ☐ | ☐ |

e. Clarify their policy and position before writing

| ☐ | ☐ | ☐ | ☐ | ☐ | ☐ | ☐ | ☐ | ☐ |

f. Discuss their piece of writing with someone to clarify what they wish to say

| ☐ | ☐ | ☐ | ☐ | ☐ | ☐ | ☐ | ☐ | ☐ |

Exhibit 10.3. (continued).

	Extreme Importance			Medium Importance			No Importance		
	1	2	3	4	5	6	7	8	9

(Please place an "X" in one box per item.)

	1	2	3	4	5	6	7	8	9
g. Research their subject	☐	☐	☐	☐	☐	☐	☐	☐	☐
h. Locate and present adequate supporting material	☐	☐	☐	☐	☐	☐	☐	☐	☐
i. Focus and then narrow their plan by recongizing the rhetorical problem(s) they wish to solve	☐	☐	☐	☐	☐	☐	☐	☐	☐
j. Identify problems to be solved that their topic suggests	☐	☐	☐	☐	☐	☐	☐	☐	☐

Organizing Goals

College graduates should be able to:

	1	2	3	4	5	6	7	8	9
a. Develop patterns of organization for their ideas	☐	☐	☐	☐	☐	☐	☐	☐	☐
b. Use knowledge of their subject matter to shape a text	☐	☐	☐	☐	☐	☐	☐	☐	☐
c. Use knowledge of potential audience expectations and values to shape a text	☐	☐	☐	☐	☐	☐	☐	☐	☐
d. Organize the material for more than one audience	☐	☐	☐	☐	☐	☐	☐	☐	☐
e. Create and use an organizational plan (e.g., outlines, lists, etc.)	☐	☐	☐	☐	☐	☐	☐	☐	☐
f. Select, organize, and present details to support a main idea	☐	☐	☐	☐	☐	☐	☐	☐	☐

Source: Jones, 1994, pp. 1–3 (out of eight pages). Used with permission of Elizabeth A. Jones, Ph.D., National Center on Post-Secondary Teaching, Learning, and Assessment.

a "pinko"; (6) obtaining agreement by stating "Every good American will agree that. . . "; (7) arguing that homosexuality must be sick because the word "gay" originally meant lewd and lascivious.

Description

This is an assortment of common misleading verbal techniques based on language usage in which a bias for or against a position is created with the connotative meaning of the words used to describe and define the concepts.

Many disciplines have also developed useful guidelines. For example, the Speech Communications Association has published *Criteria for the Assessment of Oral Communication* (1990, pp. 703, 750–953) and has other materials available. In addition, the publication *Evaluating Classroom Speaking* (Bock and Bock, 1981) contains a range of Speech Rating Forms, from which you can choose the one that most closely meets your needs.

In many instances the first place you should start looking for assistance in assessing specific goals is your school or department of education, the faculty-support center on your campus, the academic department where such skills are taught, or the units that deal with remediation on your campus. Most faculty and staff not only will be willing to help but will consider it a compliment to be asked.

Remember, the more specific your description of the performance expected from your students, the fewer problems you will have in developing student testing instruments and procedures. As a faculty member you have the option of selecting the means of assessment that is most appropriate for your course. Some methods may take more time and effort than others, but not using the appropriate approach is unfair to the students and also reduces the quality of your course or program. McKeachie (1994) provides an excellent review of the various types of tests, their uses and design, and discusses in some detail test administration, grading, and scoring.

Using Portfolios, Journals, and Simulations

When used well, portfolios, journals, and simulations combine quality instructional techniques with an assessment element. When portfolios are used, students are asked to demonstrate their growth in the course and their mastery of important skills by selecting materials they have created based on the specific goals of the course; as a result the students focus on course goals and reflect on their intellectual growth during the course. The process of selecting what to include in their portfolios becomes an important learning experience. Like portfolios, journals require students to think about course content as they make brief daily or weekly entries in a diary. Reviewing these records can allow you not only to judge student performance but to identify quickly any problems that exist.

Crouch and Fontaine (1994) have identified additional advantages of portfolios: they represent work over time; they do not penalize students for poor skills with which they enter the course; they stress reworking, rethinking, and revising; and they allow students to work toward a mastery level of performance by engaging them in the kind of activities experts carry out. Crouch and Fontaine also note that the portfolio assessment process helps students learn how to judge their own work and to develop their own standards.

Braskamp and Ory (1994) describe simulation as "central to performance testing." This approach, which can be used for almost every "skill or real-life situation," assesses the students' ability to perform in lifelike situations. Games, role playing, and computer simulations all fall under this broad category. Although time-consuming and labor-intensive to set up, simulations permit you to project how your students might perform in real-world situations. You might use several of these instruments and procedures, alone or in combination, as appropriate during the teaching of your course and also during the field-testing of specific instructional activities and materials.

Classroom Assessment

Although evaluation of students has tended to be based on major papers, mid-semester and final exams, and the like, Thomas Angelo and Patricia Cross (1993) suggested a different approach when they introduced *classroom assessment* in 1986. In this approach you collect data early and often on how well your students are learning and on their reactions to your course. The purpose is to "provide information and insight needed to adjust and improve teaching and learning as they occur" (Angelo, 1995, p. 1). Faculty using this approach have found that if problems exist, they can respond almost immediately by revising what they do in their classrooms and by improving their exams; as a result, learning improves. The effectiveness of this approach is based on the fact that you collect and use pertinent quality information as an integral part of your classroom, your course, and your program.

Assessment in a Curriculum or Program Context

When you are working in a broad context, focusing on entire programs or curricula, your purposes in collecting data will be the same as when you focus on an individual course: to determine whether the goals of the instructional program are being met, whether the assumptions being made are accurate, and whether and where gaps exist.

In curriculum and program projects, where others are involved, it is essential to ensure that the information that is collected is used. All too often excellent data are ignored and even suppressed. On too many campuses, faculty have little if any ownership or involvement in the assessment effort not surprisingly, consider it a waste of time. This problem can be avoided if everyone who will need to use the information is actively involved in designing the procedures and selecting the data that will be collected.

In "Assessing Learning in Programs," Farmer and Napieralski (1997, pp. 603–604) provide the following recommendations for ensuring that quality information will be collected and used in this broader context.

- The purpose of the assessment—to improve an academic program—should be clear and clearly distinguished from other forms of assessment such as the evaluation of teaching.
- Important quantitative data should be supplied not by the program under review but by departments in the institution better equipped to provide it, such as the alumni, planning, or registrar's offices.
- The faculty of the program to be assessed should be in charge of the self-study; they should, however, invite the active participation of constituencies that have a stake in the program, such as students, alumni, and faculty in cognate departments.
- Academic programs should include assessment information in the self-study, especially a public definition of program goals, an articulation of the relationship between these goals and the goals or mission of the institution, and indicators of the extent to which students are meeting program goals.
- The assessment design should be practical and flexible—constructed to reflect the special nature of the academic program and to serve the needs of those making subsequent decisions affecting the program.
- The assessment should include goal-free or open-ended interviews that can provide information for qualitative and holistic analysis.
- A spirit of open inquiry and communication should characterize the conduct of the assessment; the results of the assessment should likewise be broadly shared.
- Recommendations resulting from the assessment should include a list of actions to be taken, an assignment of responsibility for such actions, and a time frame.
- The assessment must make a difference and must have some impact on institutional planning and budgeting.
- The faculty of the program should find the reward for careful self-study and program assessment in action that leads to enhanced teaching and learning.

Summary

Assessment must be an integral part of any learning effort. Whether you are developing or using a new approach to teaching, designing or reviewing a course, or developing a curriculum, it is essential that you collect and use quality data. The success of your overall initiative will rest on two elements: on how well you mesh your assessment effort with your goals and on whether you effectively use the information you collect. It is not an easy process, but it is an essential one.

Useful References on Student Assessment

Assessment Update: Progress, Trends, and Practices in Higher Education. A bimonthly publication from Jossey-Bass, San Francisco.

Although it covers all aspects of assessment, this newsletter regularly includes useful information on specific classroom assessment tools and techniques.

Braskamp, L. A., and Ory, J. C. *Assessing Faculty Work: Enhancing Individual and Institutional Performance.* San Francisco: Jossey-Bass, 1994.

Although, as the title implies, emphasis is on the faculty member as teacher, the book contains excellent information on how to collect important data on the effectiveness of teaching. Includes sample instruments and suggestions for having a colleague help in the assessment process.

Cross, K. P., and Steadman, M. H. *Classroom Research: Implementing the Scholarship of Teaching.* San Francisco: Jossey-Bass, 1996.

Focusing on the ways you can collect and use data to improve your teaching and your courses, this book is loaded with practical advice. One suggestion: start with the index; it will get you to where you need to go.

Davis, B. G. *Tools for Teaching.* San Francisco: Jossey-Bass, 1993.

Although the primary focus of this high-quality and most practical volume is on teaching and various instructional strategies, the sections on testing and grading and on evaluation to improve teaching are also helpful.

Halpern, D. F., and Associates. *Changing College Classrooms: New Teaching and Learning Strategies for an Increasingly Complex World.* San Francisco: Jossey-Bass, 1994.

Included in a major section on assessing teaching effectiveness and learning outcomes is an excellent chapter on using student portfolios as an approach to teaching and assessment.

CHAPTER 11

Designing the Learning Experience

Chapter Nine described the process of moving from the overall goals of your course to more specific learning outcomes. At this point in the design process your focus shifts from the broader general issues of goals and sequence to the more practical concerns of assessment, discussed in the previous chapter, and implementation. For example, how will you facilitate your students' reaching these goals? What will be your role and the role of your students? How can the time available to you be most effectively used? How and when should assessment take place? All are critical questions that everyone of us must address in every course that we teach. You will often be working on these two areas (assessment and implementation of the design of the learning experience) simultaneously. Both are essential and which is focused on first is immaterial. This chapter discusses the design of the learning experience in your course.

In selecting the instructional approach that is most appropriate for a given course three interrelated factors must be considered (Figure 11.1):

- The specific learning outcomes you want to reach (discussed in Chapter Nine).

- The research on learning.

- The instructional options available to you. These could include both structural options (lecture, small-group activities, out-of-class experiences) and technology options (media, computers). The technology options will be discussed in Chapter Twelve.

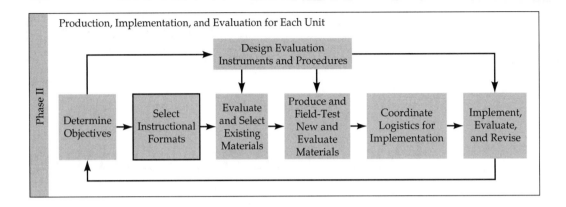

Figure 11.1 Factors to Consider When Selecting an Instructional Format.

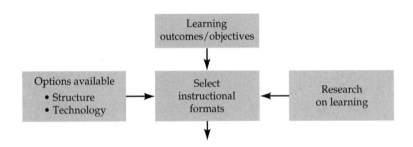

In many instances the design of our courses has been determined more by tradition, ease of implementation, or our own comfort level than by an in-depth look at these three factors.

As you design the learning experience for your course, do not let your personal preferences eliminate effective instructional options. You may have to try new techniques or get outside help, not necessarily an unpleasant experience.

Changing Role of the Faculty Member in the Learning Process

In Chapter One I mentioned briefly the shift that is under way in how we describe the role that faculty have in the learning process—the move from being teaching-centered to being learning-centered. Robert Barr and John Tagg have described this shift as a move from the "instructional delivery system," where "faculty are conceived primarily as disciplinary experts who impart knowledge by lecturing," to the "Learning Paradigm," which "conceives of faculty as primarily the designers of learning environments" where they "study and apply best methods for producing learning and student success" (1995, p. 24).

Research on Learning

Fortunately, the great amount of information on learning can provide us with an excellent starting point as we think through the design of our courses. Unfortunately, many of us have not paid much attention to this body of literature, as evidenced by our heavy reliance on the lecture, which is the most common means of instruction used on college campuses and one of the least effective and most limited instructional methods available to us (see Exhibit 11.1).

Exhibit 11.2 briefly reviews some of the significant research findings on instructional methods and learning. In Lion Gardiner's *Redesigning Higher Education* (1996), one of the books you should have in your library, you will find an excellent review of the literature and a comprehensive reference section. You should also review Barbara Gross Davis's *Tools for Teaching* (1993), which provides practical information on the various instructional options available. Using this book will save you a good deal of time.

Another excellent and brief reference is *The Seven Principles for Good Practice in Undergraduate Education* (Chickering, Gamson, and Barsi, 1989), available from Winona State University (P.O. Box 5838, Winona, MN 55987–5838). This booklet provides an excellent self-assessment checklist that you can use to compare what you are doing

Exhibit 11.1. Research Findings on the Lecture.

- The lecture is the principal method of instruction in higher education (used about 80 percent of the time).

- Lectures tend to focus primarily on low-level factual materials, with about 90 percent of all questions based on recall.

- A significant number of questions asked during a lecture (about 30 percent) result in no participation by students.

- The students who benefit most from the lecture are those with stronger academic profiles and those from families of higher socioeconomic status.

- When large lecture courses are combined with minimal out-of-class contact with other students and the faculty member, the gap between the quality of the academic experience for residential and commuting students widens.

Source: Primarily from Gardiner, 1996.

Exhibit 11.2. Research Findings on Instructional Methods and Learning.

- Although the lecture is an effective way to teach low-level factual material, discussion is far more effective for the retention of information, the transfer of knowledge to other applications, problem solving, and changes in attitude.

- Active learning is more effective than passive learning.

- Learning can take place through several sensory channels; the more channels engaged in learning, the better.

- Compared with competitive or individual learning, cooperation (cooperative learning) leads to greater reasoning ability and higher self-esteem.

- Teaching is more effective when the instructional methods used take into account the diverse ways students learn.

- The impact of college is determined largely by the student's effort and involvement in both academic and nonacademic activities.

- Students succeed best in developing higher-order learning skills when such skills are reinforced throughout the education program.

- Changes in students' ability to think critically are significantly and positively correlated with levels of praise from faculty, interaction among students and faculty, and high-level cognitive responses from students in class.

- Unlearning what is already known is more difficult than learning new information. Identifying misconceptions and correcting them through active discussion and involvement with other students is essential.

- To be remembered, new information must be meaningfully connected to prior knowledge, and it must be remembered in order to be learned.

- New information organized in personally meaningful ways is likely to be retained, learned, and used.

- There is a direct correlation between hours spent studying and all academic outcomes.

- Prior knowledge and experience generally make more difference than intellectual ability in learning success.

- High expectations encourage high achievement.

- Motivation to learn is alterable; it can be affected by the task, the learning environment, the teacher, and the learner.

- Over 50 percent of students report studying five or fewer hours per week.

- Professors rate their own teaching very highly (over 90 percent rate themselves above average or superior).

- There is a positive correlation between the frequency of out-of-class contact between students and faculty and student retention of material and social and intellectual development.

Exhibit 11.2. (continued).

- Students tend to routinely use study methods that are known not to work (such as rereading textbooks) and must be taught how to learn effectively.

- Research does not support a positive correlation between the quality of faculty research and the quality of teaching.

Source: Primarily from Gardiner, 1996, and Angelo, 1993.

in your courses with what a group of national leaders in education believe is ideal. Exhibit 11.3 contains excerpts from this inventory. The inventory is also an excellent way to review strategies you might use in your classes.

You should also read William Plater's (1995) description of the change he believes will be taking place in what we do as faculty in the years ahead; he paints a comprehensive picture of what this change of focus will mean as faculty members become "facilitators of learning" at least as much as sources of information and students take a more active role in the classroom.

The field of psychology has long been an additional source of research on effective teaching. In 1960 Goodwin Watson provided a thirteen-point review of the literature that is as relevant today as it was then. Coming from the psychological perspective, this review provides you with additional useful suggestions (Watson, 1961):

1. Behaviors which are rewarded (reinforced) are more likely to recur.
2. Sheer repetition without indications of improvement or any kind of reinforcement is a poor way to attempt to learn.
3. Threat and punishment have variable and uncertain effects upon learning; they may set up avoidance tendencies which prevent further learning.
4. Reward (reinforcement), to be most effective in learning, must follow almost immediately after the desired behavior and be clearly connected with that behavior in the mind of the learner.
5. The type of reward (reinforcement) which has the greatest transfer value to other life situations is the kind one gives oneself, that is, the sense of satisfaction in achieving purposes.
6. Opportunity for fresh, novel, stimulating experience is a kind of reward which is quite effective in conditioning and learning.
7. Forgetting proceeds rapidly at first—then more and more slowly; recall shortly after learning reduces the amount forgotten.
8. The most effective effort is put forth when tasks are attempted that fall in the "range of challenge"—not too easy and not too hard—where success seems quite possible but not certain.

Exhibit 11.3. Seven Principles for Good Practice in
Undergraduate Education.

---

1. Good practice encourages student-faculty contact
   I know my students by name by the end of the first two weeks of the term.
   I take students to professional meetings or other events in my field.

2. Good practice encourages cooperation among students
   I encourage my students to prepare together for classes or exams.
   I create "learning communities," study groups, or project teams within my courses.

3. Good practice encourages active learning
   I encourage students to challenge my ideas, the ideas of other students, or those presented in readings or other course materials.
   I give my students concrete, real-life situations to analyze.

4. Good practice gives prompt feedback
   I return examinations and papers within a week.
   I give my students the opportunity to schedule conferences with me to discuss their progress.

5. Good practice emphasizes time on task
   I clearly communicate to my students the minimum amount of time they should spend preparing for classes.
   If students miss my classes, I require them to make up lost work.

6. Good practice communicates high expectations
   I make clear my expectations orally and in writing at the beginning of each course.
   I encourage students to write a lot.

7. Good practice respects diverse talents and ways of learning
   I select reading and design activities related to the background of my students.
   I try to find out about my students' learning styles, interests, or backgrounds at the beginning of each course.

Source: Chickering, Gamson, and Barsi, 1989.

9. Students are more apt to throw themselves wholeheartedly into any project if they themselves have participated in the selection and planning of the enterprise.

10. Reaction to excessive direction by the teacher may be: (a) apathetic conformity, (b) defiance, (c) scapegoating, (d) escape from the whole affair.

11. Over-strict discipline is associated with more conformity, anxiety, shyness and acquiescence in students; greater permissiveness is associated with more initiative and creativity in students.

12. What is learned is most likely to be available for use if it is learned in a situation much like that in which it is to be used and immediately preceding the time when it is needed.

13. If there is a discrepancy between the real objectives and the tests used to measure achievement, the latter becomes the main influence upon choice of subject matter and method.

As you address this primary issue of what you and your students will be doing in and outside of your classroom, the clearer the vision of where you want to go, the more you understand what research tells us about teaching and learning, and the more you know about the advantages and disadvantages and constraints of the instructional options available to you, the better your decision will be. Reviewing Exhibits 11.1, 11.2, and 11.3 and thinking about how you might adapt these ideas in designing your course and planning for what you will be doing on a day-to-day basis may prove to be very good use of your time as you work to improve the quality of your students' learning experience.

Instructional Options

Focusing once more on the goals you have for your course and basing your decision on what we know about learning, your next challenge will be to decide exactly what your course will look like. Here you match the process of learning with the outcomes you have stated. For example, faculty developing a capstone course for the College of Agriculture at the University of Minnesota set goals that included problem solving, critical thinking, a disciplinary knowledge of crop management, interpersonal skills, and skills in oral and written communication (Simmons, 1995, p. 125). The challenge faced by the faculty was how to design this course to ensure that their students had these competencies. What type of review might be necessary? What type of assignments needed to be made? How could they and their students best spend their time in reaching these goals within the semester? To answer these questions the faculty had to explore the options available to them and the advantages and disadvantages of each.

In general, you need to make decisions about three kinds of instructional options (Figure 11.2):

- Structural options focus on the instructional setting; they include large groups and lectures, seminars, independent study, videos, laboratories, and field experiences.

- Process options focus on the design of instruction within these settings: whether you are going to use instructional time in the traditional way or provide for self-paced instruction, to offer exemptions or remediation within certain units based on students' entry-level competencies, to offer different options within

Figure 11.2. Selecting Structural Options for Each Instructional Component.

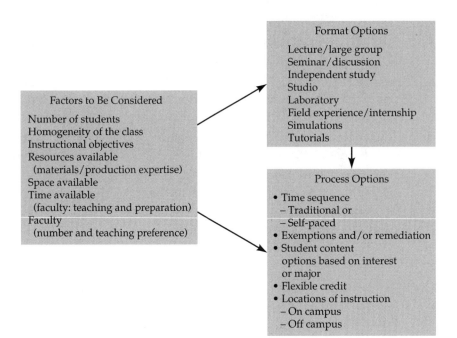

an assignment so that students can select the specific focus of their projects based on their interest or major, to allow students to earn extra credit for extra work.

- Course-management options focus on the overall organization of the course.

Structural Options

Instructional settings can be on campus or off campus. Each setting offers advantages.

New Ways of Learning on Campus

Although lectures, laboratories, seminars, and studios have been around almost from the beginning of higher education, a number of other approaches are being explored today, ranging from bringing the active learning of the laboratory and studio into the lecture hall to providing formal educational experiences within the community.

Avoiding large-group sessions may not always be possible. You may find that you have to include some lecture sections in your design for logistical reasons, or you may find the use of guest speakers, a video, or a computer demonstration valuable. Reviewing materials and administering group tests may also be appropriate and logistically essential. In *Engaging Ideas* (1996), John Bean describes a number of techniques you can use within your lectures to actively involve your students by getting away from the tradition of faculty members lecturing as students take notes. Using learning groups to improve listening, requiring related seminars, requiring student journals, and asking probing questions, these techniques can improve learning. Bean's book also contains a section on how critical thinking can be taught and reinforced through the use of writing and essay examinations.

Following is an in-depth review of the future needs of business and industry. Michael Useem (1995) makes an excellent point about the need for active learning, whether it be in the lecture hall, the seminar, or laboratory (pp. 22–23):

> First with company managers giving fewer direct orders and depending more upon subordinate initiative, team learning, and self-reliance, one wonders whether the traditional classroom is posing the wrong learning model. If students acquire knowledge by passively listening to authoritative figures at the lectern and experience no dialogue with them or among themselves, will they be prepared to acquire knowledge later in a work environment that stresses personal initiative and collaborative work? Less atomistic and more engaged learning may better model what our students are likely to face as they enter the private sector during the late 1990s.
>
> Second with company managers listening more to their subordinates and customers, one wonders whether the absence of feedback loops is also presenting the wrong paradigm. If students rarely inform faculty of what has worked and not worked in the classroom, will they later be ready to inform their boss and listen to others in a company setting that demands it?

Other increasingly popular on-campus approaches are available. While one approach may work for you, another will be more appropriate for your colleague down the hall. Indeed, no single approach will make sense for an entire course. These approaches are not independent of one another. You have the option of combining and modifying them. Davis (1993) and McKeachie (1994) provide comprehensive reviews of these options.

Learning Outside the Classroom and Laboratory

Although colleges and universities have been actively engaged in international education for some time and have provided traditional instruction in off-campus settings to meet the needs of part-time students, we have only recently begun to explore, in a comprehensive manner, the formal linking of our on-campus courses with off-campus experiences and with activities on campus but outside the regularly scheduled session. Off-campus practicums and internships are fairly common in professional schools, where practical experience has long been perceived as an essential component of the academic program, and this approach has begun to gain popularity in undergraduate arts and sciences programs.

Although we as faculty have assumed responsibility for what goes on in our classrooms, we have rarely focused on the total experience of our students and explored how we could build on and orchestrate these additional activities to improve learning. As you explore using the community in your course, you should explore three different options: community service (also called service learning), learning communities, and internships.

Community Service or Service Learning.   In her article "Bringing Community Service into the Curriculum," Barbara Jacoby (1994, p. B2) writes:

> When students engage in community service, tremendous benefits accrue to them, to the communities they serve, and to their colleges and universities. Those of us who have worked with students involved in community service repeatedly hear them say such things as: "It gave my life a purpose," "It benefited me more than any classroom experience," and "I don't take life for granted anymore."
>
> Colleges can incorporate community service into the curriculum in a variety of ways. For example:
>
> Courses in fields such as English, sociology, biology, and psychology could add a community-service component. In writing classes, for example, students could produce a newsletter or brochure for a non-profit agency. Sociology students could study at first hand such social problems as homelessness and illiteracy by working with community agencies. Biology students could study local environmental issues and work in clean-up campaigns and other projects. During and after such service, students could be required to relate their experience to course readings and to discuss whether it has made them more socially responsible citizens.

Learning Communities.   In this approach you and your students and faculty and students from other courses work together in a collaborative way. For example, students from history, geography, art, and English could work together to develop a public display depicting the evolution of a particular neighborhood, or students from a number of courses could assist a local social agency in the development of a brochure describing its services. Credits in these programs are combined. This approach can help integrate separate elements of your curriculum, build interpersonal skills, improve retention, and validate the worth of each individual. At some institutions students involved in these activities are housed together or are given lounge space for meetings. Such programs may involve only a few courses or an entire institution. In Portland State University's campuswide program, the process concludes with a senior-year experience built around a community activity. Jodi Levine and Daniel Tompkins provide an excellent overview of learning communities in "Making Learning Communities Work" (1996).

Internships.   Internships, with or without credit, can be structured into your course. The key is making sure that the internship assignment relates directly to your goals and course of study. Political science students could, as part of a course, volunteer in the office of a town supervisor, work in a political campaign, or serve as staff on a community project. A graduate student in a course on assessment or evaluation could be assigned to help another department develop a survey instrument to collect data from alumni, be involved in the design and implementation of a community survey, or help a school or college assess the effectiveness of an academic program. At a growing number of institutions special offices have as their primary purpose finding internship opportunities for students and ensuring that the supervision, feedback, and assessment needed occur. For students at Syracuse University, doctors' and lawyers' offices, newspapers, radio and television stations, governmental offices, and businesses throughout the region as well as on-campus administrative units offer internship opportunities. Often, an unpaid internship leads to a paying part-time position while the student is in school and even to employment after graduation.

Process Options

At this stage in the design process you have made all the decisions about the overall structure of your course. It is now time to decide how to structure each unit within the course. Because each process option works most effectively under certain circumstances, the decision about which of these options to use should be made after considering these factors:

- The number and quality of your students
- The instructional objectives of the unit
- The resources available (instructional technology options, production assistance, funds for new items)

- The time available for teaching, for assignments between lessons, for the production of new materials
- The individual strengths and preferences of the faculty

Several less familiar process options deserve special attention here.

Personalized instruction was introduced by Fred Keller (1968). This approach leads the student step by step to clearly defined goals. The emphasis in this method is on the design and structure of the sequence of the course; grading is based on clearly described and measurable outcomes. The approach is particularly useful where classes include students whose entry levels range from needing remediation to well prepared in the skills required for success. The materials are structured to individualize remediation.

Self-pacing enables your students to progress through a course or part of a course at their own rate on the basis of their ability to pass a specific unit or section test. This approach requires that the content be sequential, is most effective when students can be expected to learn at significantly different rates, and requires both excellent instructional materials designed specifically for independent study and the availability of one-on-one counseling or tutoring.

Simulations provide your students with an experience as close to a "real-world" situation as possible. A simulation can involve role playing, with students prepared to play a specific role in a carefully structured exercise. The exact character of a simulation is determined by the subject and the purpose. The instructor sets up the simulation exercise so that the factors the students must deal with provide them with specific challenges. Simulations can be designed by creative use of the wide range of materials made available on the computer. With technology you can provide your students with an opportunity to work through a problem while you track the questions they asked, the information they used, and the problem-solving approach they followed.

Exemption or remediation exempts your students from parts or units of a course or assigns them additional work to correct a deficiency in entering competencies. This option is most useful when prerequisite problems exist or when some students have had prior coursework or experience in the area. It requires a high-quality testing program and well-designed remedial instruction (independent study using computer-based or programmed units may be effective for this purpose).

Content options give your students a choice among assignments that are all designed to meet the same learning objective. These assignments range from writing about a topic in the student's major area of interest to solving a problem the student chooses. Content options are most appropriate when students have specific interests that can be related to the content or goals of the course.

Flexible credit allows students enrolled in the same course to earn different numbers of credits based either on additional units they are required to take or on extra work they do at their discretion. Flexible credit can be used effectively both in remedial courses, in which assignments are made on the basis of need, and in advanced or honors courses, in which students may wish to do extra work for extra credit. In a flexible-credit system the work done for each credit can be graded independently and listed in this way on the student's transcript. If this option would work for you, discuss it with your registrar. If he or she would like additional information on how such a system might be implemented, the Syracuse University registrar, at 315–443–5745, can provide specifics.

Trade-offs are always required when faculty make these decisions about structure and process. For example, the use of self-pacing can limit the time available for large-group meetings, but the availability of an outstanding lecturer may make it worthwhile to build in a number of large-group sessions, which in turn will limit the flexibility needed for individualization. If your students enter a course with academic deficiencies, these gaps must be closed by remediation if these students are to succeed. Other elements of the course may then have to be adjusted, and unless the remedial assignments are to be completed outside of class, plans have to be made to accommodate the students who do not require remedial activities.

Course-Management Options

Since the 1960s several major management systems have been introduced that you may also wish to evaluate. The first, the audiotutorial approach, uses media as the major source of instruction. It was implemented in 1961 by Samuel Postlethwait (Postlethwait, Novak, and Murray, 1972) in his first-year botany course at Purdue University. The audiotutorial system uses audiotapes, workbooks, and more recently, videotapes to provide an independent study sequence. The sequenced materials make it possible for students to repeat instruction that they find difficult and to move quickly through material that is thoroughly understood. Because it is used in connection with such other class activities as lectures, demonstrations, and tests, the course design must plan for adequate pacing through a carefully designed syllabus or course manuals, to ensure that students are prepared for these group experiences when they occur.

A second system is the Keller Plan (Keller, 1968), also called mastery learning. This system emphasizes a high level of achievement on the part of all students. In this approach, time is variable, with students required to reach a specific, clearly identified level of performance. The plan gives the student an opportunity to move from unit to unit as soon as he or she is able to meet a specific criterion (above 80 percent, above 90 percent, and so on) on individual unit tests. This approach is effective with students who enter with deficiencies in the area and for high-level students who can complete a course in less than the traditional semester. It is usually used at the lower-division level.

Unfortunately, there has been a tendency to equate both these approaches with individualized instruction. Individualized instruction is guided by the needs of the students. Class management requires that the materials be easy for the students to use, and these materials usually involve multimedia use. Such materials as diagnostic tests, self-administered tests, and carefully designed instructional materials allow for self-pacing. A comparison of both plans—in most ways they are similar—with individualized instruction reveals that they include the following elements of individualization:

- Flexible time frames for completion
- Stress on independent study
- Review sessions to meet specific problems

The following elements of individualization are usually missing in these approaches:

- Diagnostic evaluation of prerequisites followed by remediation and exemptions
- Content options based on interest or need
- Flexible sequencing (when appropriate)
- Alternate evaluation techniques
- Alternate instructional techniques

The two approaches have specific differences that must also be considered. Although both are generally linear in design—that is, every student follows the same learning sequence—the Keller Plan can be adapted to the branching concept more easily because of its more flexible approach to media. (With branching, students follow different sequences that are determined by their answers to questions posed within the instructional material.) In addition, the audiotutorial technique has generally been designed around a specific faculty member and as a result is often extremely difficult to replicate in its entirety on other campuses or with other instructors.

Several of the courses described in Chapter Seven and Resource E include excellent management systems. The freshman writing course, the introductory course in religion, the introductory economics course, and the self-paced calculus course all require carefully designed administrative procedures. What separates these from the Keller and Postlethwait approaches is that the management system was established after the course was designed. Faculty who have adopted the audiotutorial and Keller programs tend to select the management system first and then design courses around these systems.

Summary

This chapter reviewed a number of instructional design and methods options and the factors that you must keep in mind as you decide what your course will look like: what the sequence of units will be, where and when your students will have options, and which structural elements you will include. Your final design will be determined by the nature of your instructional goals, the number of and the abilities of the students you will be dealing with, the options available to you, and your own personal preferences. Underlying the entire process will be your knowledge of what we know about learning and teaching and an effort on your part to become more of a facilitator of learning and less of a fountain of information. In Chapter Twelve we will explore the use of technology and how, by selecting and using it properly, you can encourage active learning and improve the use of your time and that of your students.

CHAPTER 12

Selecting and Using Technology

"Since Gutenberg first assembled the means to mass-produce books and began printing the first pages, the printed book has continued to be the basic instructional tool in education. Nowhere is this more evident than in higher education, where textbooks and the lecture appear to continue as the norm" (Spotts and Bowning, 1995, p. 57). For decades the advocates and dispensers of instructional technology have described the "next few years" as the period in education where the wholesale adoption of one or more of the newer technologies would significantly change the structure of the classroom and the roles of faculty and students.

In his excellent report on why higher education has been slow to change William Geoghegan (1994, p.1) makes the following observation:

> Despite massive technology expenditures over the last decade or so, the widespread availability of substantial computing power at increasingly reasonable prices, and a growing "comfort level" with this technology among college and university faculty, information technology is *not* being integrated into the teaching and learning process nearly as much as people have regularly predicted since it arrived on the educational scene three or four decades ago. There are many isolated pockets of successful technology implementations. But it is an unfortunate fact that these individual successes, as important and as encouraging as they might be, have been slow to propagate beyond their initiators; and they have by no means brought about the technologically inspired revolution in teaching and learning so long anticipated by instructional technology advocates.

However, after many false starts and numerous statements and visions that were cloudy (to say the least), a period of transition may actually be here. Each of the earlier technologies—film, video, programmed instruction, and teaching machines—fell short of the potential envisioned by their supporters, perhaps because of unrealistic expectations or oversell, but more often they were badly used, poorly designed, and not integrated into the total learning experience.

Although the introduction of computers saw many of the same problems, computing should be able to overcome its less-than-promising start for several basic reasons.

- Unlike most of the other technologies, computers are both a basic tool for students and an instrument for learning.
- Unlike the other technologies, computers are already used by students, many of whom have a high level of expertise. (Each year the percentage of entering students with computer expertise grows significantly, reported to me by provosts at many universities as already reaching over 80 percent.)
- Unlike the other technologies, computers are easy to use and increasingly portable.
- Unlike the other technologies, computers are tools that all students must be able to use; computer literacy is perceived as an essential goal for students.
- Unlike other technologies, computers are strongly supported by the central administration on most campuses. (By 1994 American colleges were spending in excess of $1.75 billion annually to support the instructional use of computers; Geoghegan, 1994.)
- Unlike the other technologies, computers can significantly affect the nature and depth of what we teach and how students learn.

This chapter reviews some of the important changes that are under way, presents the questions you should be asking as you select the appropriate combination of technology for your course, and describes a number of instructionally effective approaches. I focus here on process rather than specific applications because software and hardware are often outdated in a short period of time. I have also included a number of Website references that will help you locate up-to-date information on specific techniques and exemplary projects.

Basic Uses of Technology

Steve Gilbert (1996), in his review of technology in higher education, has identified two emerging views of how technology can affect the academic life of colleges and universities. Both approaches should be examined as you think through the design of your course. In the first the focus is on improving instructional productivity, reaching more students in various settings, both on and off campus. The second focuses on what happens within the context of your courses—the teaching, learning, and content. In addressing productivity issues technology is used to reach more students, to reach a more diverse audience, or to reduce costs. In the second approach, however, technology can help you do what you do better. The focus is on facilitating learning by increasing your students' responsibility, the effectiveness of instruction and the quality of its content, and communication between you and your students. Both approaches describe making education sensitive to the range of students' abilities, interests, and accessibility. Based on the number of students enrolled in a course, where they are located, and the resources available to you, you will most likely be using technology at times both to reduce costs and to improve instruction.

As we noted earlier, selecting the most effective teaching approach to help your students reach the goals you have established is not an easy task. Your approach may involve the use of technology, or quite often it may require a change in instruction where no media will be involved. Focus on your goals and on how best to reach them. As Geoghegan concluded in his report on what happened to technology, "Technology in the service of ineffective teaching will do nothing to improve the quality of instruction; it will simply perpetuate and even amplify poor teaching. Likewise, good teaching can often be enhanced by even simple technology, wisely and sensitively applied. In either event the process begins with teaching; technology comes second" (1994, p. 21).

Specific Applications of Technology

Consider how technology can work for you as you explore ways to improve the quality of your course. Technology can enrich our teaching and allow us to reach students outside of class in effective ways. Wendy Shapiro, Katherine Roskos, and G. Phillip Cartwright note, "The college classroom has long been the solitary domain of the teaching faculty. Once that door is closed, contact with the outside world ends, . . . or so it has been until now, when the new availability of local- and wide-area networks suddenly opens the traditional classroom to the world" (1995, p. 67).

Other articles have pointed to the broadening scope of instructional applications of computers. David Soderberg (1996) describes over a dozen applications of the Web, ranging from providing students with basic information about the course and self-help materials to providing them with feedback, on-line lectures, text materials, multi-media modules, and materials for use in discussion groups.

Batson and Bass (1996, p. 44) describe how faculty are observing that as students begin to "surf the Web," the traditional four walls of the classroom begin to disappear, fostering significant changes in the student-faculty relationship and in the process of learning.

> We are finding that, for a small but growing percentage of people, new forms of communication, publications, and collaboration and the way data are accessed, represented, and manipulated are changing the way knowledge is conceived, challenged, justified, and disseminated in their disciplines, . . . changes in how we organize the process of decid-ing what is true, whose voices are heard, and how we communicate and work in groups.
>
> Because information technologies have the ability to mediate and manage this knowledge "negotiation" process more dynamically, effi-ciently, inclusively, and at a much greater scale and reach than before, teachers can now bring their students into more direct contact with the process itself. That may mean—to name just a few examples—inviting them to:
>
> - "Lurk" on a professional Internet discussion list
> - Connect to databases formerly open only to professionals in the field
> - Create simulations of reality that are almost as compelling as real-ity itself
> - "Visit" foreign countries and "talk" to natives via Internet discus-sion lists or E-Mail
> - Create learning spaces on the Net where they and fellow learners grapple with problem-solving
> - "Listen" via electronic mail or conferencing to experts in their field as they go about their daily work [reprinted with permission of the Helen Dwight Reid Educational Foundation, Copyright © 1996]

Usually the specific nature of the discipline will determine which of the many applications of technology are most appropriate. Batson and Bass observe the significant impact computers can have on the teaching of writing (1996, p. 44):

> As students worked on the networks, reworking their ideas in writing, developing a sense of audience, getting feedback on their expression of ideas, writing to an easier audience than just the teacher (who already knows all the answers, in the student's view), and strengthen-ing their sense that writing is for communication and not for evalua-tion, the process became more and more the end rather than the means. Students could be immersed in the writing process, but that process was now more public and thus was more accessible to teachers.

Computers (often in a multimedia context) are used to bring dif-ferent cultures to language courses and up-to-date news and data to natural science and social science classrooms. Students are permitted to produce their own multimedia projects instead of writing traditional papers or preparing class presentations. Recent developments in videoconferencing have permitted classes in one part of the country to see each other as they discuss national issues or developments in their fields with leaders in Washington or statesmen around the world. Faculty in the sciences are exploring applications of virtual reality as an intellectual tool, and increasingly computers are finding a place in laboratory courses.

Cartwright's review of technology projects nationwide (1996b, pp. 60–62) describes a number of institutions, including Washington State University, William Paterson College (Wayne, N.J.), Kent State University, and Miami-Dade Community College, where the effective use of technology has significantly improved the academic success of underprepared students.

On every campus some faculty on their own or with the support of other faculty and staff are using exciting applications of technology. Your challenge will be to select the specific combinations that make the most sense for you and your students.

Selecting Technology

You will be making two distinctly different types of choices regarding the use of technology in your course. In one instance you will have already decided on the general structure of your course—large group, seminar, laboratory, teams, independent study—and will be choosing the approach that will help you to facilitate learning in that context. In the second instance you will be considering how technology might affect the nature and structure of the unit or course itself. For example, a growing number of faculty are taking advantage of the availability of computer clusters and the expanding inventory of good software to move the dissemination of information from the classroom to self-paced independent study, where a mix of media can present information far more effectively than a teacher in a classroom. With this move, time is made available for those learning activities that can be accomplished only when faculty are in direct contact with their students—discussing, advising, motivating, and so on.

By now you have determined your specific goals and have decided on the general flow of your course. It now becomes possible for you to select the specific instructional options that will most facilitate your students' reaching the goals you have identified. Clearly, the list of options has never been as broad as it is today. Almost every week new software is coming on the market and effective new applications are reported regularly in the professional journals.

You have not only the traditional options of slides, overheads, audiotapes, and videotapes, but also, in a growing number of class-rooms, large-screen computer projectors with access to the World Wide Web and video down-loading from channels around the world. Games and simulations are also available in a variety of formats. Outside of class your students have many electronic resources in the library and computer access at home or on campus. The key will be matching your course goals and the tools available. At the end of this chapter you will find general references that may be helpful and also information on the Websites that provide up-to-date information on computer software and applications in higher education.

Several authors have approached the selection of media in a sequential fashion and have developed a process to help faculty make these decisions for various instructional settings. Michael Molenda, James Pershing, and Charles Reigeluth (1996) approached this task from the context of the setting and what the presentation requires (Table 12.1).

Far more detailed in his approach, Jerrold Kemp (1995) provides a step-by-step model for selecting media for each of the basic instructional settings. (Figure 12.1 is the model for presentations to regular-size classes or large groups.)

Table 12.1. Selecting a Medium.

If you have this grouping and this presentation need . . .	Then consider . . .
Large-group grouping	*Lecture only*
Verbal	Slide, overhead, computer, or
Realistic still visuals	LCD panel
Motion visuals	Video or film
Small-group grouping	
Simulation	*Simulation, game*
Graphic images	Flip chart, chalkboard, overhead
Combination of photographic and graphic images	Pictures, slides, overhead
Audiovisual, motion, interaction preferable	Computer and video, CD-ROM
Individual grouping	
Still graphics	Diagram, chart, computer
Combination of photographic and graphic images	Slides, print, video, computer
Motion image	Video, videodisc

Source: Molenda, Pershing, and Reigeluth, 1996.

Figure 12.1. Media for Regular-Size Class or Large Group.

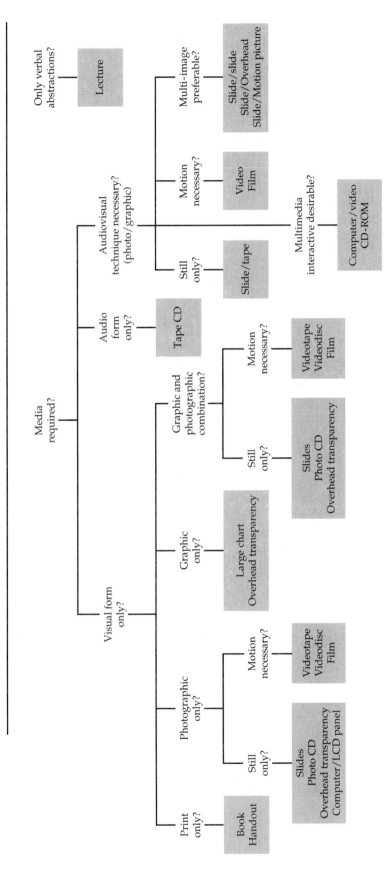

Source: Designing Effective Instruction, Kemp, 1995. Reprinted by permission of Prentice-Hall, Inc., Upper Saddle River, N.J.

As you decide which media may be appropriate, keep these factors in mind also:

- What effects do you most want to gain by using technology and what elements of your course do you cherish and not want to lose? As Gilbert (1996) has pointed out, with the use of technology there will be trade-offs.

- Before you select an option, make sure the equipment that you need is readily available. In some instances you may have to request that your class meet in a specific room where the needed capabilities exist.

- The easier a medium or sequence is to use, the more effective it will usually be. This applies to materials you must handle or coordinate and to sequences you are assigning to your students. The fancier the equipment the more things that can go wrong.

- Preview everything. Do not take anything for granted; you do not need surprises.

- If you are requiring out-of-class use of computers, make sure all your students have access; and if you are using particular software, be certain that it is available on their machines. Logistical problems in computer use and lack of compatibility between the software and the equipment your students have access to can doom a project to failure.

- If at all possible, purchase rather than develop. Despite what some software vendors say, designing your own multimedia unit is extremely time-consuming and costly (a twenty-minute multimedia sequence with some interactive design can cost well over $20,000 to develop and produce).

- Make sure all your students have the necessary support materials to complete the unit successfully. Do not make any assumptions about availability.

- Be creative and flexible. Too much of any good thing can be too much.

Low Technology

Although the focus here is primarily on complex technologies, at times the old standbys (overheads, slides, and videos) are still appropriate. In addition, programmed booklets can be effective. Providing the basic logic of computer-based instruction, far easier to produce and to disseminate, programmed materials have never been able to overcome the way they were introduced—oversold, poorly designed, and rarely used well. This technique can, nevertheless, be extremely useful when independent study is required, the number of students you are attempting to reach is modest, or the students are located in isolated areas.

Programmed booklets or manuals have been used successfully for diverse purposes:

- To teach basic vocabulary in a retailing course
- To introduce inexperienced students and staff to the basic use and operation of microcomputers and laboratory equipment
- To teach design students the use of basic drawing instruments
- To teach nonart majors to recognize various printmaking techniques
- To correct basic math deficiencies in students in an economics course
- To teach management students how to use a complex computerized accounting system
- To teach basic clinical skills to nursing students

The comments of some of the students who used programmed booklets to learn about printmaking techniques indicate how positively students respond to this approach when it is done well:

- This was of tremendous help to me. I say this because art has always been a bit confusing in that I looked but never really understood what I was seeing.
- I felt that this is a much easier way to learn the characteristics of art. If you do make a mistake, you find out exactly what was incorrect and why.
- I felt this technique of presenting the elements of art far more effective than the lecture form. I gained much knowledge from the experience as well as truly enjoying myself.

In selecting your approach, keep in mind the cost of development and the ease of use. Developing an intensive unit for a course with a limited number of students will require far too much of your time to be cost-effective. Purchasing a software package or trying another approach may make more sense. Also remember that an entire course does not have to be presented in the same format. Far from it. You should use whatever medium or combination of media is appropriate for reaching each of your goals. The most effective courses use a number of approaches and instructional techniques.

Case Study: Art History

At San Jose State University, as on most campuses, the introductory art history course for nonmajors, with an enrollment of several hundred students each semester, was taught using the lecture format, in which the instructor shows slides (often at an extremely rapid pace) and presents information about them while the students, under low-light conditions, observe and try to keep up with their note taking. With this format there is rarely time for either questions or discussions. Evaluations in these courses tend to focus on the recall of factual information with a heavy emphasis on multiple-choice, true-false, or short-answer questions.

One of the faculty members teaching the art history course at San Jose State, Kathleen Cohen, recalls the origin and early development of the redesign of the course as "innovation by accident." In a letter to the author (February 21, 1997) she writes:

> In the late 1970s, the California State University system circulated a call for proposals for innovative projects that would lead to increased student learning. I wanted to purchase the Kenneth Clark *Civilization* film series, but I knew that they would not give money just for films. Through a colleague in the Biology Department . . . I learned about an audiotutorial method that biologists had developed that would allow self-paced learning. I decided that I would have a much better chance of receiving grant funding if I proposed a self-study curriculum for art history than if I just asked for a series [of] films. . . . I received the grant and then talked with the Instructional Development office about creating the project. I learned that such projects need what were called "instructional objectives," and so I wrote them after I had completed saying what I wanted to do, which I now know is the reverse of what I should have done. However, we developed the course materials, which consisted of filmstrips, audio-tapes, and a detailed study guide and gave the course.

Fiscal Support

The $20,000 that was received provided for released time for the instructor (one full semester), a graduate student to help gather materials, the purchase of the films and equipment needed for implementation, and the production of a variety of instructional materials.

Design

Recognizing the logistical problems faced by one instructor teaching a large number of students, the design team decided to combine several instructional formats to facilitate both the delivery of information and the active involvement of students. The course that evolved by the late 1980s included three major instructional elements: large-group sessions, an audiotutorial independent-learning laboratory, and small-group discussion sections.

- Large-group sessions (ninety students each). During these sessions, general announcements were made, tests were taken, and each week the students viewed a thirty-minute film from Clark's *Civilization* series, which places the art being studied into the broader perspective of history and culture. In most instances these sessions lasted approximately forty minutes.
- Audiotutorial independent-learning laboratory. Designed for self-paced learning, the laboratory contained twenty student stations

equipped with a filmstrip viewer and an audiocassette player. Each week students were required to view two filmstrips while listening to two associated forty-minute discussions on audiocassette. To permit the students to follow the discussion and to make comparisons, the filmstrip frames were numbered, and when appropriate, split-screen images were used. As will be noted, as new technology became available this segment of the course was redesigned to take advantage of the options offered.

- Small-group discussion sections (fifteen to eighteen students each). These sessions provided the students with an opportunity to discuss the relationships among the film, the filmstrips, and the text.

The instructor moved from discussion group to discussion group, with the sections led by graduate students who also supervised the learning laboratory. These students, who were planning to become art teachers, received three "special studies" credits for their participation. At San Jose, students were allowed to take a maximum of six special studies credits, which limited the use of a single student as a small-group leader to one academic year. Funds were not available to provide regular teaching assistants for the course.

Results

As a result of the new course design, learning increased, students' attitudes toward both art and the course were more positive than they had been, and the graduate students improved their teaching skills and enjoyed the experience. The instructor has become "a course manager who works with the graduate students teaching them how to teach, . . . how to ask questions in the discussion sessions . . . [and] how to construct and evaluate various types of examinations and how to deal with difficult students" (Cohen, letter to the author, February 21, 1997). The new format not only provided the students with an opportunity to ask questions but, by using the self-paced approach, allowed them more time for taking notes and for studying the material. In addition, by using this pattern of instruction, the students' active involvement was increased, and the course reached a larger number of students without an increase in staffing.

Adding Computer Technology

With the availability of computers and their potential for adding effective learning opportunities to her class, Cohen was one of the first faculty on the San Jose campus to explore the potential of videodiscs and CD-ROMs as instructional tools. With support from sources within the California State University system and Pacific Bell, a project began in 1992 to explore the use of computer technology in the course for both on-campus and distance-education applications.

The initial step was to develop computer images of the slides that were used. At the same time a retrieval system was developed so that the faculty members could locate slides using a number of variables—type of art, period, style, artist, date, geographical location; it also included descriptive information such as a commentary by the faculty member, a bibliography, and dimensions of the depicted object. A laboratory with sixteen multimedia workstations was established, and the system was made available in the university library.

Several features of the workstations made them particularly effective. Slides were organized in sets of approximately eighty with an accompanying text. A comprehensive study guide kept the students focused on the major goal of the assignment, placing emphasis more on the recognition of style than on memorization. Students had the ability, impossible with other techniques, to enlarge any part of the image, while the faculty member could combine images as needed. Cohen found that while some students preferred an audio description of the materials accompanying the visuals, others preferred written descriptions. The flexibility of this approach is a major positive factor.

Cohen found developing the system to be a complex and challenging task:

> Trying to determine just what will happen [with technology] when and for how much [money] creates a constant challenge which at times resembles a ride of a fast roller coaster. In the meantime, we are trying to prepare our images for whatever materializes, keeping formats flexible and making certain that whatever is put in can also be taken out. Two basic rules are that technology will change and that the greatest costs are involved in preparation of the data, both the images and the related text [letter to author, February 21 1997].

> Keeping track of the progress of each image through the process of digitizing and data entry can be a nightmarish task when many people are involved in different steps in the process. To address this problem we created both Process and Location logs that are absolutely vital. We wish we had utilized such a process from the beginning, which might have prevented us from misplacing some 200 slides [Cohen, 1995].

Legal Issues

One of the goals of the project was to develop a system that could be used on other campuses and in other education settings. Here an unanticipated problem arose (Cohen 1996):

> Frustrating as the new technology might be, legal issues are still the most powerful force holding back the utilization of imaging technology. The ability to create digital copies of our materials greatly extends our capabilities to share what we do, and it also extends the problems raised by copyright protection and fair use. Discussions revolving about the Information Superhighway, the National Information Infrastructure, contrast the desire of museums to protect "their" images, and the confusions caused for museums like [the San Francisco Museum of Modern Art], who wish to share their images but are constrained by the labyrinthine copyright laws regarding works by living artists, with the obligation to share our cultural heritage with the people whose heritage it is. The issues are not easy ones, and we cannot just say let us have free access to everything since we are educators. We need to find ways to balance the interests of the creators and the users of intellectual property.

We are in the process of creating a CD-ROM with the images of art works that I have photographed both inside and outside of museums for distribution to 20 [California State University] campuses. This took longer than expected because of legal concerns. While it is clear that I own the copyright to the images which are themselves in the public domain, there could be a problem with implied licensing issues. While many museum policies permit photography for personal use but not for commercial use, they say nothing about educational use. This issue has not been tested in court, and thus remains a very gray area.

Because the definition of "fair use" is changing rapidly, particularly as it relates to segments of audio, video, and visual materials, you should check with your library's media-law expert for the latest information if you plan to rely on these materials.

Cohen's project is a fine example of how media can be utilized and how their use changes as new options become available. But the legal issues regarding the use of visual and audio materials will need to be addressed and resolved before the full potential of some of the newer applications can be realized.

Locating and Evaluating Existing Materials

As noted earlier, using commercially available materials almost always costs less, both in time and money, than designing and producing new ones. This is particularly true of computer-based units and video. You will also find that many faculty at other institutions will be happy to share with you the materials they developed.

Selecting materials involves two phases: first, locating those resources that might be useful and, second, evaluating the materials themselves. Many basic references can help locate materials quickly. Most computer stores and college bookstores offer a wide selection of software and provide preview opportunities. In addition, ads for software and related evaluations can often be found in media- or discipline-related professional journals. Most college and university offices for media or for faculty development and support also have a collection of media-company catalogues, and other faculty are often an excellent source of information about existing resources. As noted earlier, you will also find many items through the Web.

Once the specific items are located, your evaluation process begins in earnest, and at this phase many problems occur. Unfortunately, most of these problems exist because many publishers, producers, and faculty fail to provide information that faculty have been requesting for years: statements concerning the target population, prerequisites, objectives, testing data, and so on. Although some publishers do provide these data, most do not, so the evaluation of the material is up to you.

The available media (print and nonprint) selected for use should meet several specific criteria:

- The instructional objectives of your unit and of the materials must agree. Make sure the instructional materials meet established needs rather than modifying your goals and objectives so that materials currently on the market can be used.

- The media should be appropriate for the instructional method selected.

- The time required to go through the instructional materials must be within the range allocated.

- The materials must be designed for your specific student population. In the case of San Jose, for example, Cohen reports that students' response to the Clark films was disappointing, "but they very much liked the course structure and wanted to know when I would convert the second semester of the course to the new format" (letter to author, February 21, 1997).

Most materials are eliminated quickly on the basis of wrong format, wrong content, or poor quality. Also in some cases the material can be purchased, broken up into separate sequences, and used for both remedial work and review. A few sequences divided in this manner can easily serve large numbers of students when the sequences are placed in an independent-learning laboratory, in a computer cluster, or on reserve in the library.

Segments from purchased tapes, audio and video, and films also can be useful. The decision to purchase should depend on frequency of use, the number of sets required, and the quantity of the original items that will be used. Just make certain that what you select is relevant and current and that it will remain so for a reasonable period of time.

Design and Field Testing of Materials

Obviously, if existing materials are not usable, new units must be designed, produced, and evaluated. The specific format and approach selected should be the easiest to use given the constraints of time and budget. The emphasis should be on the instructional goals rather than on a specific approach or equipment system. The many language laboratories, television production systems, and off-brands of computers in storage on many campuses are mute testimony to instances in which the glamour of the hardware systems overshadowed rational decisions regarding their purchase and use.

Although I do not cover the selection and design of media in detail here, certain steps should be followed.

- State the objectives (available from earlier planning).
- Design related criterion tests (produced from the objectives).
- Review all anticipated student prerequisites. (What assumptions are made about entering student competencies, and are they accurate?)
- Select the instructional format.
- Design a preliminary draft (or an experimental edition) of the sequence.
- Field-test the preliminary draft (still in rough format) on several students who meet the definition of the population.
- Revise the preliminary draft. (Field testing often will identify differences between actual and anticipated prerequisites.)
- Continue the testing on small populations and revise as necessary.
- Produce a final field-test edition for a pilot study or field-test program. Careful pilot testing with representative students at this point will substantially reduce the problems that may occur when the materials are used as part of the formal program.

To assist in this process, a short questionnaire called the MINI-QUEST can be used to evaluate a single unit, lesson, or sequence (Exhibit 12.1). Much useful data can be obtained from such a simple instrument. Student answers to the open-ended question also prove to be invaluable.

Logistics

New programs, whether they constitute an entire course or only a three-week instructional sequence implemented as a pilot project, can be extremely complex, especially if an attempt has been made to individualize the program and to combine independent study with traditional group sessions. The scope and nature of these individualized programs make it extremely important that all of the elements be carefully coordinated and that materials be available in sufficient quantity at the right time and in the right place.

Although coordination is an obvious need, it is often overlooked. The reason for this oversight is perhaps a human one: most of us are not interested in the step-by-step analyses and preparation

Exhibit 12.1. MINI-QUEST Questionnaire for Student Evaluation of Materials.

Date _____   Material Title _____

Course Title _____   Instructor _____

Please circle the most appropriate alternative.

1. Interest
   These materials were:
   (1) Very uninteresting
   (2) Uninteresting
   (3) Interesting
   (4) Very interesting

2. Pace
   These materials were:
   (1) Much too fast
   (2) A little too fast
   (3) Just right
   (4) A little too slow
   (5) Much too slow

3. Amount Learned
   I learned:
   (1) Nothing
   (2) Very little
   (3) A fair amount
   (4) A great deal

4. Clarity
   These materials were:
   (1) Very unclear
   (2) Unclear
   (3) Clear
   (4) Very clear

5. Importance
   What I learned was:
   (1) Very unimportant
   (2) Unimportant
   (3) Important
   (4) Very important

6. General
   Generally, these materials were:
   (1) Poor
   (2) Fair
   (3) Good
   (4) Excellent

7. Please indicate any questions raised by these materials.

8. Please write at least one specific comment here about the materials. (Use the back if necessary.)

Thank you!

required to make sure all the elements are ready and available. As noted earlier, such factors as the number of students who own their own computers and the availability of computer clusters can determine the logistics necessary.

On one campus a successful program was expanded from approximately one hundred students to three hundred. In planning for this increase the staff considered the number of classrooms required but completely overlooked the need to increase the supply of independent-learning units, an integral part of the course. As a result, when the semester began, the number of sets of material on reserve in the library was not increased sufficiently, and many students found it impossible to get through the units in the required time. The result was chaos, confusion, and loss of tempers; an excellent program was damaged by careless management.

The same type of problem occurred on another campus when the faculty and support staff who had carefully designed the instructional elements, new materials, and testing procedures for a course overlooked the essential student-orientation session. Two weeks were lost as puzzled students tried to understand what they were to do and where they were to do it. Orientation is especially crucial when the program departs from tradition. Do not expect students to trust a statement of objectives, for example, when for years they have observed that faculty say one thing, teach another, and test for a third.

The logistical problems vary from project to project. Generally, however, they occur in the following areas:

• *Classroom availability.* The required number of rooms should be scheduled, and the assigned rooms must meet size and media requirements. (This is particularly important in programs that use various types of structures in a flexible pattern.)

• *Student communication system.* In large classes procedures must be established to ensure that important information, such as scheduling changes and additional class meetings, reaches the students. E-mail can be an excellent tool for this purpose. These procedures are especially important when a regular class pattern is not being followed. New course patterns and procedures are often difficult to understand for a student who is encountering them for the first time. A student manual can play a vital role in the success of a new program that breaks from the traditional approach. The design and use of a manual are described in detail in the next chapter.

• *Support system.* Be sure that support areas (library, computer clusters, and so on) are ready and able to handle the students when they arrive. Can tests and other evaluation and diagnostic instruments be scored and interpreted in the available time? Are the most efficient methods of tabulation being used, and are procedures established to collect all the evaluation data that are required?

• *Amount of materials.* Having on hand the materials necessary is particularly important if independent study is involved. The exact number of units that will be required is affected by the length of the sequence, the number of students, the number of concurrent assignments, how much time the students have between the initial assignment and its completion, the particular study pattern of the students, and various external elements, such as vacation periods and assignments in other courses. The best advice is to have more sets of materials or workstations than you anticipate needing in the beginning and then base future decisions about the amount of materials to have available on the data that are collected regarding use. Usually the ratio of sets of material to students falls between 1:10 and 1:20, and much closer to 1:4 or 1:5 if computers are involved. Experience has shown, however, that patterns of use vary substantially from course to course and may change in a single program from one semester to the next, particularly as students adjust their study patterns according to experience. For example, in an individualized biology laboratory, students tended at first to wait until the end of the week before going to the laboratory and, as a result, found themselves waiting in long lines. Within a few weeks, however, the pattern had changed, and most students completed their assignments earlier, thus improving the efficiency of the operation.

- *Availability of VCRs, computer stations, and so on.* If many students will require access to a combination of hardware and software, make sure that it is available for the hours necessary. Increasingly, a combination of student-owned equipment and institutional computer or media clusters is needed to support courses using this equipment. Check on overall computer availability on your campus.

Summary

As Ruth Colvin Clark has observed, "Any medium can be rendered ineffective by inappropriate methods" (1995, p. 5). No matter how information is presented, it will be of little use if the students are not given sufficient time to interact with it and discuss it. But a quality lesson, designed well and taught well, will be effective no matter which technology is used. As a teacher, you have available many paths that will lead your students to the instructional goals you have developed. The choice is yours, as is the quality of the experience. Today you have more options than ever before. And with more diversity in your classroom and a dynamically increasing body of knowledge you also have more challenges. Technology if used well can help you face them.

Sources of Information on Technology in Education

Electronic Sources

One source of the latest information on research dealing with the use of instructional media and on new developments in the area is the Educational Resources Information Center (ERIC) Clearinghouse on Information and Technology Resources (School of Education, Syracuse University, Syracuse, NY 13244) (Ask ERIC, http://ericir.syr.edu). This federally funded agency has been established specifically for this purpose.

Because the world of technology is ever-changing, you should spend some time searching the Web. Here you will find the latest information about computer applications in higher education, and many faculty are putting the units themselves on the system with information on the problems they were addressing and the results that they had. In Exhibit 12.2 you will find a list of forty Websites that the editors of *Syllabus* have found to be the most useful. Although some of these focus on precollege instruction, the approach used can have higher education applications.

Print Sources

Cartwright, G. P. "Technology and Underprepared Students." Part 1: *Change,* Jan.-Feb. 1996, *28*(1), 45–48. Part 2: *Change,* May-June 1996, *28*(3), 60–62.

> Case studies in the use of technology to meet the needs of underprepared students. Includes resources for additional information.

Rogers, S. "Distance Education: The Options Follow Mission." *AAHE Bulletin,* Dec. 1995, *48*(4), 4–10.

> Presenting one case study at the Rochester Institute of Technology, this excellent report describes various approaches to distance learning and the selection and use of technology in this context. Includes a glossary and some excellent and developed resources.

Halpern, D. F., and Associates. *Changing College Classrooms: New Teaching and Learning Strategies for an Increasingly Complex World.* San Francisco: Jossey-Bass, 1994.

> Part Three, "Teaching with and About Technologies," includes chapters on using the Internet, interactive video, and hypermedia, and an extremely useful chapter on ethics that has applications far beyond technology.

Soderberg, D. J. "Using the Worldwide Web for Teaching and Learning." *Focus on Teaching and Learning,* Winter 1996, pp. 8–9.

> This is a good reference with which to start. Includes references to a number of Websites that will provide you with examples of projects by faculty from various institutions.

Syllabus. A monthly publication available from Reader Services Department, 1307 S. Mary Avenue, Suite #211, Sunnyvale, CA 94087–3018.

> This monthly publication contains reports on various applications of technology with useful case studies from institutions throughout the United States. Includes a regular update on useful Websites. And the price is right—it is free to faculty and administrators. Also check out this publication's Website (http://www.syllabus.com) for up-to-date case studies and references.

Exhibit 12.2. Top Forty Education Websites.

The top forty sites were chosen based on comprehensiveness, creativity, and relevance for educators interested in technology. All contain substantive information for the education community.

1. EdWeb
http://edweb.cnidr.org:90/

2. New Media Centers
http://www.csulb.edu/gc/nmc/index.html

3. Texas Center for Educational Technology
http://www.tcet.unt.edu/

4. On the Horizon
http://sunsite.unc.edu/horizon/index.html

5. Internet Resources for Technology Education
http://ed1.eng.ohio-state.edu/guide/resources.html

6. Virtual Classroom
http://www.enmu.edu/virtual/virt.html

7. The Technology Coordinator's Web Site
http://www.wwu.edu/-kenr/TCsite/home.html

8. The Virtual Library for Information Technology
http://tecfa.unige.ch/info-edu-comp.html

9. Vancouver Film School
http://www.multimedia.edu

10. LEARNER ONLINE Home Page for Educators
http://www.learner.org/content/educator.html

11. The Galileo Project
http://es.rice.edu:80/ES/humsoc/Galileo//

12. Virtual Chemistry
http://www.chem.ucla.edu/chempointers.html

13. World Wide Art Resources
http://wwar.com

14. Developing Educational Standards: Overview
http://putwest.boces.org/standards.html

15. Computational Chemistry for Chemistry Educators
http://www.mcnc.org/HTML/ITD/NCSC/ccsyllabus.html

16. The Covis Project
http://www.covis.nwu.edu/info/covis-info.html

17. Educational News Resources
http://www.bc.edu/bc_org/avp/soe/cihe/direct2/Ed.News.html

18. Mathematics
http://pegasus.cc.ucf.edu/-ucicasio/casio.htm

19. ProfNet
http://www.vyne.com/profnet/

20. University Pages
http://isl-gamet.uah.edu/Universities/

21. Library of Congress Education Page
http://lcweb2.loc.gov/ammem/ndlpedu/

22. An Educational interface to the WWW
http://www.cis.uab.edu/info/grads/mmf/EdPage/EdPage2.html

23. The Global Campus
http://www.csulb.edu/gc/

24. WebED Curriculum Links
http://badger.state.wi.us/agencies/dpi/www/WebEd.html

Exhibit 12.2. (continued).

25. Resources for Technology Coordinators
http://www.cybergate com/-blesig/hoffman/tech/

26. Distance Learning Demonstration Projects
http://www.visc.vt.edu/succeed/distance.html

27. Global SchoolNet Foundation
http://www.gsn.org/

28. Distance Education Clearinghouse
http://www.uwex.edu/disted/home.html

29. Writing for the World
http://www2.uic.edu/~kdorwick/world.html

30. Courseware for Higher Education on the World Wide Web
http://philae.sas.upenn.edu

31. University of Michigan Online Writing Lab
http://www-personal.umich.edu/~nesta/OWL/owl.html

32. Discover NCSA: National Center for Supercomputing Applications

http://www.ncsa.uiuc.edu/General/NCSAHome.html

33. Great Lakes Collaborative Home Page
http://www.greatlakes.k12.mi.us/

34. Institute for the Exploration of Virtual Realities
http://ukanaix.cc.ukans.edu:80/~mreaney/

35. A Business Researcher's Interest
http://www.pitt.edu/~malhotra/interest.html

36. University of California-Berkeley Museum of Paleontology
http://ucmp1.berkeley.edu/welcome.html

37. SchoolNet
http://k12.school.net/home.html

38. Project EASI (Easy Access for Students and Institutions)
http://easi.ed.gov

39. International Society for Technology in Education
http://isteonline.uoregon.edu

40. AskERIC
http://erieir.syr.edu

Source: Syllabus, http://www.syllabus.com

CHAPTER 13

Developing a Learning-Centered Syllabus

The clearer the picture your students have of what you expect them to do at the end of your course and the greater their understanding of what their role will be and of the criteria that will be used to determine success or failure, the more effective the course will be. A learning-centered syllabus is based on the question, "What information will help my students succeed in my course?" Using such a syllabus can improve learning and at the same time avoid many frustrations caused by poor communication. Judith Grunnert (1997, p. xi) has observed, "Your syllabus represents a significant point of interaction, often the first, between you and your students. If thoughtfully prepared, your syllabus will demonstrate the interplay of your understanding of students' needs and interests, your beliefs and assumptions about the nature of learning and education, and your values and interests concerning course content and structure."

Throughout this book I have focused on the design of courses and curricula that will develop in our students the competencies they need to be successful in college and after graduation. The model shifts the focus away from what we teach to what students will learn, so that we as faculty serve less as disseminators of knowledge than as facilitators of learning. This shift calls for changes in how we think about the courses we teach, how we design students' learning experiences,

Portions of this chapter have been adapted from the preface to Judith Grunnert's *The Course Syllabus: A Learning-Centered Approach.* Bolton, Mass.: Anker, 1997. Used with permission of the publisher.

how we use class time and students' time, what we expect from our students, and what they can expect from us.

Technology, changing demographics, failure to engage students, and new ways of thinking about the nature of knowledge in the Information Age have prompted many instructional changes on college and university campuses. In addition, new opportunities available through the Internet and e-mail and increased use of active learning, as well as internships and extended-classroom activities, have significantly altered how we teach by requiring enhanced interaction among all members of the learning community. The traditional syllabus, designed for a teacher- or content-centered classroom, is ineffective for helping students understand their expanding role in the learning enterprise. To understand the expectations we have of them and our plans for the learning experience, students need more comprehensive information than the traditional syllabus provides. The learning-centered syllabus places students at the center of the question, "What do students need to know in order to derive maximum benefit from this educational experience?"

Many faculty have already gone far beyond the one- or two-page syllabus with which most of us are familiar. John Lough (1996), in a study of faculty members who have been recognized as Carnegie Professors of the Year, found important similarities in syllabi designed by these exemplary teachers. Most obvious was their "detailed precision." Each contained clearly stated course objectives, a day-by-day schedule identifying specific reading assignments and due dates, and clear statements regarding make-up dates, attendance, and grading standards. They also provided students with the times faculty members would be available in their offices, by e-mail, and by phone at home. Lough observes, "One gets the very clear impression the . . . award winners have extraordinary expectations for their own behavior in and out of the classroom. Perhaps it is not so surprising, therefore, that these professors might impose some of these same standards on the students with whom they share so much" (p. 223). Obviously, it is through their actions—what they do in the classroom and how it is manifested in what they say in their syllabi—that these faculty communicate these standards to their students.

As faculty we often invest a great deal of time in improving the content and structure of our courses, the quality of the materials we use, and the equity of our examinations. Despite these efforts, many of us spend countless hours with individual students reviewing content, attempting to clarify assignments, and generally helping them (and perhaps ourselves) to understand requirements, assignments, and standards.

Although many of the instructional problems we face are to be expected, others are unnecessary. If our students do not understand their assignments or if they study the wrong content for a test or are confused about how grades will be determined, they will not learn effectively. Such problems can be avoided. In a review of the problems faced by students, a course-approval committee at the University of Maryland (Rubin, 1985, p. 56) identified a series of important questions that were repeatedly not answered in the syllabi provided by the faculty to their students.

- Why would a student want to take this course?
- What are the course objectives? Where do they lead, intellectually and practically?
- What are the prerequisites? What does the faculty member assume that the students already know? Will the missing necessary skills be taught during the course?
- Why do the parts of the course come in the order they do?
- Will the course be primarily lecture, discussions, or group work?
- What does the professor expect from the students?
- What is the purpose of the assignments?
- What will the tests test? memory? understanding? ability to synthesize, to present evidence logically, to apply knowledge in a new context?
- Why have the books been chosen? What is their relative importance in the course and in the discipline?

An effectively used and carefully designed comprehensive syllabus can improve the students' learning by helping to answer these and other questions. It can improve communication, significantly reducing problems for you and your students.

Just as courses differ, no two syllabi should be alike. The final decision about the form and content of a learning-centered syllabus must be based on the structure of the course (lecture, laboratory, field experience, discussion, and so on), the number of students, the learning goals and expectations for students, and how much direction you wish your students to have. For some, the syllabus becomes a comprehensive course manual.

Why Use a Learning-Centered Syllabus?

A learning-centered syllabus serves a wide variety of functions, all designed to make your role easier and your students' roles and responsibilities clearer. Your syllabus can do the following:

- *Define student responsibilities for successful completion of the course.* One of the biggest problems students have is managing time effectively. If your students have a clear idea of what they are expected to accomplish and a time frame for completion, they are more likely to finish assignments on time and be appropriately prepared for exams. As students assume greater responsibility for their own learning, they need to know what is expected of them.

- *Improve students' note taking and studying.* Students frequently spend class time copying detailed formulas and diagrams or attempting to distinguish important from unimportant information. As a result, they often miss the major points of the presentation or discussion. By including outlines of information to be covered, essential diagrams and tables, and copies of overhead transparencies, the manual helps students organize and focus their note taking and studying.

- *Reduce test anxiety and improve test-taking skills.* Providing your students with sample questions in a manual has a positive impact on learning and reduces test anxiety. The more students know about the instructional priorities, the more effective and efficient they can be in their studying.

- *Acquaint your students with the logistics of the course.* Many courses vary significantly in the schedule of classes, the instructors for each class, and the type of sessions (guest lecturers, simulations, group projects, and so on). A learning-centered syllabus details this information so that students know what to expect at each class meeting.

- *Provide readings that are difficult to obtain.* If a course is developed before comprehensive literature on the topic is available, the manual can include copies of articles you want your students to read. (If a syllabus is used in this way, be certain that the necessary copyright clearances are obtained.)

- *Include handouts that might otherwise have been distributed individually.* We frequently distribute handouts as they become appropriate to the topics covered. If these handouts are included in the syllabus, students find it easier to keep all the course information together and accessible. Materials of this type often include important tables, charts, graphs, and diagrams that are not found in the required texts.

- *Improve your students' efficiency.* By including detailed descriptions of major assignments, you can help your students prepare for their work and improve their time management.

Faculty who have developed comprehensive syllabi have found the approach helpful for their students. Typical comments follow.

- [The expanded syllabus] provides a succinct presentation of relevant course materials, which helps the student to define what is important for this particular course.

- It helped a great deal. Faculty colleagues from other institutions have been able to easily adapt and adopt the course with limited guidance from me. In addition, I have very few requests for clarification of course requirements, time lines, grading criteria or standards, or weekly assignments. Perhaps some faculty look forward to such repeated discussions—I prefer to teach.
- A terrific idea. The students can refer to [the syllabus] throughout the semester, and they considered it to be one of the most positive aspects of the course.
- The greatest advantage for me is that it enables me to get a variety of materials in students' hands efficiently and effectively.
- [The expanded syllabus] provided necessary coherence for the class. Without it, the course would have appeared not only "experimental" but unorganized or even incoherent. The syllabus provided important information and a semblance of rationality. It gave all of us a common plan and reference.

Equally important, the very process of putting a learning-centered syllabus together can lead you to a more carefully designed course because it allows you to review, in a logical manner, the major decisions you have made up to this point.

Content and Style

The content of a syllabus varies from course to course, as does its general format. However, the following items are usually required. (The specific order in which these items are covered is not absolute.)

1. Title and number of the course.
2. Letter to the student describing the intent of the course in its present form and, if the program is experimental, asking cooperation in the evaluation that will take place.
3. Table of contents.
4. Purpose of the manual and how to use it.
5. Introduction.

   - Status of course (pilot, experimental).
   - Rationale (how this course fits into the general program and for whom it was designed).
   - General directions for the student.
   - Where notices, grades, and so on, will be posted.

6. Personnel involved in the course and how to contact them (office hours, phone). Those involved in the design of the course might also be listed. If the manual is to be used over several semesters, the names of personnel should be omitted or the manual should

be designed so the student can complete this information on the first day of class.

7. Overview of content.

   - Instructional flow diagram (introduction).
   - Course outline.
   - Module outline (may come later in explanation of each module).
   - Options.
   - General course objectives.

8. Evaluation and/or grading procedures.

   - Credits and grades.
   - Requirements/assignments.
   - Scales or forms.

9. Logistical forms.

   - To request and/or change options.
   - To notify faculty of problems and errors in the materials.

10. Specifics of each unit: objectives, options, projects, grades, place, time, personnel, flow diagram, requirements/assignments.

11. Materials.

    - Texts: where and how to get them and how to use them.
    - Bibliographies, charts, and so on.

12. Calendar—places and times for units, projects, meetings, mini-courses, deadlines, and so on (often the calendar can be combined with the flow diagram for each module). Again, if the manual is to be used over several semesters, specific dates should be omitted.

13. Facilities—learning laboratory, library, museum, and so on: where they are and how to use them.

14. Checklist of all deadlines.

15. Self-tests (with answers): designed to give the students an opportunity to see whether they can meet the stated objectives.

16. Copyright or credit notices.

17. (Optional) Readings or other materials (such as forms to be turned in) that are necessary and not available elsewhere. Also included in this section may be copies of complex diagrams or other visuals that will be used by the faculty member during lectures, chronologies, and materials on using the library or computing center.

In addition, with more and more faculty using e-mail, making assignments on the World Wide Web, and requiring that papers be completed on the computer, it is crucial that you include in your syllabus all relevant information about your expectations for computer use. In developing a course that had as one of its goals giving the students confidence that they could use computers to solve problems, Edmund Prater and Michael Smith found that providing students with key information right at the beginning of the course was essential. On the first day of class students were given the following information (1995–1996, p. 287):

- A description of how to log on to the computer system.
- Where to go for help in logging on to the computer and to get general questions answered (usually a computer-center support desk).
- How to print out an on-line set of directions for using e-mail.
- The instructor's e-mail address.
- Where to find on-line postings of the class syllabus and schedule and how to view them on-line or print them out.
- Where to find the announcement file for class messages. This file includes announcements, reminders, and corrections of and addenda to material presented in readings and lectures.

They also provided their students with a list of courses offered by the library on using electronic research tools. Using e-mail for all official communication, they found in time that regular office hours became unnecessary because all student appointments with faculty were arranged via this process.

Faculty at Syracuse University have found that all this information—how to use e-mail, a list of appropriate workshops and courses—can easily be included in their syllabi.

Because your syllabus will be used by students, it should be written to students, using "you" whenever possible. It should be clear and precise, especially for courses with complex structures. Flow diagrams, if used well and designed with care, can outline the scope of the course and provide logistical information. If complex drawings are to be used in large lecture sections, reduced copies should be included. Also effective is leaving space for taking notes if the syllabus is to be referred to during the lecture. Grunnert (1997) is an excellent guide to writing a learning-centered syllabus; it includes representative pages from a number of syllabi in various disciplines.

Getting Your Syllabus Prepared, Printed, and Distributed _____

A comprehensive syllabus can run anywhere from twenty to well over a hundred pages. Therefore, before work begins on putting your syllabus together, a process that can take a great deal of time and effort, the basic logistics of production and distribution should be worked out.

Obtaining Permission to Reproduce Copyrighted Material

At times you may want to include materials from other sources in your syllabus. In most instances you are permitted to quote words, tables, figures, and other material as long as the quotation is accurate and appropriately credited. However, depending on the source, length, and nature of a quotation, permission from the copyright holder may be needed. Some quotations do *not* require permission:

1. Quotations from any work published before 1906.
2. Quotations from most federal government publications.
3. Any quotation from nonfiction of fewer than three hundred words or less than 1 to 2 percent of the total word count, whichever is less, provided that it is (a) clearly presented as a quotation, (b) not taken out of context, (c) not used as an epigraph, or (d) not "qualitatively substantial"—that is, it does not go to the heart of the work or quote from the most moving or interesting parts; and provided that full credit is given.

Some quotations and paraphrases do require permission:

1. Any table, checklist, or other list taken entirely from another source.
2. Quotations from nonfiction in excess of three hundred words or 1 to 2 percent of the total, whichever is less. Permission is required for both single long quotations and multiple quotations from a single work that add up to more than three hundred words.
3. Quotation of *any* length from a work of fiction.
4. A paraphrase of more than three hundred words from nonfiction whose wording and sequence of ideas are similar to the original.
5. Any quotation used as an epigraph.
6. Quotations of any length from information publications including speeches, position papers, corporate in-house documents, mission statements, questionnaires, and unpublished dissertations.

7. Quotations from personal letters and documents (the recipient owns the letter, but the copyright is retained by the author).

In some instances paraphrasing an author's ideas is as effective as a direct quote, and doing so relieves you of the obligation to get permission (except in the case of item 4 above). You may want to consider this option. Of course, you still need to provide thorough information on the source.

Fees charged by publishers for the use of materials vary greatly, and they are often negotiable. Make sure publishers have a clear understanding of the amount of material you want to use, and if you feel the charge is excessive, call and negotiate. For a single table or chart or citation of three hundred words, charges may range from nothing to $35. If you are selling your manual at cost and with a limited run, you can usually negotiate no charge or a low fee. But do get permission.

For the latest and most detailed information on copyright, contact the National Association of College Stores, Inc., 500 E. Lorain St., Oberlin, OH 44074.

Production by an Outside Publisher or Printer

If you have more than one hundred or so students each semester, you can use publishers who, in addition to printing and distributing your syllabus, will take care of obtaining the necessary clearances from other publishers and authors. The following three publishers, among others, will help obtain permissions and print your syllabi:

Copley Publishing Group
138 Great Road
Acton, MA 01720

Ginn Press
160 Gould Street
Needham, MA 02194

Kendall/Hunt Publishing Company
4050 Westmar Drive
P.O. Box 1840
Dubuque, IA 52004

In addition, small printing/duplication stores located on or near college campuses will both print and sell such manuals. These stores copy directly from your materials and do not generally provide editorial or graphic assistance. Many college bookstores are now also providing this service.

Production Within Your Institution

Some institutions have staff available who will help with layout, graphics, and editing. If you are planning to develop a syllabus, find out whether such resources are available. Is there a center for instructional development or faculty development with staff who can help in layout and editing? What kind of help can you get from your department? Many chairpersons or deans can provide clerical assistance and, as noted earlier, can pay some salary in the summer to assist you during this period of heavy writing. In other instances summer stipends come directly from the central administration. On some projects a portion of this money can be used to pay a graduate assistant for help.

Costs

Most academic departments have funds set aside to cover the printing of classroom handouts and short syllabi. However, these monies usually are not adequate to support the free distribution of a more complete syllabus. Depending on the quantity and the number of pages, printing these more detailed syllabi may cost well over $1,000 for a class of several hundred students. For this reason I recommend selling these syllabi/manuals to the students through your college bookstore, other normal textbook channels, or local duplicating stores.

The advantages of selling these manuals through one of these outlets are many:

- There is no fiscal risk to the faculty or to the department.
- Some bookstores, as well as duplicating stores, are willing to handle the printing as well, significantly reducing the faculty member's production concerns.
- It is possible to pay royalties to the authors or, if fiscal support has been given, to the department or institution.
- If the quality is high, students accept paying for the syllabus as they would for any other course-related resource.

The selling price of a syllabus produced within the institution can be determined by adding together the production costs, the royalties (usually about 15 percent), the cost of desk copies and overruns (usually about 10 percent), and the bookstore markup (usually about 25 percent) and dividing by the number of copies produced.

Printing small quantities of materials is expensive. Even though the students will usually purchase the manual (since note taking in the syllabus is encouraged), attempts should be made to minimize the cost. The cost can be lowered substantially by either separating the unique semester information (calendar, faculty, office hours, specific options, and so on) from the main body of the material and giving it to the students separately as a handout or by leaving space for students to fill in this information. Doing so allows more copies of the syllabus to be printed at one time for use during several semesters. In addition, you can cut the costs to your students significantly by forgoing royalties. Because a bookstore will mark up the price by 25 percent or more, forgoing a 15 percent royalty can result in a nearly 19 percent reduction in the selling price.

Royalties and Copyright

As noted previously, writing a high-quality learning-centered syllabus takes time and effort—time that you could devote to research, to other writing, or to other financially rewarding activities. Collecting royalties on the sale of a syllabus recognizes the value of the effort and, in one small way, helps to balance the reward system for teaching, research, and publication. The key is how much new material is in the final product. If it contains extensive original work, you may want to discuss with your chair or dean the possibility of collecting royalties. Some faculty are comfortable doing so; others are not.

Because a syllabus may contain important new material, some consideration should be given to copyrighting it. At Syracuse University, where many syllabi are produced with the assistance of the Center for Instructional Development, a formal royalty and copyright policy is in place. See Resource H for a sample copyright agreement. If sales are anticipated outside the institution or if significant new material is contained in the manual, you can hold the copyright or it can be held by the institution if you were awarded funds for the project. If the syllabus does not contain much new material and it is for use only in a specific course, you can simply include a notice of copyright on the title page. No other formal action on your part is required.

Putting Your Syllabus On-Line

Although an increasing number of faculty are placing their syllabi on-line for easy retrieval and to cut costs, others are finding that this approach can actually reduce the effectiveness of the document. They report that because the student-centered syllabus is an outstanding reference, it should be used in class on a regular basis. When it is placed on-line, students do not have it available for use in class. Their approach: have it on-line (for enrolled students and others who wish to learn more about the course), but require that it be purchased by the students and brought to class.

Summary

This chapter has described the kind of material you might include in your syllabus and ways of preparing, producing, and distributing it. However, no matter how good a syllabus is, its contents should always be reinforced in your classroom. The best of syllabi are effective only if you refer to them on a regular basis and make bringing them to class an integral part of your approach to teaching.

CHAPTER 14

Cultivating a Respect for Diversity

Most higher education institutions include on their list of major goals some reference to developing in their students a respect for diversity, an understanding of different cultures, and the ability to work constructively with others who have different backgrounds, goals, and priorities. The growing movement in this direction is as significant as it substantial. A study of thirty-four thousand faculty noted, "Perhaps the most striking shift between 1989 and 1995 has been the increased commitment to diversity and multiculturalism among faculty and their institutions" (Astin, 1991).

Schneider (1995) discusses issues of diversity in our society and how diversity should relate to the goals and processes of higher education. "In its commitment to diversity, higher education assumes . . . both a distinctive responsibility and a precedent-setting challenge. While other institutions in the society are also fostering diversity, higher education is uniquely positioned, by its mission, values, and dedication to learning, to foster and nourish the habits of heart and mind that Americans need to make diversity work in daily life" (p. xvi).

Unlike most of the other basic goals for all students, cultural diversity cannot be addressed within one course or curriculum. Reaching this goal presents faculty and institutions with a unique challenge, and for that reason it is discussed here in more depth than all others.

Developing in our students the ability and willingness to work effectively in a multicultural environment is a complex task for a number of reasons. First, to do it successfully we must actively involve the entire campus community and reach far beyond the classroom. We cannot successfully teach our students to deal with diversity if they find intolerance and bigotry in their residence halls and in offices around campus. Second, few issues create more tension in our classrooms because in this instance students are asked to question beliefs that have been developed since childhood. Third, until we deal with prejudice directly, a significant portion of students will find that the environment of our classrooms is simply not conducive to learning. Wlodkowski and Ginsberg (1995, p. 2) have observed that "people who feel unsafe, unconnected, and disrespected are unlikely to be motivated to learn. This is as true in college as it is in elementary school. Such a conclusion does not explain all the issues and barriers related to the progress of people of color in postsecondary education settings, but it is fundamental to what happens among learners and teachers wherever they meet. In education, perhaps more so than in work, it is the day-to-day, face-to-face feelings that make people stay or go." Fourth, most of us are not particularly comfortable addressing these issues in our courses, in our classrooms, or in conversations with our students. Nor have we been prepared to do so.

Specifying Outcomes

I will respect the dignity of all persons [Carolinians Creed, University of South Carolina].

We the students, faculty, staff and administrators of Syracuse University will promote a culturally and socially diverse climate that supports the development of each member of the community [Compact, Syracuse University].

Students will have a heightened awareness of and sensitivity to gender issues, diverse cultures, international perspectives, and a variety of issues calling for social justice [Instructional Mission Statement, Holly College].

Hartwick graduates will be noted as being able to thrive in the webbed world of the next millennium; a world in which people of the broadest range of national, ethnic, social, and personal backgrounds will interact personally and technologically.
To thrive in this context will require that Hartwick students learn to: understand the world from a variety of perspectives; work constructively with people from a variety of backgrounds [Hartwick Signature, Hartwick College].

Although each of these statements sets as a goal developing in students a sensitivity to others with different backgrounds and perceptions and an ability to work constructively in a pluralistic society, the statements do not provide enough specificity to be useful to those responsible for the design of instruction. Earlier chapters pointed out the need to state such goals in operational terms so that we can determine how successful we and our students have been in reaching them.

Paula Rothenberg (1996b, p. 59) describes the educational outcomes of such goals as follows:

> Students need to learn to identify and reject narrow oppositional thinking that teaches them to see the world in terms of good and bad, right and wrong, black and white, male and female, winners and losers. They need to know that there are always more than two sides to an issue and that alternatives can often be situated on a continuum rather than framed as diametrically opposed. They need to explore the liberating possibility that a number of conflicting and even contradictory things can be true at the same time and to examine models for thought and analysis that are more like spider webs than railroad tracks. Similarly, students need to acquire a respect for diverse styles of writing and arguing, which will in turn affirm the diversity not merely among us but within us—diversity (richness) that has been suppressed by the imposition of categories of both gender and race as narrowly oppositional and hence mutually exclusive.

A national panel made five recommendations for meeting diversity goals (Schneider, 1995, p. xii):

- Create a level playing field on which everyone holds an equal stake in explorations of societal experiences, identities, and aspirations;
- Impart knowledge of the diverse cultures, communities, and histories that comprise United States society;
- Connect these diversities to a continuing engagement with democratic ideas and aspirations;
- Provide experiential as well as formal knowledge of these topics; and
- Prepare students for a world in which unitary agreement does not now exist and is not likely ever to exist.

More specifically, the panel recommended four kinds of courses and experiences (p. xxi):

1. Experience, Identity, and Aspirations: The study of one's own particular inherited and constructed traditions, identity communities, and significant questions, in their complexity.
2. United States Pluralism and the Pursuits of Justice: An extended and comparative exploration of diverse peoples in this society, with significant attention to their differing experiences of United States democracy and the pursuits—sometimes successful, sometimes frustrated—of equal opportunity.
3. Experiences in Justice Seeking: Encounters with systemic constraints on the development of human potential in the United

States and experiences in community-based efforts to articulate principles of justice, expand opportunity, and redress inequities.

4. Multiplicity and Relational Pluralism in Majors, Concentrations, and Programs: Extensive participation in forms of learning that foster sustained exploration of and deliberation about contested issues important in particular communities of inquiry and practice.

Most of us would agree that every college graduate should be able to identify the significant contributions to our culture made by minorities, women, and individuals from other countries. We want the graduates of our institutions to be sensitive to how individuals from other cultures and backgrounds might see the world differently and as a result act differently in similar situations. Moreover, we believe our students should understand how the society in which they live has affected their own beliefs and how these perceptions affect their perceptions of and reactions to others.

Agreeing on Structures

Although most faculty support these outcomes, there is far less agreement on how they can be achieved. Should one or more courses on multiculturalism be recommended or required, or should a multicultural perspective be built into all courses? What are the trade-offs? If a diversity goal is to be added, what will it replace? We have a limited amount of time, and for every element or exercise we add, something else must be dropped. As Joan Stark and Lisa Lattuca (1997, p. 368) observe, "The struggle to include pluralistic views in the curriculum faces battles quite similar to those faced in previous eras by disciplines as they emerged from parent fields such as natural philosophy. Pluralistic views must compete for scarce curricular space. . . . Although the change to multiculturalism may be on the near horizon, the decisions about sequence needed to fully achieve a global curriculum may require totally new thinking about the content included in undergraduate education."

For some institutions the solution will be to add several requirements to their programs and to encourage faculty to address the topic of diversity whenever possible, as, for example, a topic that lends itself well to developing thinking skills. For others, reaching the goal of cultural diversity will require major changes in the total curriculum, as Rothenberg (1996a, pp. 13–14) suggests:

Curriculum transformation on a large scale, the kind that gets talked about beyond the halls of the academy, occurs periodically and in response to dramatic changes in our society, changes that prompt us not merely to reappraise the utility of a particular text but to question the very worldview that informs the perspective from which we teach and write.

Those of us teaching and learning at the close of the twentieth century find ourselves caught up in one of those moments when the foundations of knowledge have been called into question. As a result of the scholarship that has been produced by women's studies, black and other ethnic studies, and lesbian and gay studies, profoundly disturbing questions have been raised about what we have always considered to be knowledge in any field. By focusing on the ways in which this knowledge has been socially constructed, such scholarship has raised revolutionary questions about the way we have defined objectivity, truth—even reality. These questions shape this historical moment in education and frame the intellectual and social context in which we function as educators.

Institutional Initiatives

Although this book focuses on courses and curricula, ideally the goal of multiculturalism should be addressed from an institutional perspective with the establishment of an all-campus task force or committee. This committee should include representatives from the faculty selected for the role they can play in developing and implementing the academic side of the initiative, key staff and administrators from the office of student affairs, and on a residential campus, leaders from the office of residential life. From a political viewpoint, others may need to be involved: faculty and staff who are already doing work in this area or who have related expertise, representatives from key student groups (do not forget fraternities and sororities), and representatives from religious units. In addition, a community advisory committee could include representatives from organizations in your region who are dealing with issues of cultural diversity. Not only can this group provide you with resources, resource people, and excellent advice, but their participation might open up internships and other course-related experiences for your students that could prove invaluable.

The purposes of such a task force are many:

- Articulating the institutional goal.
- Educating the college or university community about the importance of and rationale for this goal.
- Informing other members of the community about actions taken, about what others outside the institution are doing, and about lessons learned.
- Reviewing materials, approaches, games, and exercises that are available on campus.

- Providing a training base for faculty and staff who are willing to address these issues within their courses or programs.
- Coordinating initiatives to produce maximum impact with minimal overlap and duplication.

This task force could, if it is successful, make your life as a faculty member much easier not only by helping you understand what you might expect in your classroom and helping you prepare for these experiences but also by providing you and your students with resources and opportunities that would otherwise not be available.

Classroom Initiatives

Deciding how to address diversity issues within your academic program will not be easy. For most of us it will be necessary to study developing areas and philosophies that were not even in our textbooks when we were in college. In addition, as many faculty are finding out, including the topic of diversity in our teaching can have a far greater impact on the dynamics and climate of our classroom than we anticipate. We must focus not only on what we teach but on how we teach, and prepare ourselves to handle the stresses that our students will feel as perceptions and long-held basic beliefs are challenged, often for the first time.

When Glen Jacobs led his undergraduate students in a discussion of race relations, a well-intentioned scholarly dialogue soon turned into a shouting match, resulting in anger, insults, and tears (Readon, 1992, p. 10).

> "The incident began innocently enough," says Jacobs, who is entering his seventeenth year as a professor of sociology at the University of Massachusetts at Boston. A white student [who] was expressing his interest in black culture inadvertently offended several African-American classmates. "The discussion gained momentum very quickly and I lost control of it," Jacobs says. "That was the scariest thing. I started to realize how powerful this subject is and began to question my own ability to manage a classroom symposium."

As Wlodkowski and Ginsberg have observed (1995, p. 287), your students need to feel safe and secure if they take a stand with which others might not agree or if they are anxious about having their beliefs challenged. In this regard you may find it helpful to acknowledge that doubt and anxiety are signs of change in personal and professional development.

In almost any course you will have the opportunity to make your students aware of the contributions of different cultures to your discipline. In many courses, but particularly in those with a historical dimension, teams can be assigned to identify how and why different groups of individuals perceive the same action so differently. You can assign students to teams in which they will work closely with people of different backgrounds and beliefs, being sensitive to the difficulties some students may have in such a setting. Such assignments will succeed only where respect for difference has already been nurtured.

The resources listed at the end of this chapter include practical suggestions for teaching and learning in this most complex area and information on how other faculty and institutions around the country are doing so.

Case Study: University of Massachusetts at Boston

In May 1991, a coalition of faculty, students, and staff at the University of Massachusetts at Boston won approval for a universitywide diversity requirement; diversity was defined as differences based on race, gender, social class, culture, age, disability, and sexual orientation. This initiative was led by faculty member Esther Kingston-Mann, a professor of history, who in 1988 was disturbed to find that her students believed that Africans had not made contributions to civilization. Also playing major roles were Estelle Disch, associate professor of sociology, who focused on building campuswide support for the initiative, and Wornie Reed, chair of the Black Studies Department, who argued that a multicultural curriculum elevated academic standards by making them more honest and reflective of world history. The initiative began in 1989, with the establishment of a Diversity Awareness Working Group of students, faculty, and staff, which held twenty Diversity Awareness Workshops in that academic year. The group grew from six or seven people to over sixty by 1991. A basic principle of the group was that whenever someone criticized part of the initiative, he or she was asked to join. As Kingston-Mann (1992) observed, "It was very important to us that nobody sees us as a group of outsiders trying to impose something, but that people see this as a group inclusive in its process as well as its goal, so that people would really buy it and not see it as external."

With released time and full support from the top administration the three leaders focused on the diversity requirement from an intellectual perspective and won wide faculty support with this approach. By including age, social class, gender, and disability, they also astutely included almost every student and faculty member in their definition, providing a bridge for people "who might not have understood it in other ways."

Under the proposal no one is required to teach a diversity course. Faculty can propose new courses or transfer existing ones into the curriculum. "We were trying to create a situation where when you teach a course in economics or history or psychology, thinking about issues of diversity and inclusion would be a normal part of what you do when you are planning the course. For example, whose voices are you listening to? What authorities? Are they only white? Are they only male and European? Or are they multicultural and diverse? We're encouraging people to think about a new way of teaching," says Kingston-Mann (quoted in Deitz, 1995, p. 11).

Undergraduates must take two courses that are primarily concerned with the intellectual contributions of historically marginalized cultures; courses in such diverse fields as literature, art, history, anthropology, nursing, business, and economics as well as core courses are designed specifically to meet this requirement.

Debate about the initiative was often surprisingly positive. As Kingston-Mann observed (1992, p. 30), "At a time when the national and local media were reporting on a national crisis over political correctness and multiculturalism, . . . faculty members debating multicultural curricular change [at the University of Massachusetts at Boston] did not ever accuse their reforming colleagues of 'political correctness.' Instead, a wide range of 'traditional' and 'non-traditional' faculty members came to agree that diversity and multiculturalism should be taken seriously as academic issues and made a sincere effort to decide how this was to be done."

In his anthropology course Childhood in America, a course meeting the diversity requirement, Tim Sieber includes a number of writing assignments. Exhibit 14.1 is one of them. Notice how carefully the assignment has been constructed and how clearly Sieber describes the ground rules and the process that should be followed. For this assignment students have the option of comparing their own childhood experiences with the experiences of those in other cultures they have studied.

The University of Massachusetts initiative has expanded to include a number of institutes, various publications, and outreach to the community (including the public schools in the region) and to other colleges and universities.

The Boston experience provides a great deal of insight into the political process of change. Although the change process could easily have become explosive and counterproductive, it did not. Faculty were actively involved from the beginning; efforts were made to support faculty in learning about the topic; and in-service training was provided on how to handle classroom problems that might occur. Effective leadership among faculty and the top administration made a significant difference.

Looking back, Kingston-Mann (1992, pp. 30–31) observed:

> The history of multicultural curriculum initiatives at [the University of Massachusetts at Boston] carries five important lessons about the political correctness controversy, and more importantly, about curricular reform itself.

> - A faculty that is relatively diverse is likely to recognize the academic legitimacy and importance of a wide variety of cultural perspectives.
> - A personnel process that rewards faculty members who take teaching seriously will encourage them to invest time and energy in rethinking and reorganizing courses to take account of multicultural issues.
> - A diverse student body may find a greater emphasis on diversity long overdue rather than "novel" or "alien."

Exhibit 14.1. Pluralism Assignment.

Anth L301—Childhood in America   Tim Sieber
Short Paper Assignment: Due May 10

Childhood is a subject everyone can relate to personally, since each of us has been a child. However vivid and intense our personal childhood experiences are, and however strong the feelings that we have about them, on the other hand, experience itself does not usually give us intellectual tools for its own understanding. Typically, we resort to learning and employing specialized, often formal, frameworks of inquiry and analysis in order to understand the full meaning of our own experience. Important among these frameworks are some we have been learning about in this course: those offered by the social sciences, and by history.

Your second writing assignment for "Childhood in America" is to complete a short paper that analyzes (1) your own childhood, and/or (2) your own family history in light of the issues and questions about American childhood that we have studied in this course. This is a very open assignment, and there are many different ways that you could fulfill it. Here are just some of the possible examples and suggestions; there are many others.

1) We have read about many different kinds of childhood and many different kinds of child-rearing strategies that have been employed by people in different social groups in the USA. How do your own childhood experiences compare and contrast with some of the others that we have read about? Where does your childhood fit in among the diverse variety we have considered?

2) Perhaps there was one variety we studied that, on the surface, ought to apply to your own childhood. For example, maybe your father was a blue-collar worker or a professional white-collar worker of the sort discussed by Melvin Kohn. Do the reading materials in question seem to illuminate your experience?

Remember this is not an exercise in criticism of the reading materials; be sure to use any such criticism or agreement as a departure point for discussing your own past, which should be the real focus of the paper.

3) Maybe you want to focus on a small analytic point or insight from one of the readings, and explore it in some depth in relation to your own background. For example, Kohn says that adults' experiences at work help them define their goals for rearing their own children. Perhaps you could question your own parents, and/or some other adults in your family to explore this idea.

4) If this applies to you, how did the experience of being a member of a racial, linguistic, or cultural minority affect how your parents brought you up? Or how did it affect the way your grandparents brought up your parents? As a child, what kind of awareness did you have of your minority status?

5) Perhaps you want to focus on discipline as an issue. According to what principles were you disciplined as a child? How did you feel about it then? How do you feel about it now? How did your experience compare with others we have read about?

Exhibit 14.1. (continued).

6) Perhaps you could focus on the relations between the sexes. How much cooperation was there between men and women in rearing you? How was the role of mother or father conceived of in your family and group? Did your parent or parents ever question ideas of what was considered proper in child rearing? Why? This would be an ideal topic calling for interviews of your parent or parents about their experiences in bringing you up.

7) When you were brought up, did your parent or parents feel a need to deliberately try to depart from the models of child-rearing they themselves had been subject to in their own childhood? Why?

8) How were boys and girls treated differently within your family? Why?

9) If you are not American, or were not brought up in the United States, or your family history lies outside of it, this opens up many other good possibilities! How does your own experience as a child or your own family history, compare with what you understand to be the more common American patterns?

There are a few rules you should follow:

1) You have to do some serious thinking and investigation here. Essays written off the top of your head will read as such.

2) What kind of sources should you use for information? Your own memory is an important source, but also very selective and faulty; so, do not depend on it entirely. Few of us have very extensive documentary materials on our childhoods and family histories. This means, in other words, that to do this paper, *you must interview some other people*—preferably people in your family, if they are available to you, who can give you other perspectives on the past. In class, I'll talk about procedures for interviewing.

3) In writing your paper, be sure to mention explicitly what course reading or issues you are trying to relate to your own past, or the past of your family. Be clear about what problems or questions concern you the most. Don't just jump into a long discussion about your past or your family, without first explaining what facets of your past you are looking at, and what in the course materials is helping you to understand or investigate them.

4) Five to eight pages, double space typed, is the length. You can go over this limit if you like, but don't go too far over. Doing something meaningful in less than nine pages (when we are talking about ourselves), I think you will see, can take discipline!

- Linking multicultural curriculum change with academic excellence and higher standards appeals to a wide range of faculty members who see a commitment to excellence as the primary goal of any academic institution.
- "Grass-roots," faculty-based initiatives are particularly effective because they respect and build on the skills and insights which a number of faculty already possess, and make it impossible to portray reforms as changes "imposed from above" or inspired by outside experts. Encouraging faculty to take ownership of multicultural curriculum initiatives is crucial to their realization.

For more information contact Esther Kingston-Mann, Center for the Improvement of Teaching, University of Massachusetts at Boston, Wheatley 5–013, Boston, MA 02125–3393; 617–287–6767; kingstonmann@umb-sky.cc.umb.edu. A booklet describing the various initiatives on the campus—"A Guide to Diversity Resources"—is also available.

Summary

This chapter has reviewed the importance the developing in our students a willingness and ability to work with individuals of different backgrounds and priorities. We have described ways in which this goal can be addressed and thee importance it has in our institutional context. We have considered how your success might be measured. Few agreed-upon goals require us to test our own beliefs and biases more directly than does this one. As a result this goal, as important as it is, can be among the most difficult to address.

Additional Resources

Diversity Connections, available on the World Wide Web (http://www.inform.und.ed/connections/) or by writing to *Diversity Connections*, Judd Hall, Wesleyan University, Middletown, CN 06459.

Designed to provide an up-to-date, comprehensive look at how institutions throughout the United States are addressing diversity issues. Covers course curricula and campuswide initiatives.

Friedman, E. G., Kolmar, W. K., Flint, C. B., and Rothenberg, P. (eds.). *Creating an Inclusive College Curriculum: A Teaching Sourcebook from the New Jersey Project.* New York: Teachers College Press, 1996.

With some excellent overview chapters this report on a statewide initiative begun in the mid-1980s contains over thirty descriptions of courses from many fields of study and from a wide variety of institutions—from community colleges to research universities—as well as information on the statewide program that supported the initiative.

Project Three: Curriculum and Faculty Development Network, Teaching Diversity and Diversifying Teaching. Association of American Colleges, 1818 R Street NW, Washington, DC 20009; 202–387–3760.

Sponsored by the Ford Foundation, this network of sixty institutions has been established to develop new courses about American pluralism and to share ideas.

Wlodkowski, R. J., and Ginsberg, M. B. *Diversity and Motivation: Culturally Responsive Teaching.* San Francisco: Jossey-Bass, 1995.

Provides some practical suggestions on how to bring multicultural issues into your classroom while recognizing that there are many places to begin. Includes a wide array of possible directions and approaches.

CHAPTER 15

Implementing, Evaluating, and Refining the Course or Curriculum

Previous chapters emphasized the direct relationship between a statement of learning outcomes and student assessment. This chapter focuses in depth on this relationship and on the final phase of your effort: implementing, evaluating, and revising your course or curriculum. The primary emphasis is on courses and on the use of capstone courses to determine the success of the overall program.

Throughout the design process you have been collecting, analyzing, and using information. Before you even began, data were collected to determine need and to identify the problem. Data were collected to help design the "ideal" program and then to modify the design so that it could be implemented with the resources available. During the early production phase you evaluated existing instructional materials and may have had the opportunity to field-test new ones.

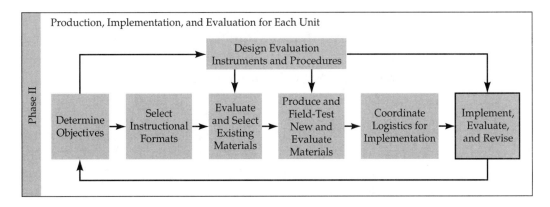

Production, Implementation, and Evaluation for Each Unit

Phase II

Design Evaluation Instruments and Procedures

Determine Objectives → Select Instructional Formats → Evaluate and Select Existing Materials → Produce and Field-Test New and Evaluate Materials → Coordinate Logistics for Implementation → Implement, Evaluate, and Revise

In this, the final stage, you will be implementing your new course or program and collecting data on logistics, coverage, methods, and most important, student learning. Because data are important, make sure that all your assessment instruments are ready before you begin implementation so that you will be able to collect essential information at the ideal time. During this stage you will be able to determine how successful your effort has been.

In a course design project the initial implementation and evaluation stage will take only a single semester. In the case of an entire undergraduate curriculum, however, it will take much longer, as each element of the program is phased in and implemented. Because curriculum projects usually require significant changes in the freshman year, the first complete assessment will follow that first cohort through their entire four years and even into the job-interviewing and placement activities that follow. For a professional program students will be followed into their early years on the job. In projects of this magnitude individual courses will be evaluated as they are implemented so that they can be modified and improved even before the first group of students completes the entire sequence. You can build in other comprehensive evaluation efforts at key points in the program—at the completion of a required course or at the end of a sequence of courses where there is a focus on a specific discipline or skill (that is, writing, speaking, computer skills, and so on) and in a capstone course. Your primary challenge in this stage is to determine which data will provide you with the best information for determining whether you have been successful.

Implementation Guidelines

When you are implementing a new design for the first time, whether it be for a single unit, a course, or an entire program, it is best to try to limit the number of students involved, although doing so is sometimes impossible. Large numbers of students (several hundred) constrain your ability to find rapid solutions to problems that may occur. With smaller numbers, design deficiencies can be corrected as they are identified, significantly reducing frustration for you and your students. Dealing with a large number of students can create major headaches for you if your estimate of the time required is inaccurate or if an unexpected problem occurs. The case studies later in this chapter show that surprises are to be expected. Every project will go through several design–field-test–revision sequences before it is considered fully operational. As problems in the program are identified and solved, you can gradually increase the number of students enrolled. Resist trying to accomplish too much in too short a time.

Improvement and modifications of the program can be expected to continue as students change, additional faculty become involved, the content changes, and new methods become available. Although it can be far less comprehensive than the earlier efforts, a modest evaluation effort should be continued.

Outcomes and Assessment

In the long run your success as a faculty member will be determined by the performance of your students. The more successful they are in reaching the goals that you have established, the more successful you will have been as a teacher. As basic as this relationship is, it creates a fundamental problem in higher education: there is often a significant difference between the goals we establish and the methods and criteria we use to judge and grade our students. As noted earlier, our goals include higher-order reasoning abilities, but the assessment techniques we most frequently use focus on recall and recognition. As you select the approaches to assessment and the specific items you will use, make certain that each of the major goals and outcomes you have identified is addressed.

Useful Publications and Other Resources

As we move from basic recall and recognition goals to focus more on process and complex behaviors, assessment becomes increasingly difficult. In addition to the help you can obtain from other faculty, particularly the experts in learning and assessment found in schools or departments of education, various publications can provide you with a starting point as you develop the kinds of student assessment you will use for certain outcomes. These publications are reviewed here.

Angelo, T. A., and Cross, K. P. *Classroom Assessment Techniques: A Handbook for College Teachers.* (2nd ed.) San Francisco: Jossey-Bass Publishers, 1993.

This extensive and comprehensive publication offers practical advice on and concrete examples of most current assessment techniques.

Evers, F. T., and Rush, J. C. *The Bases of Competence.* San Francisco: Jossey-Bass, 1996.

This book provides useful descriptions of basic skills, which can be of great help as you develop assessment protocols. In Exhibit 15.1 you will find an example that outlines the skills needed by managers.

Greenwood, A. (ed.). *The National Assessment of College Student Learning: Identification of the Skills to be Taught, Learned, and Assessed.* NCES #94–286. Washington, D.C.: National Center for Education Statistics, U.S. Department of Education, 1994.

Exhibit 15.1. Basic Skills Needed by Managers.

1. **Mobilizing innovation and change:** conceptualizing as well as setting in motion ways of initiating and managing change that involves significant departures from the current mode.

   • **Ability to conceptualize:** involves the ability to combine relevant information from a number of sources, to *integrate information* into more general contexts, and to apply information to new or broader contexts.

   • **Creativity/innovation/change:** involves the ability to *adapt* to situations of change, at times it involves the ability to *initiate* change, and provide "novel" solutions to problems. Also involves the ability to *reconceptualize* roles in response to changing demands related to the firm's success.

   • **Risk-taking:** involves taking reasonable job-related *risks* by recognizing alternative or different ways of meeting objectives, while at the same time recognizing the potential negative outcomes and monitoring the progress toward the set objectives.

   • **Visioning:** involves the ability to conceptualize the future of the company and to provide innovative paths for the company to follow.

2. **Managing people and tasks:** accomplishing the tasks at hand by planning, organizing, coordinating, and controlling both resources and people.

   • **Coordinating:** involves being able to coordinate the work of peers and subordinates and encourage positive group relationships.

   • **Decision-making:** involves making timely decisions on the basis of a thorough assessment of the short- and long-term effects of decisions, recognizing the political and ethical implications, and being able to identify those who will be affected by the decisions made.

   • **Leadership/influence:** involves the ability to give direction and guidance to others and to delegate work tasks to peers and subordinates in a manner which proves to be effective, and motivates others to do their best.

   • **Managing conflict:** involves the ability to identify sources of conflict between oneself and others, or among other people, and to take steps to overcome disharmony.

   • **Planning and organizing:** involves being able to determine the tasks to be carried out toward meeting objectives (strategic and tactical), perhaps assigning some of the tasks to others, monitoring the progress made against the plan, and revising a plan to include new information.

Source: Evers and Rush, 1996, p. 280.

Jones, E. A. *Essential Skills in Writing, Speech and Listening and Critical Thinking for College Graduates: Perspectives of Faculty, Employers and Policy Makers.* University Park: National Center on Post-Secondary Teaching, Learning, and Assessment, Pennsylvania State University, 1994.

Jones, E. A. *National Assessment of College Student Learning: Identifying College Graduates' Essential Skills in Writing, Speech and Listening, and Critical Thinking.* NCES #95–001. Washington, D.C.: National Center for Education Statistics, U.S. Department of Education, 1994.

Limited to four basic competencies—writing, speaking, listening, and critical thinking—these three reports are published by the National Center for Education Statistics and the National Center on Post-Secondary Teaching, Learning, and Assessment at Pennsylvania State University. Included in these reports are detailed descriptions of each skill and of how specific performances can be used to determine whether the competency has been achieved (see Exhibit 15.2).

Jones, E. A. *Writing Goals Inventory.* University Park: National Center on Post-Secondary Teaching, Learning, and Assessment, Pennsylvania State University, 1994.

As Exhibit 10.3 showed, this inventory specifies four categories of writing competence expected of college graduates and lists subskills under each. The instrument provides a means of reaching agreement on what we mean when we say our graduates are competent in writing.

Pedersen, P. *A Handbook for Developing Multicultural Awareness.* Alexandria, Va.: American Counseling Association, 1988.

Written for individuals who, like most faculty, will be counseling in multicultural environments, this handbook describes the awareness, knowledge, and skills that an individual needs to be successful and then provides questions that could be asked to assess whether these competencies are being reached (Exhibit 15.3). These same questions could be asked as you assess any student's ability to work and live effectively in a multicultural environment.

Assessment Update, published bimonthly by Jossey-Bass, 350 Sansome Street, San Francisco, CA 94104–1342).

This is a most useful publication. In the July–August 1996 issue, for example, an article by Trudy Banta describes how a simple matrix can be a powerful tool in helping you plan and organize your approach to assessment. The same issue includes a review of a standardized objective test for assessing critical thinking (the Watson-Glazer Critical Thinking Approach) by Gary Pike, and one on critical thinking by Joseph Shaelwitz that focuses on assessing capstone courses.

"Teaching Goals Inventory," developed by Thomas Angelo and K. Patricia Cross, *Classroom Assessment Techniques.* San Francisco, Jossey-Bass, 1993; see Resource I.

This is another excellent resource, designed specifically to help you list your goals in order of importance. By adding your discipline-focused goals to the list, you will have a broad base from which to select appropriate assessment techniques.

Exhibit 15.2. Decision-Making and Problem-Solving Skills.

Category description: The skills used in decision making and problem solving are those involved in the generation and selection of alternatives and in judging among them. Many of these skills are especially useful in quantitative reasoning problems.

Skill	Description	Examples of Use
a. Listing alternatives and considering the pros and cons of each	Every problem and decision involves selecting among alternatives. This is a systematic way to consider the advantages and disadvantages of various alternatives.	Several ways of increasing sales are described. CT (critical thinker) combines the advantages and disadvantages of each and adds his own alternatives and combination of alternatives.
b. Restating the problem to consider different sorts of alternatives	Most real life problems are "fuzzy"; that is, there are many possible goals and ways to achieve them.	Several ways of increasing sales are described. CI redefines the problem as too little profit and considers other ways to increase profits.
c. Recognizing the bias in hindsight analysis	Hindsight analysis is the reevaluation of a decision after it has been made and its consequences known, with the belief that the consequences should have been known with greater certainty when the decision was made.	After a parolee goes on a killing spree, the townspeople want to fire the parole board. CT knows that the decision to release the parolee may have been reasonable given the information available at the time it was made.
d. Seeking information to reduce uncertainty	Decisions based on more information are likely to be better than those made with greater uncertainty.	A company is deciding whether to increase its advertising budget. CT gathers relevant information about the effect of increased advertising before making the decision.
e. Recognizing decision based on entrapment	Entrapment is a situation in which much money, time, or effort has been invested and the decision to continue with a course of action is based on this investment.	The Pentagon argues that the government needs to continue spending money on a new weapon because it has already invested large sums of money on its development.
f. Producing graphs, diagrams, hierarchical trees, matrices, and models as solution aids	Graphic representation of problems can be useful in solving them.	A problem is described verbally. The task for the CT is to depict the information in a graphic display in order to solve it.

Exhibit 15.2. (continued).

Skill	Description	Examples of Use
g. Understanding how worldviews can constrain the problem-solving process	There are limitations on the way individuals approach problems placed upon them by social class or other group membership.	A company president is confronted with a takeover. The possibility of cooperating with the competitor does not occur to the president because of the individual's worldview.
h. Using numerous strategies in solving problems, including means-ends analysis, working backwards, simplification, analogies, brain storming, contradiction, and trial-and-error	This is a collection of common strategies that every problem solver should know and use. They all require the planning and monitoring of solution strategy.	Several stages of action need to be completed by a due date. CT works backward from the due date to decide how much time should be spent on each stage.

Source: Greenwood, 1994.

Using Portfolios as an Assessment Technique

One assessment approach that you may wish to explore is the student portfolio, which has a number of purposes. As noted earlier, developing a portfolio can help students reflect on what they have learned and link what they are doing to the goals of your program; it can help improve their writing skills; it can lead to self-reflection and self-evaluation; and as at Alverno College (Resource A) it can provide you with an in-depth and holistic view of the student's growth over a period of time. Portfolios can also be submitted for review during the semester, which enables teachers to monitor student progress and provide support when it is most needed and most useful.

Portfolios contain the actual work that the students have done in a course. Braskamp and Ory (1994, p. 219) describe them as "purposeful and systematic collections of the students' work, which will demonstrate students' efforts and progress and achievement to a variety of audiences, particularly their teachers. . . . Portfolios contain samples of work from different types of assignments, . . . work completed under different conditions. They may include work in progress, such as term papers. Often portfolios represent the best work of a student's accomplishments and include student self-evaluations and reflections." Many of us are familiar with the use of portfolios in art and writing classes, but they are finding their way now into other courses with equal success.

Exhibit 15.3. Multicultural Competencies for Counselors.

The student should be able to describe a situation in a culture so that a member of that culture will agree with the student's perception of it. Such an awareness would require an individual to have:

Required competencies:
- Ability to recognize direct and indirect communication styles;
- Sensibility to nonverbal cues;
- Awareness of cultural and linguistic differences;
- Interest in the culture;
- Sensitivity to the myths and stereotypes of the culture;
- Concern for the welfare of persons from another culture;
- Ability to articulate elements of his or her own culture;
- Appreciation of the importance of multicultural teaching;
- Awareness of the relationships between cultural groups; and
- Accurate criteria for objectively judging "goodness" and "badness" in the other culture.

Guidelines for measuring assessment
- Does the student have specific knowledge about the culturally defined group members' diverse historical experiences, adjustment styles, roles of education, socioeconomic backgrounds, preferred values, typical attitudes, honored behaviors, inherited customs, slang, learning styles, and ways of thinking?
- Does the student have information about the resources for teaching and learning available to persons in the other culture?
- Does the student know about his or her own culture in relation the other culture?
- Does the student have professional expertise in an area valued by persons in the other culture?
- Does the student have information about teaching/learning resources about the other culture and know where those resources are available?

Guidelines to measure skill development
- Does the student have appropriate teaching/learning techniques for work in the other culture?
- Does the student have a teaching/learning style that will be appropriate in the other culture?
- Does the student have the ability to establish empathic rapport with persons from the other culture?
- Is the student able to receive and accurately analyze feedback from persons of the other culture?
- Does the student have the creative ability to develop new methods for work in the other culture that will go beyond what the student has already learned?

Exhibit 15.3. (continued).

Guidelines to measure awareness

- Is the student aware of differences in cultural institutions and systems?

- Is the student aware of the stress resulting from functioning in a multicultural situation?

- Does the student know how rights or responsibilities are defined differently in different cultures?

- Is the student aware of differences in verbal and nonverbal communication styles?

- Is the student aware of significant differences and similarities of practices across different cultures?

Source: Reprinted from P. Pedersen, *A Handbook for Developing Multicultural Awareness,* 1988, pp. 9–11. © ACA. Reprinted with permission. No further reproduction authorized without written permission of the American Counseling Association.

In her report "Student Portfolios for Academic and Career Advising," Laurie Schultz Hayes (1995b) describes in some detail how the contents of student portfolios used in the University of Minnesota College of Agriculture are linked to the specific instructional goals of the program. These fourteen outcomes include demonstrating fundamental knowledge of the biological and physical sciences; communicating effectively; retrieving, analyzing, and managing information; evaluating and integrating diverse viewpoints; managing human resources; and working effectively as part of a team (the complete list is in Exhibit 6.4).

As Angelo and Cross (1993) point out, although portfolios have major advantages, using this technique requires a great deal of time and careful integration of the portfolio and your objectives.

Using Before-and-After Comparisons

If your curriculum or course is replacing a program that existed previously, you have an excellent opportunity to collect data that focus on change. In deciding to begin your project you identified a need, justified the project as important, and collected data about what was and was not working with the existing program. You may also have collected data about attrition, student attitudes toward the course or program, and job placement. As you plan your assessment, an effort should be made to see whether these problems have been resolved.

- If instructional elements were missing from the original program, have they been included?

- If there were attendance problems, have they been reduced or eliminated?
- If job placement was a problem, are employers actively seeking your graduates?
- If student attitudes were negative, have they improved?
- If attrition was high, has it been reduced?
- If few students were majoring in your field, has the number of majors increased?
- If faculty teaching follow-up courses complained about the quality of student preparation, have their needs been met?
- If the line of students wishing to drop the course went around the block, has it been reduced or eliminated?
- If students and their parents were constantly complaining about the course or program, have these complaints been reduced or eliminated?

Information of this type can be extremely powerful and most useful to you as the instructor, to administrators, to alumni, and to outside funding agencies.

Unanticipated Assessment Results

Every project will have results you do not anticipate. In many instances these surprises are positive. Perhaps your students are performing far beyond your expectations or have attitude changes you could only have hoped for. Perhaps you are spending instructional time more efficiently. These outcomes may become apparent during the course of the program or may come to the surface from data collected at the end or from students' perceptions or from comments made later by students, their parents, other faculty, administrators, or employers. Be sensitive to this feedback; it may provide you with important information that you can use to improve your course or program and other courses as well.

Sample Results

As an example of the kind of detailed results you can expect from assessment, here are some from Prater and Smith's efforts to use e-mail and electronic postings. They made the following observations based on their assessment of this practice (1995–1996, pp. 287–288):

- The availability of an easy-to-learn text editor for composing messages removes a great barrier to e-mail use. The default text editor of our e-mail system, which is called "vi," has many useful functions but is difficult to learn. This distracts students from our goal of having them use the technology. We advise the students to change their default text editor to an alternative program called "pico." Pico has fewer functions than vi but is much easier to learn. Students who already know another text editor or wish to learn one are free to do so.

- Good documentation is essential. Some students come into our classes having used e-mail rarely, if at all, and with little knowledge of the Unix commands necessary for using the computer system. Students quickly grow frustrated and petulant when they cannot figure out how to accomplish a task. Unable to find a suitable e-mail manual, Michael [Smith] simply wrote his own and placed it in a postscript file where students can print it out. This manual has also proven useful to grad students and some faculty.

- Using electronic posting cuts down on the time spent in "administrivia" in several ways. It reduces the time required to make and distribute paper copies. This also eliminates the competition for time on the copy machines. Electronic postings can be made from any terminal through which the computer system can be accessed, even from home. Also, the computer system often proves more reliable than the copies. All of these things simplify the dissemination of information to the class.

- E-mail also helps protect the students from carelessness on the part of the instructor. Having students send copies of their assignments to themselves at the same time they e-mail their work to the instructor produces a time-stamped "receipt" for their work. If the assignment is misplaced, the student(s) always can produce their own copy of the message, exactly as it was first sent.

Keeping Students Informed

At times, particularly during the initial trial of a program, it is essential that the students involved in the experimental or pilot group be kept informed of what is happening and what you are finding out. Providing information to the students during this period serves several purposes. First, it gives the program credibility. Students know that you are listening to them and that you care. Second, as a result, they are willing to tolerate the intrusion of evaluation and may improve the quality of the information they provide. And third, if problems occur, they tend to forgive and to be far more positive toward the whole experience than they might otherwise be. In one new project the students were willing to overlook an unrealistically heavy workload when they were informed that as a result of their feedback, the assignments and time schedule were being changed for the next semester. A memorandum sent to students involved in the pilot run of the music course described later in this chapter not only covered test results by level and described the student attitudes toward the test and individual units but also discussed the changes that were being made based on their input. Finally, the memorandum stressed the importance of the information the students had provided to the development team and thanked them for their assistance.

The one-minute paper is also an excellent technique for collecting data and reporting to students. In this approach, you ask your students, near the end of your course, to write a brief paper listing what they got from the course and what they did not understand. You then begin the next class by referring to their comments, answering questions, and addressing concerns. Remember, a course may not always proceed as you had hoped, and your students are usually most affected by any problems.

Case Study: Evolution of an Introductory Psychology Course

In the fall of 1983, the psychology department at Syracuse University, building on an earlier project, introduced a new first-year course that was designed to provide all students with the same basic program. Previously, individual sections had been taught by different faculty, each using textbooks supporting his or her own approach to psychology. As a result, the faculty teaching the courses that followed could make few if any assumptions about what the students already knew, causing major problems in the department.

Recognizing the potential problems associated with having faculty and nearly a dozen graduate students offering a single course to approximately eight hundred students, the department asked the Center for Instructional Development to formally evaluate the new program and to make recommendations based on the findings. An evaluation protocol was cooperatively developed and administered, and student performances on tests and examinations were analyzed.

To collect these data, several steps were taken. Staff attended lectures, a random number of recitation sections, and meetings of faculty involved with the course. Interviews were conducted with the recitation leaders (graduate students), the large-group lecturers, other faculty, the department chair, and the course coordinator. The students were surveyed in the middle and at the end of the course.

Although the course generally ran smoothly for a first offering of this type, several specific problems were identified.

- The course, while crucial to the department, was perceived by many as not covering the content considered essential.
- The lecturers (four different faculty members) were not equally well prepared and their presentations were uneven in quality and lacked continuity.
- The room in which the lectures were held was poorly suited to the use of the visuals (vital to the course) and had an inadequate sound system.

- The readings assigned by the four lecturers were uneven in both length and difficulty.
- There was too much emphasis on "word lists" and definitions and too little emphasis on important concepts.
- The role of the course coordinator was not clear.
- Quizzes and examinations were based primarily on textbook materials and did not include questions related to the lecture topics or the recitation discussions; consequently, the students perceived the lectures and recitations as unimportant.
- There was some disagreement about the role of the recitation leaders.

To address these concerns, a number of actions were taken.

- The location of the lectures was changed.
- To provide greater continuity, the department tried to reduce the number of new lecturers from semester to semester and to improve the quality of materials used. Greater effort was also made to ensure that the content of the lectures meshed with the specific goals of the course.
- A comprehensive student manual was produced. This manual, in addition to describing the general operation of the course and the role of each of its components, spelled out grading procedures and instructional objectives and provided representative questions and vocabulary lists. The manual also provided content guidelines to faculty responsible for the large lectures. (In the latest version, selected readings have also been added.)
- Quizzes and examinations were restructured to be more comprehensive, to stress the major objectives of the course, and to include elements covered in both lectures and recitations as well as in the text. Scored items were analyzed, and poorer items were replaced or rewritten.

The results were positive. Ratings of the lectures improved significantly; students found grading to be fairer and exams to better indicate knowledge and relate more to coursework. In addition, and perhaps most significant, enrollment increased from eight hundred to thirteen hundred students. In addition, the student manuals were rated extremely useful and clear. In the following semester the student survey indicated an improvement of the lectures but increased concerns about the recitation sessions. Improvements in the recitation sessions were made during the following year, and a major revision of the entire course is now under way to meet the significant increase in student enrollment.

A comment from the course coordinator best describes the success of this project. "During the current fall semester, attendance at the lectures runs about 90 to 95 percent (up from about 50 percent in its first year). In addition, there is close cooperation, and weekly meetings are held among the TAs [teaching assistants] and lecturers. Although a fair amount of experience with this format would inevitably tend to improvement, the contributions by CID [Center for Instructional Development], I feel, in terms of diagnoses of problems and specific recommendations, were invaluable in the speed with which the course has improved and reached this status. I also found the data extremely valuable as I trained new teaching assistants entering the program."

Case Study: Revision of a Music Course for the Nonmajor

Figures 15.1 and 15.2 are the field test and revised outlines of the first four-week module of a music course for nonmajors at the State University of New York College at Fredonia. (Although this project was completed some time ago, the process that was used in its development and modification is almost identical to the model described in this book.)

The introductory module was designed to provide each student with an orientation to and framework for the entire course and with the prerequisites that were necessary for the units that follow. Because the student population was extremely diverse—some students had as many as eight years of formal music training while others had none—three tracks were used, with assignments based on the performance of the students on the pretest. Level #1 students had the most comprehensive music background; Level #2 students had some musical experience or coursework; and students assigned to Level #3 had little, if any, background in music.

The changes that were made as a result of the field test and the reasons for them are as follows (notice how these changes affected the operational sequence):

- The course overview and the pretest were separated to improve the orientation session. *Rationale:* the course was such a major departure from traditional courses, with its emphasis on independent study and options, that many students found the transition to it difficult. As a result, additional time had to be spent reviewing how to use the student manual as well as explaining to students how they could use the statements of instructional objectives to improve learning and increase the effectiveness of study time.
- The sequencing of seminars within the module had to be substantially changed. *Rationale:* for a seminar to be effective, a certain amount of background information is essential. The original sequence did not provide students with enough study time to complete the necessary units before they were discussed in the seminars. The seminars therefore were rescheduled later in the module.
- New instructional units were required. *Rationale:* on the posttest, students did not perform at the anticipated level in their ability either to read scores or to discriminate aurally. Two additional independent-study units, a tape and slide sequence on score reading and a programmed booklet with audio, were added. As a result, students' deficiencies were corrected.
- One unit had to be completely redesigned. *Rationale:* the original multiscreen presentation on style proved to be instructionally ineffective and disliked (an understatement) by the students. This approach also proved cumbersome and inefficient as it forced all students to move at the same pace. It was replaced by a far more effective tape and slide sequence used in conjunction with written materials.
- The number of seminars was reduced. *Rationale:* as sometimes happens, the fall and spring semesters did not have the same amount of time available for instruction, forcing a modification in design. By placing the seminars later in the sequence and scheduling more seminars for the Level #3 students and fewer for the well-prepared

Figure 15.1. Fall Field-Test Version of Introductory Module for Music in the Western World.

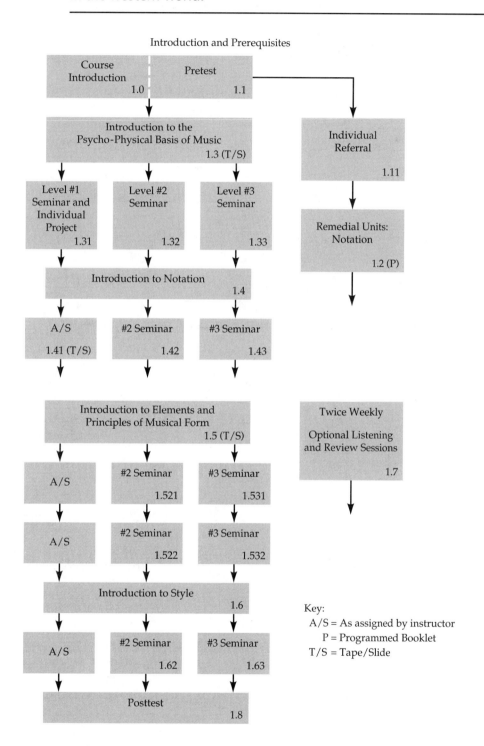

Credit: Thomas Regelski and Robert M. Diamond.

Figure 15.2. Spring Revision of Introductory Module for Music in the Western World.

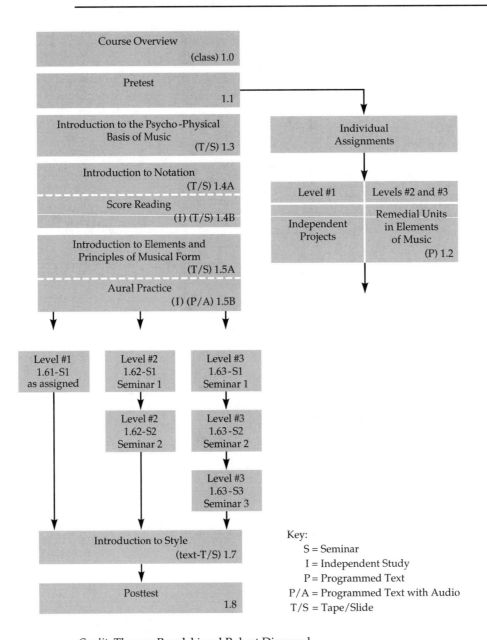

Credit: Thomas Regelski and Robert Diamond.

group, the number of seminars was reduced from fourteen (including three optional ones) to six. This decrease did not appear to have a negative effect on either attitudes or achievement. In addition, to permit maximum flexibility, this three-hour course was scheduled for an hour a day (five hours each week) so that every student could attend any session scheduled during that period. However, the maximum number of live meetings a student would attend during the four-week module was six.

- The twice-weekly optional listening and review sessions were replaced by oral practice, optional audiotapes placed in the Independent Learning Laboratory. *Rationale:* because of a heavy assignment load, students did not attend the regularly scheduled, optional, faculty-led review sessions.

In addition, minor modifications were made in the pretest, in some of the tape and slide sequences, and in the remedial units that were used. Several remedial assignments were also eliminated, and a more realistic time frame was established. The effectiveness of the new remedial module made it possible to eliminate grouping the students by entering levels of proficiency once this unit was completed.

Case Study: Improving Teaching Effectiveness in Economics

The two previous case studies focused on collecting data for course improvement, but sometimes questions are designed to collect data about teaching effectiveness. This technique is particularly helpful in multisection courses in which teaching assistants or junior faculty teach the sections, laboratories, or discussion groups, usually coordinated or supervised by senior faculty members.

In the microeconomics and macroeconomics courses discussed in Chapter Seven, a single faculty member supervised more than a dozen teaching assistants responsible for approximately twenty discussion sections. To assist the supervising faculty member in this role and to provide information that could help these beginning teachers improve their teaching, questions focusing specifically on their performance in the classroom were added to the student end-of-course questionnaire (Exhibit 15.4).

Other sections of the questionnaire dealt with such areas as course objectives, the student manual, the remedial mathematics sequences, course materials, the evaluation procedures, and instruments that were used. It also included a number of open-ended questions focusing on strengths and weaknesses of the course as students perceived them.

To make the questions about the discussion leaders particularly useful, the information collected was presented to the course coordinator and the discussion leaders in three different ways. (See Exhibit 15.5.)

- For each question the course coordinator received an analysis of the data for every discussion section. Because most teaching assistants were responsible for two sections, specific problem areas were easy to identify, and counseling could begin.

Exhibit 15.4. Selected Portion of Questionnaire Regarding Small-Group Discussion Leaders.

A one (1) represents *Not at All*, a three (3) represents *Somewhat*, and a five (5) represents *Very much*.

Please indicate the degree to which you perceive your instructor as:

	N		S		V
14. Prepared	1	2	3	4	5
15. Organized	1	2	3	4	5
16. Understandable in terms of level of presentation	1	2	3	4	5
17. Understandable in terms of language	1	2	3	4	5
18. Being open to questions	1	2	3	4	5
19. Treating students with respect	1	2	3	4	5
20. In control of the class	1	2	3	4	5
21. Enthusiastic	1	2	3	4	5
22. Answering questions effectively	1	2	3	4	5
23. Caring about the subject	1	2	3	4	5
24. Making students interested in the subject	1	2	3	4	5
25. Providing high-quality instruction	1	2	3	4	5
26. Motivating you to perform well in this course	1	2	3	4	5

Exhibit 15.5. Selected Portion of Report to Individual Discussion Leaders.

Class/section/prof: ECN20204

Overall Mean Score = 4.4

Rank over all classes = 3 of 19

Enroll = 2

Item/Question

	Score			
	This Class	All Classes	STD	N
27. Instructional pace about right	3.7	3.6	0.9	31
28. Required workload about right	4.0	3.6	0.8	31
32. Degree exam questions were fair	3.4	3.4	1.2	31
33. Degree exam grading was fair	3.5	3.6	1.0	31
34. Degree exams covered what was taught	3.9	3.7	1.1	31
35. Degree exam time to finish was right	2.5*	3.7	1.3	31
36. Feedback was timely	3.5	3.7	1.0	31

*Problem area.

- All discussion leaders were provided with a summary mean ranking of all sections.
- Each discussion leader also received his or her own summary for all items on the questionnaire and could then compare that data with the data for all discussion leaders.

As a result of reporting information in this way, the coordinator was able to meet with individual discussion leaders to review the specific problems identified and suggest how they could be resolved.

Case Study: Orientation Program for New Teaching Assistants

This project, undertaken at Syracuse University, indicates the importance of collecting base data before an important new program is implemented. The orientation program was a major departure from the way the university trained and supported its teaching assistants and would involve a major commitment of financial and other resources if it were continued after pilot testing. Data collection was imperative to show the impact of the program on the participants and the institution.

To provide this information, a survey instrument was developed and administered to all teaching assistants at the university the semester before the new program was to get under way (spring 1987). The questions on the survey pertained to the needs of teaching assistants and the support they were receiving. The same instrument was administered again in the spring of 1988, which provided a comparison of the replies from first-year teaching assistants and indicated how participants in the program differed from their counterparts from the year before.

In addition to interviewing the participants during the program and the experienced teaching assistants who served as group leaders, the university collected data in a number of other ways. Mid-program and end-of-program questionnaires were administered, deans and faculty supervising teaching assistants were interviewed during the fall semester following the program, and data on the effectiveness of the teaching assistants as teachers were collected in several large-enrollment courses.

The data collected proved invaluable in ensuring the continuation and institutionalization of the program and in identifying areas that needed improvement. Although the first offering of the program was highly successful, change was necessary in some areas. The program that was offered in the summer of 1988 incorporated these changes: more time was set aside for the students to find housing, international students who had studied previously in the United States could be excused from the international program, the amount of time spent in small groups was increased, and the number of large-group lectures was substantially reduced. The length of the program was also slightly reduced, and a number of other scheduling changes were instituted. The evaluation protocol was repeated once again to measure and identify the impact of these modifications.

Based on additional data from the teaching assistants and their departments, the program is now a year-round support system for the teaching assistants with increased participation by the academic units. Results have been positive. Although the scope and intensity of the evaluation effort will be reduced, the program will always include an evaluation component.

Summary

The collection and use of data are essential to the success of this model. Clear and concise outcome statements combined with an assessment program that measures how well your students reach these goals and that collects information on the individual elements of your course or program, on student attitudes toward the program, and if appropriate, on job placement and success after graduation are essential to a quality education system. This process will ensure that your program will improve over time.

Without planned information collection and evaluation, the three courses described in this chapter would not have reached the level of effectiveness that they have. Although some of the evaluation focuses on structure, other questions focus on the effectiveness of a single lesson or on the materials that are used or on the content and goals of the course. Similarly, in peer projects, projects on which students work together, a wide range of questions can be asked, but limited time and resources require focusing on the essential ones. It is your responsibility and that of those working with you to identify which information is most important to collect and which questions should be asked. The assessment of your students' performance will be based on the goals that were established at the beginning of the design process.

The course-evaluation protocol in Resource A is designed to make this process less complicated and more efficient. The detail level of the questions asked and the questions themselves will vary depending on the reason for the evaluation, the problems that are perceived, and the resources and time that are available for the evaluation itself. What is important is that essential questions not be overlooked simply because no one thought of them when the evaluation was being designed.

CHAPTER 16

Learning from Experience

The challenges we face today as teachers at colleges and universities are more complex than ever before. Our students are more diverse and often come to us inadequately prepared (academically, emotionally, and socially); there are more and more demands on our time; resources are often diminishing; and the critics of higher education are convinced that we place our highest priorities on everything but the education of our students. In addition, if our students are to be prepared for the next century, they will require a wide range of additional competencies beyond what has been traditionally taught in our classrooms—competencies that John Abbott, director of the Education 2000 Trust, has described as "the ability to conceptualize and solve problems that entail abstraction (the manipulation of thoughts and patterns), system thinking, experimentation, and collaboration" (1996, p. 4).

To reach these goals will require major changes in what we do as faculty, in how we design the instructional experience of our students, in the role of our students in the learning process, and in where this learning takes place. More and more teaching and learning will occur outside the traditional classroom, and the teaching that does take place in the familiar classroom setting will be increasingly different from what it is today. There will be far fewer lectures and more student participation, and our role will shift to being facilitators of learning rather than disseminators of information. As these trends continue we will find ourselves focusing more on our teaching, using technology more frequently, interacting more with our students and the community, and in most instances enjoying our role more. In addition, change in how we teach and in the materials we use will become a constant rather than occurring from time to time when we get bored with what we are teaching. The stereotype of senior faculty reading from yellowed and somewhat brittle notes almost as old as many of the students in the class will be an image of the past.

A Respected, Honored Activity

For several decades those faculty who spent their energies on teaching-related activities were viewed on many campuses either as being incapable of doing research or as caring little about promotion, merit pay, and at some institutions, tenure. On these campuses the message was clear: spend your energies on teaching at your own risk.

Fortunately for our students, for our institutions, and for many of us, the situation is changing. Teaching and the type of course and curriculum activities described in this book are not only becoming respectable but are encouraged, even at the most prestigious of our research institutions. Each year more campuses are establishing instructional-support centers (a growing number of which are endowed), internal monies are being set aside to fund course and curriculum activities, and the promotion and tenure system is being modified to include these endeavors under the rubric of scholarly work. These changes do not imply that research is no longer important. Rather, faculty reward systems must recognize a far wider range of activities than has been recognized in the past and must be sensitive to the differences among the disciplines and among individuals. The strongest academic units and the most effective institutions recognize that their vitality comes from individuals with different, but equally strong and important, interests and strengths.

It is one thing to have an activity supported; it is another to do it well. A successful effort in course and curriculum design requires a complete approach. The elements of your course or curriculum must be carefully orchestrated to interrelate and connect. The most talented teacher on your campus will not be successful if what he or she teaches is out of date or if essential goals or elements are missing. The best software program in the world is useless if students do not have computer access, and discussion sessions are ineffective if some of your students cannot attend when they are scheduled. An excellent course providing a crucial and required competency is limited by the inability to enroll all the students who need it and the lack of space. The approach described in this book was developed to avoid these problems so that once you begin you can design the best possible program.

Characteristics of Successful Innovation

Heeding the important lessons learned over the years will enable you to reduce the problems you have to face and to improve your end product in a reasonable amount of time.

- *Have a plan and follow it.* This book has proposed a specific model for course and curriculum design. There are others. More important than the model selected is that before you begin you select one model and follow it. Do not skip steps or change models.

- *Do not do it alone.* Having someone from outside your department facilitate the design process not only will result in a better product but also will improve the efficiency of the process itself by reducing the time required. Using a staff member from your faculty-support or instructional-support center or a faculty member who can ask questions, test assumptions, and explore options with you will make your life much easier by eliminating the problems that occur when you have the dual roles of content expert and facilitator. The design process is far more efficient when you are supported by an objective individual whose primary function is helping you get where you want to go.

- *Strive for the ideal.* Do not focus on what exists; focus on what ideally could be. Not only does this approach reduce "turf" wars, particularly in curriculum projects, but it will lead to exciting new approaches and structures that would, under other conditions, rarely even be discussed.

- *Collect information before you begin.* Whether you are designing a course or a curriculum, collect information for three purposes: to establish need, to test your assumptions about your students, and to provide base data so you can document the significant changes that occur. All too often we wait until we are almost finished before we think about writing a report about our accomplishments. As a result the information is no longer available. If you are going to work on a course, collect data before you begin on attrition, student attitudes, learning styles, and so forth. In a curriculum project look for enrollment data, information on the quality of applicants, job-placement data, number of transfers out, and so forth.

- *Create ownership and keep key individuals informed.* Before you begin a project, make sure you have the necessary support. In a course project your chair, dean, and other key faculty should be kept informed. In a curriculum project every department that will be involved must participate. If appropriate, ask them for advice or suggestions. Do not surprise anyone. The more people involved, the greater your support. Key administrators and faculty often are extremely helpful. Share information and seek advice as you move through your project.

- *Be sensitive to human problems.* At times design projects can significantly affect others. These people may be faculty, secretaries, custodians, technicians, or administrators. Remember that change can be an emotional process, and be sensitive to the feelings of others. If you know where problems might occur down the line, bring everyone who may be affected into the conversation as early as possible. And if you are going to need more or different kinds of space or a different credit structure, talk to your registrar. Few administrators can open more doors for you or give you more problems in certain areas; registrars are always complaining, usually for good reason, that faculty members do not advise them early enough of what they have in mind. Do not forget your students either. Be sensitive to the problems of students who are in a course or program that is being offered for the first time or that is being revised. Schedules may not be working well, the workload may be excessive, and every other day someone collects evaluation data. Keep the students informed. Let them know that their assistance, responses to your questions, and patience are extremely important, and be prepared to adjust and modify the course on the basis of their responses.

- *Do not reinvent the wheel.* Whenever possible, use some of the course and curriculum designs and evaluation instruments presented in this and other books for reference. Using existing media, software, and publications is a lot cheaper and certainly faster than trying to develop these items yourself. However, do not try to use material designed for a different purpose or for a different population of students. Keep abreast of what is new, what is being tried, and if it is helpful in the project, use it, borrow it, and where appropriate give credit. Do not waste resources by doing what has already been done or trying things that have failed again and again. Throughout this book, relevant printed materials and World Wide Web sites have been listed; they should prove helpful.

- *Pay attention to support systems and logistics.* As noted earlier, the registrar's office, perhaps more than any other, can encourage or discourage academic innovation by being supportive or obstructive. The library can also play a large role. We as faculty have a tendency not to worry about logistics, but you need to keep on top of details if your project is to succeed. Make out schedules and room assignments. Make sure that book orders have been processed, that multiple sets of materials are ready, that you have the necessary computer terminals available. Keep students informed of any changes, and be sure your secretary and any other staff members who need to respond to questions from students seeking help have accurate, up-to-date information. Leave nothing to chance.

- *Keep media in perspective.* Do not select the media solution before identifying the problem and exploring the alternatives. When technology is used, make sure it is the most effective solution. If computers are to be used, make sure the hardware will support the software you have chosen. Careful selection is essential. When properly used, technology can be a major asset in improving instructional quality and effectiveness. All too often we find faculty and staff starting with the answers and then attempting to modify the project accordingly, a process that usually leads to poor results and failure.

- *Build in evaluation and assessment.* An effective data-collection program can significantly improve the quality of your course or curriculum. Data provide a base for good decision making throughout a project. Determine what information is needed, and develop an evaluation system that provides this information. The data can also be used for your tenure and promotion portfolio as evidence of your teaching effectiveness and efforts in this area.

- *Sometimes, when more than one faculty member is involved, agree to disagree and move on.* Problems of this type do occur, but they are rare. They are most common when goals for curricula are be set because fundamental differences can occur on a specific issue. For example, a task force at the University of Northern Iowa, in an effort to describe the "qualities of an educated person," posed the following questions: Is there one ideal of an educated person, or are there many ideal types? If there are multiple types, to what extent is it feasible to identify common, desired qualities of an educated person (University of Northern Iowa, 1996)? As the task force obviously anticipated, in answering such questions, faculty will have some basic areas of disagreement, but there will be far more areas of agreement. These common goals should become the focus of the conversations that follow. You cannot allow disagreement on one topic to stall the implementation of initiatives.

- *Expect the unexpected.* There are power failures, people get sick, boxes get lost, students may not listen to what they are told or read materials they are given. A snowstorm can play havoc with a schedule, and a computer system always manages to be down on the most crucial day of the year. We have had guest speakers miss their planes and the faculty member scheduled to handle the major course orientation end up having a baby on that day, two months early. At times like these, one can only do his or her best, be creative, and maintain a sense of humor.

Summary

Obviously, a list like this is never complete. Many of the suggestions, once one thinks about them, are obvious. Unfortunately we often find that we have created many of our own problems by rushing, by not worrying about details, by not listening, or by not being as sensitive to the feelings of others as we should be. However, as difficult as the process of course and curriculum design can be, it is also challenging, exciting, and rewarding. Few things we do in our careers will have more significant impact on the lives of more students or will make us feel as good. Enjoy the experience.

Questions for Evaluating a College Course

RICHARD R. SUDWEEKS
ROBERT M. DIAMOND

No two evaluation designs will be the same. In each instance the evaluation must be structured to serve the information needs of those involved in the decision-making process. However, some general questions tend to recur in the evaluation of courses and other programs of instruction. The following list has been designed to assist faculty and administrators who are or will be charged with the task of evaluating a course. Although no list can ever be considered complete, this one has been developed from efforts on several campuses that have designed and implemented new courses and programs and have evaluated existing courses and curricula. The list is intended to be a guide in the design stage of an evaluation. It should serve as a checklist for making sure that all relevant questions have been considered.

All the questions in this list may not be appropriate in a single project because of limitations in time, staff, and money. Those involved must select the specific questions that should be addressed and prioritize them. This list is intended to be comprehensive so that those involved can omit questions intentionally rather than by accident. The evaluation methodology selected should match the questions that are being asked.

Participants in the evaluation process should consider each of the following questions and check those that are appropriate for the specific course they are evaluating:

I. RATIONALE
- [ ] A. What population of students is the course intended to serve?
- [ ] B. What student needs is the course intended to meet?
- [ ] C. What institutional, community, or societal needs is the course intended to meet?
- [ ] D. What other defensible reasons exist for offering this course?
- [ ] E. What other courses fulfill these same needs?
- [ ] F. To what extent does this course overlap with or duplicate these courses?

II. DEVELOPMENT AND CURRENT STATUS
- [ ] A. When and under what circumstances was the course developed?
- [ ] B. How frequently and how regularly has the course been offered?
- [ ] C. How much has enrollment increased or decreased from year to year, or has it remained stable?
- [ ] D. What problems have been associated with the course and how have they been resolved?
- [ ] E. To what extent is the course intended to be replicable from instructor to instructor or from term to term?
- [ ] F. To what degree do the plans or design for the course exist in a written or documented form? In what documents (course-approval forms, course outlines or syllabi, memos, and so on) do these plans exist?
- [ ] G. How does the current version of the course differ from earlier versions? Why?

III. CREDIT AND CURRICULAR IMPLICATIONS
- [ ] A. What credit is awarded for successful completion of the course? On what basis is this credit allocation justifiable?
- [ ] B. How does this course fulfill graduate and degree requirements?
- [ ] C. At what level (lower division, upper division, or graduate) is the course classified? On what basis is this classification justified?
- [ ] D. How does the course fit into the overall curriculum of the department and college?
- [ ] E. In which departments is the course cross-listed? Why? How does it fit into the curriculum of these departments or colleges?
- [ ] F. What prerequisite skills or experiences are needed in order to succeed in this course?

☐ G. What problems are experienced by students who do not have these prerequisites?

IV. OBJECTIVES

☐ A. What are the formal, stated objectives of the course?

☐ B. How feasible and realistic are these objectives given the abilities of the target population and the available time and resources?

☐ C. How are the stated objectives related to the competencies students will need in everyday life outside of school?

☐ D. How are the objectives related to the competencies students will need in their subsequent academic careers?

☐ E. If the course is designed to prepare students for a specific professional or vocational field, how are the objectives related to the competencies they are likely to need in their future careers?

☐ F. What values are affirmed by the choice of these objectives as goals for this course?

☐ G. What other purposes or goals do the faculty, administrators, and other interested audiences have for the course?

☐ H. What goals and expectations do students have for the course?

☐ I. To what extent are these additional goals and expectations compatible with the stated course objectives?

V. CONTENT

☐ A. What (1) information, (2) process, and (3) attitudes and values constitute the subject matter or content of the course?

☐ B. How are the various content elements related to the objectives?

  ☐ 1. Which objectives receive the most coverage or emphasis? Why?

  ☐ 2. Which objectives receive only minor coverage? Why?

☐ C. How is the content sequenced or arranged? Why is this sequence appropriate/inappropriate?

☐ D. How are the various content elements integrated into a coherent pattern or structure? To what extent does fragmentation or lack of coherence appear to be a problem?

☐ E. What values and assumptions are implicit in the content selected and emphasized?

VI. INSTRUCTIONAL STRATEGIES
  ☐ A. What kinds of learning activities are used?
      ☐ 1. What activities are the students expected to engage in during class sessions?
      ☐ 2. What assignments or projects are students expected to complete outside of class?
      ☐ 3. In what ways are these activities appropriate or inappropriate in light of the course objectives?
      ☐ 4. How could these activities be made more effective?
  ☐ B. What instructional materials are used?
      ☐ 1. How and for what purpose are the materials used?
      ☐ 2. How accurate and up to date are the materials?
      ☐ 3. In what ways do the materials need to be improved?
      ☐ 4. How could the materials be used more effectively?
  ☐ C. What instructional roles or functions are performed by the teacher(s)?
      ☐ 1. How could these roles be performed more effectively?
      ☐ 2. What important instructional roles are not provided or are performed inadequately? Why?
  ☐ D. What premises and assumptions about learning and the nature of the learner underlie the selection of instructional strategies? How and to what extent are these assumptions warranted?
VII. PROCEDURES AND CRITERIA FOR EVALUATING STUDENTS' ACHIEVEMENTS
  ☐ A. What instruments and procedures are employed to collect evidence of the students' progress and achievement?
  ☐ B. What criteria are used to assess the adequacy of the students' work and/or achievement? On what basis were these criteria selected?
  ☐ C. How well do the assessment procedures correspond to the course content and objectives? Which objectives or content areas are not assessed? Why?
  ☐ D. Are the assessment procedures fair and objective?
  ☐ E. What evidence is there that the assessment instruments and procedures yield valid and reliable results?
  ☐ F. How are the assessment results used? Are the results shared with the students within a reasonable amount of time?

☐ G. How consistently are the assessment criteria applied from instructor to instructor and from term to term?

☐ H. Is the amount of assessment excessive, about right, or insufficient?

VIII. ORGANIZATION

☐ A. How is the course organized in terms of lectures, labs, studios, discussion sections, field trips, and other types of scheduled class sessions?

☐ B. How frequently and for how long are the various types of class meetings scheduled? Is the total allocation of time sufficient or insufficient? Why?

☐ C. If there is more than one instructor, what are the duties and responsibilities of each? What problems result from this division of responsibilities?

☐ D. What outside-of-class instruction, tutoring, or counseling is provided? By whom? On what basis?

☐ E. How well is the student workload distributed throughout the course?

☐ F. Are the necessary facilities, equipment, and materials readily available and in good working condition when needed?

IX. OUTCOMES

☐ A. What proportion of the enrollees completed the course with credit during the regular term? How does the completion rate vary from instructor to instructor or from term to term?

☐ B. What proportion of the enrollees withdrew from or stopped attending the course? Why?

    ☐ 1. To what degree does their withdrawal appear to be related to factors associated with the course?

    ☐ 2. How does the attrition rate vary from instructor to instructor or from term to term?

☐ C. At the end of the course, what evidence is there that students have achieved the stated objectives?

    ☐ 1. Which objectives does the course help students meet the most and the least?

    ☐ 2. For what kinds of students is the course most and least successful?

☐ D. What effects does the course have on students' interest in the subject matter and their desire to continue studying and learning about this subject?

☐ E. What other effects does the course have on the students?

☐ 1. How are their values, attitudes, priorities, interests, or aspirations changed?

☐ 2. Are their study habits or other behavioral patterns modified?

☐ 3. How pervasive and/or significant do these effects appear to be?

Case Studies in Developing Learning Outcomes

Alverno College

Alverno College, a small Catholic liberal arts college in Milwaukee with a student body of twenty-two hundred, has long been a national leader in its coordinated effort to describe the instructional goals of the institution, in the development of an academic program to meet these goals, and in the design of a program to measure each student's progress.

As a first step in the curriculum design process, the college identified and then described in detail eight basic abilities:

Communication: Make connections that create meaning between yourself and your audience. Learn to speak and write effectively, using graphics, electronic media, computers, and quantified data.

Analysis: Think clearly and critically. Fuse experience, reason and training into considered judgment.

Problem Solving: Define problems and integrate a range of abilities and resources to reach decisions, make recommendations, or implement action plans.

Valuing: Recognize different value systems while holding strongly to your own ethic. Recognize the moral dimensions of your decisions and accept responsibility for the consequences of your actions.

Social Interaction: Demonstrate ability to get things done in committees, task forces, team projects, and other group efforts. Elicit the views of others and help reach conclusions.

Global Perspectives: Act with an understanding of and respect for the economic, social, and biological interdependence of global life.

Aesthetic Responsiveness: Appreciate the various forms of art and the context from which they emerge. Make and defend judgments about the quality of artistic expressions.

Effective Citizenship: Be involved and responsible in the community. Act with an informed awareness of contemporary issues and their historical contexts. Develop leadership abilities.

For each area the faculty then developed specific levels of performance. For example, the Effective Citizenship goal had these four levels:

Level 1.   Assess own knowledge and skills in thinking about and acting on local issues.
Level 2.   Analyze community issues and develop strategies for informed response.
Level 3.   Evaluate personal and organizational characteristics, skills, and strategies that facilitate accomplishment of mutual goals.
Level 4.   Apply developing citizenship skills in a community setting.

The faculty then went one step further and described in detail each of these four levels. The following example is from Level 2 of the Analysis goal.

Level 2 . . . focuses on the student's ability to *draw reasonable inferences* from her observations and requires her to distinguish between fact and inference, evidence and assumption.

For example, a student in a science investigative learning laboratory might learn to hypothesize about possible results of an experiment she designs herself. A student in a psychology course on life span development might learn to infer theories of human development by interacting with people at differing stages of life—by taking a young child to lunch, for example, or interviewing a grandparent. After carefully examining her observations and inferring the subject's stage of development, the student would review theories of human development which she had learned in class to see how her experiences reinforced her understanding and how her inferences corresponded to the theories.

Built on these goals are the discipline-specific outcomes. For every course faculty at Alverno develop a syllabus outlining the ability levels available in the course, the means by which they will be taught, and the methods used for validating attainment. This detailed documentation is the basis on which the educational experience at Alverno rests.

One of the major strengths at Alverno is the approach to assessment—specifically, the use of video and written portfolios to record the development of each student as a communicator and a learner.

The Alverno approach in its totality may be unique for an institution of its size and character. The systematic approach that was used to develop an integrated curriculum, the documentation required, and the assessment protocol used have applications far beyond the institution. (For additional information, write to Kathleen O'Brien, Academic Dean, Alverno College, 3401 South 39th Street, P.O. Box 343911, Milwaukee, WI 53234–3922.)

Southeast Missouri State University

Southeast Missouri State University in Cape Girardeau was established in 1873. It has a current enrollment of over eight thousand students and offers undergraduate liberal arts, teacher preparatory, and professional programs. It also offers graduate study beyond the master's level but does not offer doctorates. The university was one of the first institutions to bring coherence to its basic academic program by developing a comprehensive set of academic goals to serve as the underpinnings of its core curriculum. In 1981, nine overarching objectives were developed for the University Studies, or core, program. This program is described as follows:

> The University Studies program at Southeast Missouri State University is designed to provide all students with the knowledge, concepts and competencies necessary for them to assume productive leadership roles in a pluralistic society. The purposes of the University Studies program are to ensure the acquisition of knowledge common to educated people; the ability to process, synthesize and evaluate such knowledge for use in making intelligent decisions; and the ability to use such knowledge in everyday life for a more rewarding, fulfilling existence and to disseminate such knowledge to others in one's society and world.
>
> The entire undergraduate program at the University encourages students to develop an intellectual orientation—to build reasoning powers capable of integrating personal experience with collective human experience. In particular, students educated by a coherent University Studies program learn ultimately how to discover and comprehend, how to create and communicate, how to appreciate and use knowledge for themselves and for others. Reason fostered by education thus prepares them for their future academic, professional, personal, and societal lives.

The core program had as its goal "equipping students to make sound choices by critically thinking through a problem and assessing its implication in the world at large. By integrating the various disciplines and thus identifying the interconnections of thoughts and ideas, students will increase their understanding of their physical, social, political, economic, psychological and cultural and intellectual environment." As you read the nine goals of Southeast Missouri State University presented here, notice that although they overlap considerably with the Alverno statements, they are different in both character and description.

> Objective No. 1. Demonstrate the ability to locate and
> gather information

The explosion of knowledge in the twentieth century and the variety of formats in which information is being presented have resulted in the need for more sophisticated tools and capabilities to access that information. At the same time, the need for information has accelerated. Information is necessary for making intelligent decisions and informed judgments and for the enrichment of personal life. The ability to locate or retrieve this information efficiently is an important component in the preparation for living a fulfilling life and for assuming a responsible/creative role in society.

> Objective No. 2. Demonstrate capabilities for critical
> thinking, reasoning and analyzing

Since information exists in a wide variety of formats, students often encounter it as disjointed and disparate facts. Thus, it is necessary for students to learn to evaluate, analyze, and synthesize information in order to make intelligent use of it. Students need to learn that there are numerous ways of discovering and processing information, and applying it to a given situation. The University Studies program should equip students with the ability and the desire to think critically and to reach well-reasoned conclusions about specific issues. Only as students become skillful in evaluating, analyzing, and synthesizing information, will they be able to engage in the level of intellectual activities required for critical thinking.

> Objective No. 3. Demonstrate effective communication
> skills

The mastery of verbal and mathematical symbols is an essential component of the University Studies program. The ability to understand and manipulate such symbols is a fundamental requirement in any society which encourages and thrives upon the free interchange of ideas and information. In this context mere functional literacy can never be an adequate goal; students must attain a level of proficiency which will enable them to become informed, effective citizens in their society and world.

Objective No. 4. Demonstrate an understanding of
human experiences and the ability to relate them to
the present

One important characteristic of human beings is their ability to understand and transmit the accumulated knowledge of the past from one generation to another. This ability enables each generation to build on the experiences of the past and to understand and function effectively in the present. The degrees to which individuals and societies assimilate the accrued knowledge of previous generations is indicative of the degree to which they will be able to use their creative and intellectual abilities to enrich their lives and the culture of which they are a part.

Objective No. 5. Demonstrate an understanding of
various cultures and their interrelationships

Understanding how other people live and think gives one a broader base of experience upon which to draw in the quest to become educated. In the University Studies program, students explore the different interrelationships among cultures that must be understood in order to appreciate the differences and similarities in customs throughout the world.

Objective No. 6. Demonstrate the ability to integrate the
breadth and diversity of knowledge and experience

The educated person is not one who possesses merely isolated facts and basic concepts, but one who can correlate and synthesize disparate knowledge into a coherent, meaningful whole. Even though modern society encourages a high degree of specialization in some areas, students should be encouraged and empowered to perceive connections and relevancies within the multiplicity of data experience.

Objective No. 7. Demonstrate the ability to make
informed, intelligent value decisions

Valuing is the ability to make informed decisions after considering ethical, moral, aesthetic, and practical implications. Valuing is a dynamic process that involves assessing the consequences of one's actions, assuming responsibility for them, and understanding and respecting the value perspectives of others. As a result, valuing is a natural dimension of human behavior and an integral component of the University Studies program.

Objective No. 8. Demonstrate the ability to make
informed, sensitive aesthetic responses

A concern for beauty is a universal characteristic of human cultures.
Although the term aesthetic is usually associated with such fine arts
as literature, theater, art, music, dance, and architecture, in actuality
the term need not be so narrowly defined. All areas of human
endeavor—science, history, business, and sport, for example, as well
as the arts—contain elements of beauty. Toward the end of exercising
an informed sensibility, students should be exposed to various definitions of beauty, equipped with the appropriate methods of investigation and evaluation, and encouraged to make independent judgments.

Objective No. 9. Demonstrate the Ability to Function
Responsibly in One's Natural, Social and Political
Environment

The existence of mankind depends on countless interrelationships
among persons and things. Students must learn to interact responsibly with their natural environment and with other citizens of their
society and world. The University Studies program should help students to realize that individual freedoms may necessarily be limited
and that natural, social, and political harmony begins with the individual. Further, the University Studies program should foster a
desire for a political and social system based on a concern for human
rights and just public policy determined through reasoned deliberation. Such an ideal presupposes an educated, enlightened citizenry
that accepts its responsibility to understand and participate in the
governance process.

A particularly powerful aspect of this approach is that clear and
concise guidelines and procedures have been developed for proposing courses within the program. These guidelines are provided to the
faculty committee that will make the decision:

University Studies courses may be developed by individual faculty
members, committees within a department or discipline, committees
representing clusters of departments or disciplines, or faculty teams
aided by consultants from outside the area(s) of specialization. It will
be the responsibility of the individual faculty member(s) or group(s)
proposing the course to demonstrate the level of the course, the number of credit hours, which of the nine objectives . . . will be addressed,
and the methods to be employed to ascertain how well the objectives
have been met.
In considering these matters, the University Studies Committee
will examine the proposed course syllabus and cover sheet designed

253

by the committee to be submitted by the course proposer(s). The committee will also review the proposal in relation to the overall structure of the University Studies program. In some cases the committee may wish to interview the individual(s) who has (have) submitted the course proposal.

In determining whether a course may be included in the University Studies offering, either as a requirement or an elective, the committee shall evaluate the course proposal in relation to the nine objectives. While it would be impractical—and perhaps undesirable—to expect any single course to focus equally on each of the nine objectives, the committee believes that, as a general rule, a course should effectively address and integrate as many objectives as possible and that, ideally, every course approved for the program should effectively address and integrate, in some fashion, all nine of the objectives.

In considering the extent to which the nine objectives will be met in a given course, proposers should demonstrate whether each objective will receive *significant, considerable,* or *some* emphasis in the course. *Significant emphasis* shall be determined by having an objective effectively met by all four of the following course components: content, teaching strategies, student assignments (including texts and/or other resources), and methods of evaluating student performance. *Considerable emphasis* shall be determined by having an objective effectively met by three of the course components. *Some emphasis* shall be determined by having an objective effectively met by two course components.

The distinction between lower- and upper-level University Studies courses will not be based on the nine general education objectives. Rather, that distinction will be based on such factors as difficulty of course content, types of assignments, stringency of evaluation procedures, and possible use of prerequisites. This manner of classification is similar to the current practice of distinguishing between lower- and upper-levels for non-University Studies courses.

This effort has led to the development of a basic core program for all students at the institution (see Exhibit B.1). (For additional information, write to John B. Hinni, Dean, School of University Studies, Southeast Missouri State University, One University Plaza, Cape Girardeau, MO. 63701–4799.)

Monmouth University

A Masters I institution located in New Jersey, Monmouth University began curriculum redesign, as did Indiana University, Bloomington, by focusing on outcome assessment prior to its Middle States accreditation review in 1995–96. From this effort, in 1993 the institution evolved a strategy for the formative assessment of academic majors and concentrations (Figure B.1) that included such elements as the

Exhibit B.1. Structure of the University Studies Program at Southeast Missouri State University.

I.   GS–101: Creative and Critical Thinking...3 hours

II. The 100–200 Level Core Curriculum:

One course is required from each of the twelve categories.

Artistic Expression ....3 hours

Literary Expression ....3 hours

Oral Expression...3 hours

Written Expression ....3 hours

Behavioral Systems...3 hours

Living Systems ....3 hours

Logical Systems...3 hours

Physical Systems..3 hours

Development of a Major Civilization ....3 hours

Economic Systems ....3 hours

Political Systems ....3 hours

Social Systems ....3 hours

III. The 300–400 Level Interdisciplinary Curriculum

300 Level Interdisciplinary...6 hours

400 Level Senior Seminar...3 hours

TOTAL	48 hours

development of departmental objectives, assessment indicators, feedback, and criteria for interpretation.

Monmouth also developed this set of learning objectives:

Health	Collaborative problem solving
Writing	Experiential learning
Reading	Historical perspective
Speaking	Global perspective
Quantitative reasoning	Cross-cultural perspective
Critical thinking	Diversity perspective
Research	Aesthetic perspective
Information literacy	Scientific perspective
Scientific method	Ethical perspective
Systems thinking	Depth of knowledge in a major field

Figure B.1. Formative Assessment of Academic Majors and Concentrations.

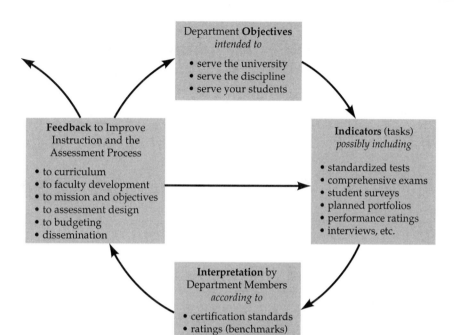

As part of this initiative, each academic area developed a comprehensive statement defining the goals of the program, the relationship of these goals to the mission of the institution, and a description of the assessment strategies that would be used to determine success. In addition, the agreed-upon learning objectives were assigned to specific required courses in the core program (Exhibit B.2). (For additional information, write to Thomas S. Pearson, Provost and Vice-President of Academic Affairs, Monmouth University, West Long Branch, NJ 67764–1898.)

Exhibit B.2. Learning Objectives Assigned to Core Courses.

Course	Code	Credits	Learning Goals Addressed
1. Foundation courses			
College English	EN101–102	6	Writing, reading, reasoning, research
World Masterpieces	EN201–202	6	Reading, writing, diversity, aesthetics, ethics
Western Civilization in World Perspective	HS101–102	6	Historical perspectives, reading, writing, cross-cultural, diversity, global
Information Technology	IT100	3	Research, problem solving, reasoning, information literacy, ethics
Critical Discourse	HU201	3	Critical reasoning, speaking, research, system thinking, collaborative problem solving
Physical Education	PE101	1	Health
2. Foundation distribution			
Discovery and Thinking in Natural Science (a)	SC100	3	Scientific method, problem solving, technology, ethics
Mathematics and Problem Solving (b)	MA100	3	Mathematics, quantitative reasoning, problem solving in collaborative groups

Mathematics Prerequisites and Student Success in Introductory Courses

Final Report

WILLIAM J. HARDIN

Introduction

In the fall of 1986, The Center for Instructional Development (CID) in cooperation with the Economics department undertook a pilot project to see if addressing mathematics prerequisite deficiencies could reduce the course failure rate. The project demonstrated that for some students, a brief review could in fact, improve their success rate in an introductory courses (Evensky, 1991). This project explores the possibility of using this approach in other introductory courses.

This study was a pilot effort to determine what mathematics skills are assumed in selected freshmen courses at Syracuse University and to determine to what extent, weaknesses in these prerequisite mathematical skills adversely effect the academic performance of students. It was our hypothesis that if such a relationship exists, special attention could remove certain mathematical barriers for "at risk students," resulting in academic success and reduced failure rate. If this approach was successful, the university could improve its overall retention rate of students while maintaining academic standards.

Selected passages from this document are reproduced here. The author is at the Center for Instructional Development, Syracuse University. The document was written in 1987.

The courses selected for this study were Anthropology 101, Astronomy 201, Chemistry 103, Chemistry 106, Geography 105, Physics 101, Political Science 121, and Psychology 205.

The study consisted of three phases: (1) math prerequisite identification, (2) course specific prerequisite test generation, and (3) test administration and data analysis.

Phase I: Mathematics Prerequisite Identification

Instructional materials from introductory undergraduate courses were collected and evaluated to determine which mathematical skills or concepts are assumed. A basic skills mathematics inventory defined in CID was used as a frame of reference for reviewing course tests and associated materials as well as for discussions with the faculty member. After conversations with the appropriate Dean and Department chairs, faculty responsible for several courses were asked, and agreed, to participate in the project. These courses and the materials that were reviewed in each were as follows:

ANT 101, Introduction to Cultural Anthropology

> Exams, review questions and text, Kottak, *Cultural Anthropology*, 5th ed., McGraw-Hill. (Faculty: Dr. Michael Friedman)

AST 201, Introduction to Astronomy

> Text, Robbins and Jefferys, *Discovering Astronomy*, 2nd ed., Wiley. (Faculty: Dr. Mark Bowick)

CHE 103, General Chemistry for nonscience majors

> Exams, lab assignments and text, Joesten, Netterville, and Wood, *World of Chemistry Essentials*, Saunders Golden Sunburst Series. (Faculty: Dr. Joe Chaiken)

CHE 106, General Chemistry

> Exams, lab assignments and text, Umland, *General Chemistry*, West Publishing. (Faculty: Dr. Roger Hahn)

GEO 105, World Geography

> Text, English and Miller, *World Regional Geography: A Question of Place*, 3rd ed., Wiley. (Faculty: Eric Miller)

PHY 101, General Physics for nonscience majors

> Exams, homework assignments and text, Kirkpatrick and Wheeler, *Physics: A World View*, Saunders. (Faculty: Dr. Karl Rosenzweig)

POL 121, American National Politics

> Text, Patterson, *The American Democracy*, 2nd ed., McGraw-Hill; text, Schwarz and Volgy, *The Forgotten American*, Norton. (Faculty: Dr. Joe Cammarano)

PSY 205, The Foundations of Human Behavior

> Text, Baron, *Psychology*, 2nd ed., Allyn & Bacon. (Faculty: Dr. Bruce Carter)

It was our basic assumption that:

1. There are certain basic mathematics skills assumed for all courses.

2. An understanding of mathematical processes and products would improve understanding of course material.

3. When advanced mathematics skills are used in texts, it is assumed that the students have the prerequisites. For example, to solve algebraic equations a text assumes the students understand basic operations, fractions, the concept of variable and (perhaps) the concept of a constant.

4. That while our list of basic skills was developed over time and is extensive, there is a possibility that for some first year courses additional mathematics skills may be required. For example, in GEO 105 students were expected to know the meanings of certain vocabulary terms such as per capita, and six fold decline.

To provide a check on the process, the faculty member and the project coordinator reviewed the materials independently and generated two independent lists. Then they met to discuss and resolve discrepancies between these two lists. The lists were then combined to resulted in one list.

It should be noted that while some prerequisite skills were assumed in every course others were course specific. For example, fractions and percents were assumed in all courses. Only Chemistry 106 assumed linear interpolation, the ability to solve inequalities and word problems using decimals (see Table C.1).

Reference

Evensky, J. "Dealing with Skill Prerequisites: Extending the Margin of Success and Accomplishing Affirmative Action in Introductory Economics." Unpublished report, Syracuse University, 1991.

Table C.1. Prerequisite Mathematics Skills Identified by Course.

Course	ANT 101	CHE 103	CHE 106	PHY 101	POL 121	PSY 205	AST 201	GEO 105
Basic skills								
Arithmetic	x	x	x	x	x	x	x	x
a) Basic arithmetic operations		x	x	x	x	x		
i) Order of operations			x					
ii) Prop. of addition		x	x	x				
iii) Prop. of multiplication		x	x	x	x		x	
b) Place value								
c) Exponents		x	x	x			x	
d) Fractions	x	x	x	x	x	x	x	x
e) Percents	x	x	x	x	x	x	x	x
f) Decimals	x	x	x	x	x	x	x	x
g) Significant digits			x					
h) Powers	x		x	x			x	
i) Roots			x	x				
Measurement systems	x	x	x	x		x	x	
a) Unit conversions		x	x	x			x	x
b) Scientific notation		x	x	x			x	
c) Orders of magnitude							x	
Calculator skills								
a) 4-Function calculators		x	x				x	
b) Scientific calculators								
c) Statistics calculators								
d) Graphic calculators								
Other general skills								
Probability	x	x	x	x	x	x	x	
a) Naive definition of probability	x	x	x	x	x	x		
b) Probability distributions			x			x		
c) Normal distribution			x			x		
d) Uniform distribution								
Statistics	x	x	x	x	x	x	x	
a) Descriptive statistics	x	x	x	x	x	x	x	
i) Measures of center of distribution (mean, mode, median)	x	x	x	x	x	x	x	
ii) Measures of the spread of a distribution (sample variance)							x	
b) Infernal statistics								
i Z-test								
ii) T-test								
iii) Confidence interval estimation								

Table C.1. (continued).

Course	ANT 101	CHE 103	CHE 106	PHY 101	POL 121	PSY 205	AST 201	GEO 105
Estimation and approximation	x	x		x			x	
a) Estimation								
b) Approximation	x		x				x	
Working with graphs		x	x	x	x	x	x	x
a) Rectangular coordinates		x	x	x			x	
b) Polar coordinates							x	
c) Graphing points		x					x	
d) Graph lines								
e) Graph algebraic expressions								
f) Bar graphs				x	x	x		
g) Pie charts		x	x		x	x		
h) Line graphs		x	x	x	x	x	x	x
Working with tables	x	x	x	x	x	x		x
a) Reading data from tables	x	x	x	x	x	x		x
b) Making tables		x	x					
c) Linear interpolation			x					
d) Linear extrapolation			x	x				
Logic and set theory						x		
a) Baby set theory						x		
i) unions and intersections								
ii) DeMorgan's laws								
iii) Venn diagrams						x		
b) Logic-conjctn, disjctn								
c) Notion of proof								
Map skills	x						x	x
Translate symbols	x	x	x	x			x	
Categorization	x	x					x	
Genetic addition	x							
Algebra								
Real numbers:	x		x			x	x	
a) Basic definitions								
b) The number line			x	x				
c) concept of variable			x	x			x	
d) concept of constant			x	x			x	
e) Equality and inequality	x	x	x	x	x	x		
f) Operations on real numbers				x				
g) Numbers in other bases (base 2, octal, hexadecimal) and conversions							x	
h) Scientific notation		x	x	x			x	

Table C.1. (continued).

Course	ANT 101	CHE 103	CHE 106	PHY 101	POL 121	PSY 205	AST 201	GEO 105
Linear equations and inequalities			x	x			x	
a) Solve linear equations in one variable			x	x				
b) Sove linear inequalities in one variable			x					
c) Absolute value inequalities								
d) Compound inequalities					x		x	
e) Absolute value inequalities								
Exponents and polynomials		x	x	x				
a) Integer exponents		x	x	x			x	
b) Properties of exponents								
c) Multiplication of polynomials								
d) Greatest common factors; factoring by grouping								
e) Factoring trinomials								
f) General methods of factoring								
g) Solving equations by factoring								
Rational expressions	x	x	x	x	x	x	x	x
a) Basics of rational expressions								
b) Ratios and proportions	x	x	x	x	x	x	x	x
c) Multiplication and division of rational expressions			x					
d) Complex fractions								
e) Dividing polynomials								
f) Synthetic division			x	x				
g) Solve equations with rational expressions								
h) Solve inequalities with rational expressions								
Rational exponents and radicals								
a) Rational exponents			x					
b) Radicals								
c) Simplifying radicals								
d) Adding and subtracting radical expressions								
e) Multiplying and dividing radical expressions								
f) Equations with radicals			x					
g) Complex numbers								

Table C.1. (continued).

Course	ANT 101	CHE 103	CHE 106	PHY 101	POL 121	PSY 205	AST 201	GEO 105
Quadratic equations and inequalities			x					
a) Solve quadratic expressions by completing the square								
b) The quadratic formula								
c) Non-linear inequalities								
The Line		x					x	
a) The slope of a line		x						
b) The equation of a line								
i) Slope intercept form								
ii) Point slope form								
iii) Standard form								
c) Linear equations								
d) Linear inequalities								
Systems of linear equations								
a) Linear systems of equations in two variables								
b) Linear systems in three variables								
c) Matrices and determinants								
d) Solutions to linear systems with determinants								
e) Solutions of linear systems of equations by matrix methods								
Conic sections							x	
a) The parabola							x	
b) The circle and ellipse				x			x	
c) The hyperbola							x	
d) Nonlinear systems of equations								
e) Second degree inequalities								
Functions								
a) Definition of function								
b) Functional notation		x	x	x				
c) 1-1 functions and inverses of functions								
d) Domain and range								

Table C.1. (continued).

Course	ANT 101	CHE 103	CHE 106	PHY 101	POL 121	PSY 205	AST 201	GEO 105
Exponential and logarithmic functions								
a) Exponential functions								
b) Logarithms								
c) Properties of logarithms								
d) Calculating with logarithms								
e) Logarithms and exponential equations								
f) The natural logarithm								
Trigonometry			x					
Sequences and series								
a) Sequences								
b) Series								
c) Arithmetic sequences								
d) Geometric sequences								
e) The binomial theorem								
Vectors				x				
a) Definition								
b) Vector operations								
c) Graphing								
Geometry								
Lines				x			x	
Angles				x			x	
Area							x	
Perimeter								
Concept of congruence								
Concept of similarity							x	
Geometric figures in the plane							x	
a) Triangles								
b) Quadrilaterals								
c) More general polygons								
d) Circle							x	
Solid geometry				x			x	
a) Cube								
b) Sphere				x			x	
c) Pyramids								
Applications (word problems)								
Problems involving decimals			x					
Problems involving percents			x					
Problems involving interest								
Problems involving geometry								
Problems involving mixture			x					
Problems involving motion								
Problems involving loans								

Sample Alumni Survey for Evaluating Program Effectiveness and Needs

Syracuse University
College for Human Development
112 Slocum Hall
Syracuse, New York 13210

Dear Graduate:

We are seeking your help as we begin a comprehensive study to determine the relevancy of our programs in the College for Human Development at Syracuse University. Your views as a graduate of this college are very valuable to us as we seek input from the profession.

There has been increasing discussion of late regarding the rapid changes in our society, the shift from industry to technology and communication, and the need for strategic planning. These are of common concern to industry, social service organizations, and education alike. We must project at least five years ahead in order to best prepare our students for their future careers. Therefore we are asking you to share your perspectives and visions and become part of our team as we seek to accomplish this goal.

We have attached a survey which is divided into four sections:

1. General professional skills and personal traits of undergraduates relevant at the entry level in your profession.

2. Topics and experiences specific to your specialization which you think should be included in the undergraduate curriculum.

3. An opportunity for you to share your vision of the future to help us anticipate changes in your profession for which we need to prepare students.

4. Background information so that we may share the results of our survey with you and also update our records of alumni.

Please know that all information you provide us will remain strictly confidential. If you have any questions about the survey, don't hesitate to call me at 315–423–2033, or write to me. I have enclosed a stamped envelope for your convenience. Please return the survey by April 15, 19XX, a date that should be easy to remember! And, if you complete and return the enclosed lottery ticket with your survey by April 15th, you will be eligible to win one of five exciting prizes such as a Syracuse University ceramic mug, paperweight or letter opener.

In closing, I would like to once again stress how very important your input is to us. You are in a unique position because of your education and professional experience to directly affect the quality of the educational experience provided by our college. Thank you for your help!

Sincerely,
Jane M. Lillestol
Dean

Alumni Survey
College for Human Development
Syracuse University

Section I

There are some things that students learn that are not part of the formal academic curriculum. These include general professional skills. In addition, there are personal traits that can be important in one's success in a given area. In response to the following items, please indicate (1) if the skill or trait is important for people in your area, and (2) its prevalence among those people who, like our undergraduates, are just entering your area.

Professional Skills

| Skills | Importance for People in Your Area | | | | Prevalence Among Those Entering Your Area | | | |
	None	Low	Medium	High	None	Low	Medium	High
Professional writing	0	1	2	3 (7)	0	1	2	3 (16)
Professional speaking	0	1	2	3	0	1	2	3
Basic mathematics	0	1	2	3	0	1	2	3
Microcomputer use	0	1	2	3	0	1	2	3
Resource management	0	1	2	3	0	1	2	3
Planning	0	1	2	3	0	1	2	3
Decision making	0	1	2	3	0	1	2	3
Leadership	0	1	2	3	0	1	2	3
Interpersonal skills	0	1	2	3 (15)	0	1	2	3 (24)

Personal Traits

| Traits | Importance for People in Your Area | | | | Prevalence Among Those Entering Your Area | | | |
	None	Low	Medium	High	None	Low	Medium	High
Loyalty	0	1	2	3 (25)	0	1	2	3 (34)
Common sense	0	1	2	3	0	1	2	3

Alumni Survey (continued)

Traits	Importance for People in Your Area				Prevalence Among Those Entering Your Area			
	None	Low	Medium	High	None	Low	Medium	High
Ethics	0	1	2	3	0	1	2	3
Persuasiveness	0	1	2	3	0	1	2	3
Creativity	0	1	2	3	0	1	2	3
Enthusiasm	0	1	2	3	0	1	2	3
Willingness to take risks	0	1	2	3	0	1	2	3
Industriousness	0	1	2	3	0	1	2	3
Appearance	0	1	2	3 (33)	0	1	2	3 (42)

Section II

A. There are many topics that could be included in the undergraduate curriculum. From your point of view, how valuable are the topics listed under each of the following categories in the education of an undergraduate preparing to enter your field? Please *circle* the number which most accurately reflects the value you place on each topic.   2 (43)

Categories/Topics

Value (Circle appropriate number)

	None	Low	Medium	High
RETAILING				
(Please rate the following if this is your field.)				
Retailing fundamentals	0	1	2	3 (44)
Merchandising mathematics	0	1	2	3
Merchandising management	0	1	2	3
Visual merchandising	0	1	2	3
Salesmanship	0	1	2	3

Section II (continued)
Categories/Topics

Value (Circle appropriate number)

	None	Low	Medium	High	
Retailing problems & policy	0	1	2	3	
Small business administration	0	1	2	3	
Advertising principles	0	1	2	3	
Visual arts	0	1	2	3	
Retail advertising	0	1	2	3	
Financial accounting	0	1	2	3	
Computer applications	0	1	2	3	
Data processing	0	1	2	3	
Introduction to the legal system	0	1	2	3	
Marketing and society	0	1	2	3	
Consumers and the marketplace	0	1	2	3	
Elementary statistics	0	1	2	3	*(60)*

CONSUMER STUDIES
(Please rate these topics if this is your field.)

	None	Low	Medium	High	
Individual/family resource management	0	1	2	3	*(61)*
Personal finance management	0	1	2	3	
Consumer behavior	0	1	2	3	
Consumer economics	0	1	2	3	
Consumer protection	0	1	2	3	
Current consumer issues	0	1	2	3	
Consumer education	0	1	2	3	
Consumer problems of the elderly	0	1	2	3	

Alumni Survey (continued)

Section II (continued)

Categories/Topics — Value (Circle appropriate number)

Categories/Topics	None	Low	Medium	High	
OTHER CONSUMER STUDIES RELATED TOPICS (Please rate these topics if this is your field.)					
Organizational behavior	0	1	2	3	(69)
Advertising principles	0	1	2	3	
Introduction to the legal system	0	1	2	3	
Marketing and society	0	1	2	3	
State and national legislative process	0	1	2	3	
Computer applications	0	1	2	3	(74)
HUMAN DEVELOPMENT TOPICS (Please rate if you are in either field.)					
Child and family studies	0	1	2	3	(75)
Human behavior	0	1	2	3	
Human nutrition	0	1	2	3	(77)
ARTS AND SCIENCES (Please rate if you are in either field.)					
History	0	1	2	3	(78)
Higher mathematics (e.g., algebra)	0	1	2	3	
Psychology	0	1	2	3	(80)
English literature	0	1	2	3	(6)

Section II (continued)

Value (Circle appropriate number)

Categories/Topics	None	Low	Medium	High
Expository writing	0	1	2	3
Foreign language	0	1	2	3
Economics	0	1	2	3
Sociology	0	1	2	3
Anthropology	0	1	2	3
Fine arts	0	1	2	3
Philosophy	0	1	2	3
Religion	0	1	2	3
Chemistry	0	1	2	3
Physics	0	1	2	3
Biology	0	1	2	3 (17)

Section II. (continued)

B. Entry Level Criteria
1. What are the basic requirements and the outstanding or unique factors that you use to assess an entry level *portfolio?*

Basic requirements: _____(28)

_____(29)

_____(30)

Outstanding/unique factors: _____(31)

_____(32)

_____(33)

2. What are the basic and outstanding or unique *design capabilities* that you look for in assessing an entry level applicant?

Basic capabilities: _____(34)

_____(35)

_____(36)

Outstanding/unique capabilities: _____(37)

_____(38)

_____(39)

C. Additional Topics
Are there other topics related to any of the above categories that you feel should be covered in our programs? (Please list them below).

_____(40)

_____(41)

_____(42)

_____(43)

_____(44)

D. Practical Experiences

The curriculum also consists of practical experiences as part of a field internship or some other practicum. Please answer the following questions about the field based part of the curriculum.

How important is a field experience in a undergraduate's preparation? (circle one)

Not very important	Important	Very important	(46)
1	2	3	

In your opinion what are the most important elements of a practical field experience?

a._____ *(47)*

b._____ *(48)*

c. _____ *(49)*

d._____ *(50)*

e. _____ *(51)*

E. General Comments and Suggestions

Please make any additional comments or suggestions which you think would help us strengthen our programs for the preparation of undergraduates who will enter your field.

(52)

(53)

(54)

(55)

(56)

Section III

Your View of the Future

Next year's freshmen will enter your field five years from now. Therefore, we need to be aware of trends that will have an impact on the field when these students graduate. Please respond to each of the following questions so that we can have the benefit of your perspective as we continue to improve our curriculum to make it relevant to the future.

1. In what direction do you see your profession moving during the next five years?

(57)

(58)

(59)

2. What new knowledge, skills and attitudes will be needed by people entering your field?

(60)

(61)

(62)

3. What skills, attitudes or knowledge will become obsolete and, therefore, no longer needed?

(63)

(64)

(65)

4. What do you see as the essential philosophy and/or components of a program preparing undergraduates to enter your field?

(66)

(67)

(68)

5. Please make any additional comments or suggestions which you think will help us understand your perspective.

(69)

(70)

(71)

Section IV

Information About You

Please provide the following information so that we may update our records and share the results of the survey with you. Of course, your response to the survey will be kept confidential.

Name _____

       Last   First   Middle   Maiden

Home Address _____Telephone _____

      Street   City   State   Zip

Current Business
Address _____Telephone _____

      Street   City   State   Zip

Undergraduate Major _____*(72)* Year Graduated _____ *(73–74)*

Degree Received _____Institution _____

Additional Degrees—Indicate Major, Institution, and Year Received

_____

Information on Present Status

Please check appropriate category:

_____Student *(1)*   _____Full-time homemaker *(2)*   *(75)*

_____Employed *(3)*   _____Retired *(4)*

_____Other (Please explain): _____*(5)*

Please complete below in regard to most recent employer.

Organization _____

      Name   Address   City   State   Zip

Period worked for this organization _____

Job Title _____ *(76–77)*

Describe briefly the nature of the organization's operation and your position.

_____*(78–79)*

_____

_____

Thank you for your help! Please return this survey in the enclosed, stamped envelope or send it to:

> Dr. Peter J. Gray
> Associate in Evaluation
> Syracuse University
> Center for Instructional Development
> 115 College Place
> Syracuse, New York 13210

RESOURCE E

Additional Case Studies in Course Design

Expanding the Course Time Frame to Compensate for a Lack of Prerequisites: Introductory Calculus

The basic sequence in calculus as traditionally taught at Syracuse University consisted of four sequential three-credit courses taken during the freshman and sophomore years. The sequence was required of all engineering, mathematics, economics, and science majors. Over the years, faculty teaching the course had become increasingly concerned with a high failure rate. In addition, studies had shown a direct and high correlation between achievement on the mathematics placement test taken by all entering freshmen and success in the traditional course. In other words, those students who entered with a solid mathematics background tended to pass; others did not. To address these issues, a self-paced program based on the mastery concept of learning was developed and introduced. This program used the continuous-registration and flexible-credit systems implemented earlier for use in other courses.

Students enrolled in the initial field-testing version of the course slightly over four months after design work began. The design and implementation phase was short because the content and the sequential materials presented were traditional (not open to significant review) and the course was built around an available commercial text. Student guides, manuals, and some instructional materials, however, were developed specifically for the new program.

The goal of self-paced calculus is to permit students to master the materials covered in an introductory college calculus course at a

277

pace most comfortable to them. The subject matter is divided into units (or blocks of material) that each take about one week to cover and learn thoroughly. The students use a standard calculus textbook and a set of detailed study guides to learn the material in each unit. Regularly scheduled tutorial periods are also available. Problem-solving sessions are provided on an optional basis, and two programmed booklets were written to teach content not covered adequately or effectively in the available materials. A page from the student manual describing the courses is shown in Figure E.1.

For each unit a series of equivalent tests was prepared. When the students believe they have mastered the material in a unit, they may request a test. A student who passes at a prespecified level of mastery may begin to prepare for the next unit test. Students who do not pass are given tutorial help or remedial assignments and must then take another version of the test for that same unit. Again, a pass is required before proceeding to the next unit. Unit tests may be taken as often as needed with no grade penalty for not passing. Tests for all units are available from the beginning of the course so that any student who has prior preparation in calculus may receive credit by passing the appropriate unit tests.

Figure E.1. Self-Paced Calculus (MAT 295, 296, 397, 398) Course Sequence.

- Tests for all units will be available during the tutorial periods and may be taken when you become prepared for them.

- Failed unit tests may be retaken until passed, with no penalty.

- Satisfactory completion of each unit test is required before proceeding to the next.

- There is no limit to the number of credits that you may earn in any semester.

Math 295, 296, units 1–24 (4 unit tests = 1 credit)

4-credit pace: Completion of 16 units per semester

3-credit pace: Completion of 12 units per semester

2-credit pace: 8 units per semester

Math 397, 398, units 25–42 (3 unit tests = 1 credit)

4-credit pace: Completion of 12 units per semester

3-credit pace: Completion of 9 units per semester

2-credit pace: 6 units per semester

In the early weeks of the course, to earn one academic credit students must pass four units successfully; eight units passed earns two credits; and so on. As students advance to the more difficult concepts, they must pass three unit tests to earn one credit. The speed at which the students progress through the course and the number of credits individuals earn depends on how rapidly they can master the material. A separate letter grade is earned and recorded for each credit hour.

A follow-up study of 248 students, 60 in the self-paced program and 188 in the conventional course, showed that the primary goals were reached. First, for those in the self-paced course the direct correlation between entry-level test results and performance in the course was significantly reduced as entry-level problems were dealt with and corrected. In the conventional course, placement-exam results had a direct relationship to semester examination scores (see Figure E.2). Second, there was a major improvement in overall student performance.

As in any self-paced course, it was necessary to build into the program a minimum pace—a rate of movement below which students could not fall—although there was no maximum pace. Students were required to complete eight units in their first semester—a two-credit-per-semester pace.

One caution about materials should be noted. Because the course relies on a published text, it is necessary to rewrite all the associated materials with each revision of the text. This has become a problem because the publisher has tended to publish new editions every two or three years. To reduce the need for extensive rewriting

Figure E.2. Correlation Between Mathematics Preparation and Performance in Introductory Calculus.

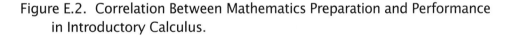

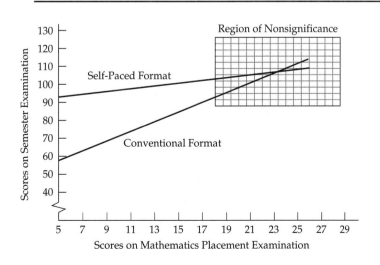

of associated materials, the university has stockpiled extra copies of the text that can be used after new editions are published.

Expanding the Course Time Frame to Compensate for a Lack of Prerequisites: General Chemistry

Another interesting and successful project in which time, rather than content, was the significant variable was the redesign of the introductory general chemistry course at the University of Rhode Island.

The problem was not unusual: a high failure rate (30 percent) and a related frustration level on the part of both the faculty and many students. From an analysis of student profiles, faculty learned that the majority of those who failed or dropped the course could be identified even before the course began by analyzing their entering SAT scores, high school class rank, and standardized test scores in mathematics.

The instructor, Jacklyn Vitlimberger, proposed an experiment that was implemented with the approval of her chair during the 1985–86 academic year. A number of high-risk students were enrolled in a new two-semester general chemistry course that had the identical content, assignments, instructional objectives, and instructor as the existing one-semester program. The additional time was used to provide the students with an increased opportunity to practice the problem-solving skills that were identified as necessary for success in general chemistry. The examinations in both courses were also identical; the midterm in the traditional program became the first-semester final in the experimental two-semester program, and both sections took the same final examination. The performance of students in the two-semester program was then compared with that of students in the one-semester program who had the same range of SAT scores, class rank, and math-test scores.

The results were positive:

- Seventy percent of the high-risk students in the two-semester program passed the course and the final examination.

- Each of the students in the experimental section who completed the two-semester sequence scored above the median score of the students in the traditional sections on the final examination.

- The overall failure rate in the course was significantly reduced (from 30 percent to approximately 10 percent).

- Students who completed the two-semester sequence also performed satisfactorily in subsequent science and math courses.

As a result of this project, the experimental two-semester course was regularized, and entering students who are identified as being in the high-risk category are encouraged to enroll in this option.

In the experimental course, students received no credit for the first semester and three credits for the second. This approach placed a hardship on students. Because they had to earn twelve credits to maintain full-time academic standing for purposes of financial support, work-study, and so on, they were forced to enroll in five courses the first semester rather than four, an academic load too heavy for high-risk students. These issues were resolved by granting three credits for each semester of the revised course but with the stipulation that only the second-semester credits count toward a degree. Grades for the first semester are, however, included in the student's grade point average. Awarding credit in this manner allows an institution to meet the needs of academically disadvantaged students without lowering the academic standards of the course, the department, or the institution.

Expanding Course Content to Account for Different Student Backgrounds and Interests: Introductory Course in Religion

Chapter Six described the data collected during this project, which indicated a wide diversity in backgrounds and areas of interest. The structure developed was based on this information and other priorities of the department. Several key goals for the course evolved:

- A common framework for the course had to be set, and appropriate vocabulary had to be introduced.
- The course had to include major interest areas of the students.
- Because the course is the initial contact the students have with the department, it had to serve as a recruiting vehicle for majors and for enrollments in other religion courses.

The unique course design that was developed proved most effective in meeting these objectives (Figure E.3). Seminars and programmed materials were used to introduce the term *religion* and religion as a field of study. From this point, students were required to take one four-week option from each of three major areas: Forms of Religious Expression, Forms of Religious Issues, and Methodologies. Additional options could be taken for extra credit. An advantage of this design (referred to by some as the "Chinese-menu" approach) was that it allowed freshmen to have direct contact in small-group sessions with senior faculty teaching in their areas of specialization. Options with higher enrollments were repeated as needed.

An interesting sidelight is that when the new course was first taught, some students in the class felt strongly that religion as a formal subject did not belong in a university. For this reason the optional unit Objections to the Study of Religion was built into the program. As the political climate of the country changed during the l970s, the number of students enrolling in this option declined significantly, and the option was dropped.

Figure E.3. Structure of Introductory Course in Religion.

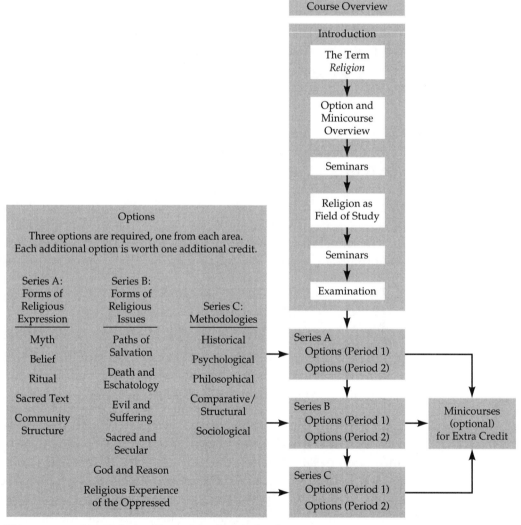

This course provides students with a variety of required options and an opportunity to earn extra credit by taking additional options or minicourses. Classes are scheduled for two hours, twice weekly, with a different series of options offered each hour, permitting a student to complete two option credits in any four-hour period.

Credit: Ronald Cavanagh, Robert Diamond.

Developing an Institutional Assessment Culture at Truman State University

BRONWYN ADAMS

At Truman State University (formerly Northeast Missouri State) an assessment culture was cultivated over the nineteen-year tenure of institution president Charles J. McClain. When McClain arrived at Northeast Missouri State University in 1970, he brought with him a commitment to institutional quality and accountability that was not to become a national concern for at least a decade. Along with a new dean of instruction, Darrell W. Kreuger, McClain worked though the 1970s to focus the institution's attention on measuring—so as to improve—student learning. Working along with faculty, McClain and Kreuger developed an assessment core as the center of the university initiative to improve student learning. Their efforts attracted the attention of external constituencies. In 1985 the Missouri General Assembly designated the university as the public liberal arts and sciences university for the state. In 1995 the General Assembly renamed the institution Truman State University. Truman State is an excellent example of planned institutional change and illustrates some of the features of successful change initiatives. This case also reminds us that "successful assessment is much more than techniques, processes, or even outcomes; it is a cultural issue that affects how a community of scholars defines its work and its responsibilities to its students" (Magruder, McManis, and Young, 1996, p. 1).

Administrative Leadership

The transformation of Northeast Missouri State was undeniably a presidential initiative; however, McClain was careful to build community ownership in the change process by involving faculty and challenging them to answer difficult questions about how well the university was accomplishing its mission and goals. McClain worked to create a consciousness of the need for change by demonstrating to faculty that they had no way of assessing how well they were preparing students for life after college.

Because Truman State's roots were as a teachers' college, placement records and feedback from school districts who worked in partnership with the college provided an information base from which to begin thinking about the assessment of student performance. The first attempt to collect additional data on which to base improvement initiatives came in 1972, when graduating seniors were invited to take nationally standardized mastery examinations in their majors. For a number of years these exams were taken voluntarily. The results were reviewed with faculty, allowing them to consider the outcomes and their implications as they were asked to make recommendations about which examinations were most appropriate for assessing knowledge in the field. Additional means of assessing outcomes were used, including student-satisfaction surveys and value-added tests, so as to provide feedback from multiple sources and perspectives.

McClain's nineteen-year tenure as Truman's president was certainly an important variable in this case. Consistent leadership as the assessment culture evolved undoubtedly contributed to the transformation of this institution.

A Community Effort

Another important variable was the purposeful manner in which McClain involved faculty in developing and implementing the assessment plan. Making this initiative a community effort, involving multiple measures of students' knowledge and perceptions, and supporting this effort over a period of years fostered a receptive climate for institutional change.

Faculty are often wary of assessment initiatives; however, McClain's careful, consistent efforts reassured faculty that the data collected about student learning would not be used in punitive ways. This assurance made it possible for assessment to become part of the ongoing improvement processes under way at Northeast Missouri

State University. Performance data were shared, and occasions were provided for faculty to analyze the data publicly. Moreover, the president and dean modeled for the campus community the ways in which assessment data would be used for ongoing improvement. Their public and private communications with faculty consistently indicated that decisions about existing and future programs and initiatives needed to be informed by assessment data. Faculty also came to take for granted that the focus on student learning goals would be paramount at the institution.

Staged Implementation

Having established a climate accepting of assessment as the means to a mutually desirable end of improvement, the university developed an assessment system. By 1980 all students were required to take pre- and posttests of general education, to pass a locally designed writing assessment, to complete three surveys, and to take a nationally normed examination in the major. There were no negative consequences for individual students to taking the various examinations. In fact, there was a benefit for individual students insofar as mentoring and advising were available to refer them to campus services based on assessment results.

Group scores were considered as information and feedback about how well the institution was achieving its goals and objectives. By 1990 new qualitative measures were added to the evaluation design, incorporating such methods as capstone experiences in the major and student portfolios. In 1992 an annual initiative was launched to interview students concerning their undergraduate experience.

Truman State University continues to explore methods for gathering good data on which to make improvements. Although recognizing the centrality of such data collection, Truman's success demonstrates the importance of institutional climate in change initiatives, particularly those in the assessment domain. A campus culture that accepts assessment as part of the business of teaching and learning and supports self-evaluation makes ongoing improvement possible. Magruder, McManis, and Young (1996) identified four essential factors in developing this culture: (1) administrative clarity and commitment, (2) timing and motivation for the assessment initiative, (3) integration of assessment into the management and operation of the institution, and (4) reliance on faculty to develop and implement the assessment.

Making Good Things Visible _____

Sustaining any change initiative is difficult if participants in the process do not see tangible outcomes and experience the impact of those outcomes in positive ways. "Part of the successful strategy used by McClain and Krueger was to assure that good things happened because of assessment" (Magruder, McManis, and Young, 1996, p. 4). Faculty received generous, positive reinforcement for their work in improvement efforts. Moreover, as the university's reputation changed, better-prepared students were attracted to Truman, and students responded to the institution's interest in their success and became more engaged in academic life. Finally, the university's strong benchmark data attracted support for a number of focused initiatives to improve the academic environment and ultimately led to the state's designation of Truman as a selective statewide liberal arts university. Assessment has paid off for Truman State University.

An important factor for faculty was that over time they came to trust that assessment would pay off for them more personally as faculty—or at least that it would not hurt them in any way. Faculty and staff evaluations were never linked to the assessment plan. The institution was careful to provide opportunities for dialogue and input and to introduce change systematically.

Making changes visible to outside constituencies was also accomplished purposefully. Truman was in the advantageous position of being ahead of the accountability movement, allowing the institution time and freedom to explore options and find measures that worked within the institutional culture. The public-policy environment in Missouri was supportive of Truman's efforts and recognized and rewarded the institution for its self-study. The rewards the university received for its efforts were a strong pay-back to members of the campus community.

Sustaining the System _____

Higher education enjoys little stability in terms of major stakeholders. Students rotate out of the system continuously, and faculty and administrators turn over, although certainly with less frequency or regularity. Keeping the culture in tune with the assessment system requires ongoing socialization. Keeping the system fresh and current requires consideration of new ways of measuring, displaying, and using data. New people need to become involved in order to bring fresh perspectives to bear, and "veterans" need to be reinvigorated. Maintaining the energy that comes with innovation is a challenge. Because Truman's success has been so highly dependent on the assessment culture as opposed to the assessment program, this aspect of the Truman case cannot be underestimated. Magruder, McManis, and Young note that "new leaders have to be socialized to understand the use of data. The temptation for leaders to delegate the assessment processes to others can quickly make assessment just one more report" (1996, p. 15). It remains an ongoing challenge for the institution to maintain the cultural ethos that enabled its successful transformation.

At a time when many in academe are haggling over questions about the assessment of student outcomes, Truman State University has a long history of measuring student learning. To quote Peter Ewell, an assessment expert with the National Center for Higher Education Management Systems in Boulder, Colorado, "The experience that this university has had is astonishing in terms of the amount of change which has occurred in a small period of time. I know personally of no other institution—and I work with about 120 at this point—which has changed so much, so consciously, so single-mindedly and so successfully" (oral report to the Board of Governors, Truman State University, November 1991).

Ewell's remarks highlight a key reason for Truman's success—focused, conscious efforts to involve a campus community in assessing student learning. The culture of assessment at Truman State University has made great strides in helping the institution understand how teaching and learning take place in its institutional context. This case has much to teach us about the importance of community and culture in institutional change.

For more information, contact Michael McManis, University Dean, 816–785–4695.

Reference

Magruder, J., McManis, M., and Young, C. *The Right Idea at the Right Time: Development of a Transformational Assessment Culture.* Kirksville, Mo.: Office of the President, Truman State University, 1996.

RESOURCE G

Qualities of the Liberally Educated Person

A Description of Important Competencies

THE TASK FORCE ON THE STUDENT EXPERIENCE, FACULTY OF ARTS AND SCIENCES, RUTGERS UNIVERSITY-NEWARK

Members

Lion F. Gardiner, Zoology and Physiology, *Chairman*

John Faulstich, Dean of Instruction, NCAS

Richard H. Kimball, Business Administration

Cassie E. Miller, Dean of Students, UC

Vincent Santarelli, Physics

Harold I. Siegel, Psychology

Raymond T. Smith, Director, Educational Opportunity Fund Program

Cecile R. Stolbof, Dean of Instruction, UC

Linda Swanger, Student, NCAS

Elena E. Thompson, Student, UC

Former Members

Henry A. Christian, English

Mary C. Segers, Political Science

Olga J. Wagenheim, History

April 1986

Introduction

Liberal arts colleges have historically taught a broad range of traditional studies in the humanities, social and natural sciences, and mathematics. This curriculum has recognized the central importance for success in life of broad development of the "whole person" as contrasted with acquisition of career-oriented knowledge and skills alone. Thorough personal development can enable us effectively to plan, control, and enjoy our lives, and it can significantly enhance the probability of professional success and satisfaction as well.

The major human dimensions—intellectual, moral, emotional, and social—all require development. Truly liberal learning can help us develop each of these dimensions, illuminate their interconnections, and reveal their relevance for our lives. When such learning occurs in college, it is accomplished by active involvement with members of the faculty and staff, peers, and others; in and out of class; and on and off campus.

Becoming liberally educated can enable us to identify alternative goals for our lives. It can accelerate our progress in achieving clear and mature personal values and enhance our ability to plan our lives and solve personal and professional problems. Perhaps most important, liberal education can catalyze a process of continuous learning and personal development throughout life.

The more closely the qualities of the liberally educated person are identified, the more easily they can be observed and measured. The description below can guide faculty members and administrators in decision making as they plan, implement, and evaluate curricular and cocurricular activities and assess student achievement. This description can guide students in planning their educational experiences and in assessing their personal change and growth.

The Qualities

These qualities, characteristics, abilities, or competencies involve the whole person and are teachable and measurable. These competencies, although they may be developed in one context, are transferable to other settings and situations and are broadly applicable in life. They are stated in language that permits their observation and measurement.

The qualities are grouped together in four clusters of related competencies. The number of competencies classed together in a cluster in no way signifies the relative importance of the cluster; other classifications are possible.

Specifically, the liberally educated person engages in the following activities:

Cluster I.
Higher-Order Cognitive Skills

These skills involve the ability to move beyond knowledge requiring memory alone, comprehension, and low-level application of concepts and principles. These skills involve the ability to engage in abstract problem-solving behavior in many settings and contexts.

A. Analytic thinking
    1. Draws reasonable inferences from observations and logical premises.
    2. Independently discerns internal structure, pattern, and organization using frameworks or models from various disciplines and fields of inquiry to comprehend the natural world, social and cultural relations, and artistic products.
    3. Recognizes and analyzes problems in a variety of situations, both independently and cooperatively with others; views issues from a multiplicity of perspectives.
    4. Analyzes and describes the value structure of a specific area of knowledge, both in theory and practice.

B. Synthetic-creative thinking
    1. Identifies problems, perceives associations, and constructs relationships that are novel.
    2. Uses one's intellectual skills effectively to construct original ideas and products.

C. Evaluative thinking
    1. Identifies assumptions and limitations in problem solving and evaluates the adequacy of one's own and others' approaches to problems.
    2. Evaluates one's own and others' ideas, behavior, and cultures using criteria from various disciplines and fields of inquiry.

D. Scientific reasoning
    1. Demonstrates an understanding of the scientific method of inquiry, including accurate measurement based on observation and the use of controlled experiment.
    2. Identifies the assumptions and limitations of the scientific method of inquiry and distinguishes

the extent to which this method is applicable in various situations and contexts in all disciplines and fields of inquiry.

3. Distinguishes first- from second-hand information, facts from opinions, and hypotheses from substantiated conclusions; identifies the need for and role of appropriate evidence in providing support for or in falsifying testable hypotheses or points of view.

4. Evaluates the quality of evidence, distinguishing appropriate and significant evidence from inadequate evidence, and discriminates between pseudoscientific explanations.

E. Using numerical data

1. Uses numerical data effectively to provide support for positions taken.

2. Responds in a sophisticated manner to arguments and positions depending on numerical support; recognizes the misuse of numerical data and their manipulation to mislead in the presentation of issues.

Cluster II.

Active Awareness of One's Natural Environment

A. Structure and function

Perceives and describes the complex relations of the structures and functions within the physical and organic environment and the relative stability of these relations through time.

B. Human-environment interactions

Observes and analyzes the impact of individuals and groups on the environment, including the role played by technology, and how the environment affects individuals and groups.

C. Problem solving

Constructs effective solutions to environmental problems.

Cluster III.

Active Awareness of Oneself

A. Self-identity

1. Articulates a clear and integrated sense of one's own personal identity, place in the world, and potential as a person.

2. Recognizes and names one's own emotional states in various contexts, situations, and circumstances.

        3. Demonstrates ability to function effectively under conditions of ambiguity, uncertainty, and conflict.

        4. Demonstrates ability to empathize with others who are substantially dissimilar from oneself and to communicate effectively this empathy to others.

        5. Demonstrates awareness of the structure and function of one's own body and the conditions that will maintain and ensure its well being.

B. Values

        1. Identifies one's own chosen values, and employs consciously these values in decision making in one's own life to take and defend reasoned stands on significant social issues.

        2. Demonstrates facility in recognizing and evaluating values expressed in discourse such as casual conversation and in philosophical, political, artistic, and humanistic works and implied by scientific and technological developments.

C. Learning

        1. Identifies one's own preferred learning styles and one's strengths and weaknesses as a learner.

        2. Demonstrates active, diverse, and effective learning behaviors appropriate to various disciplines and fields of inquiry as an individual and in group settings.

        3. Learns independently, both to satisfy one's own curiosity and to achieve practical ends; has an active, consistent, and life-long orientation toward learning.

Cluster IV.

Awareness of and Effective Action in One's Social and Cultural Environment

A. Communication

        1. Analyzes oneself as a communicator and identifies one's own strengths and weaknesses.

        2. Communicates effectively both abstract concepts and feelings and emotions in writing, speaking, reading, and listening, using words or quantified data, and with other media, including the computer.

        3. Identifies and effectively uses the tactics of skilled persuasion; recognizes attempts at manipulation such as hucksterism and demagoguery in various settings, contexts and situations.

B. Interpersonal interaction

1. Identifies and evaluates one's own behaviors and emotional responses experienced when interacting with others, both in one-to-one and group settings and contexts, and can analyze the behavior of others.

2. Employs effective interpersonal and intragroup behavior when interacting with others in a variety of situations, within one's own culture and in intercultural settings, contexts and situations.

3. Facilitates effective interpersonal and group interactions both within one's own culture and in intercultural settings, contexts, and situations.

C. Leadership

1. Demonstrates independence of thought in decision making and implements these decisions in an effective way.

2. Demonstrates knowledge of leadership skills and can identify one's own strengths and weaknesses as a leader.

3. Uses effective leadership behaviors confidently in relating to others.

4. Identifies values implicit in political views espoused and methods employed.

D. The contemporary world

1. Demonstrates insight into the psychodynamic forces at work in individuals and groups and utilizes these insights to interpret human events and comprehend their causes, effects, and implications.

2. Demonstrates perception and knowledge of contemporary world conditions and events and the capacity to analyze the complex interrelationships of these conditions and events in their historical contexts.

3. Demonstrates understanding of the growing interdependence of nations, especially concerning natural resources and economic development, and analyzes the impact of events in one area or culture on others.

4. Demonstrates understanding of the structural and functional differences among cultures, Western and Eastern, industrialized and less developed.

5. Based on one's own values, takes and defends effectively a reasoned personal position concern-

ing the implications of contemporary events on various social groups and on one's own personal life.

   E. Cultural change

     1. Describes the process of cultural change and analyzes specific cultural changes.

     2. Evaluates (1) the significance of these cultural changes for individuals and groups, both within a culture and as it relates to other cultures, and (2) the effects of individual and group change on culture.

     3. Identifies and evaluates one's own changes over time and one's own response to cultural change.

     4. Demonstrates intellectual flexibility and the capacity to adapt to change in one's own life and in various settings, contexts, and situations.

   F. Artistic response and expression

     1. Expresses personal response to the literary, performance, and visual arts in terms of their formal elements and one's own personal background.

     2. Distinguishes among artistic forms in terms of their elements and one's personal response to specific works.

     3. Relates works to their philosophical, historical, and cultural contexts.

     4. Makes and defends judgments of the artistic quality of specific works.

     5. Expresses creatively both abstract concepts and feelings and emotions using various artistic modes.

Using the Qualities to Develop Curriculum

College faculties and their curriculum committees today are increasingly specifying in considerable detail the learning "outcomes" they desire for their students. The use of "behavioral" language wherever possible increases significantly the probability of actually assessing (measuring) learning, no small advantage today, with a sharply increased awareness of the need for assessment and the demand for accountability.

The "qualities" listed above describe major competencies we consider characteristic of all liberally educated men and women. Although most of these characteristics have been considered important by thinkers for millennia, following increasingly common modern academic practice, they are today written down and couched in precise language to guide the planning and assessment of learning, not to mention the thinking of students themselves.

The curriculum (and today the cocurriculum as well) is the vehicle for actualizing or developing competencies in students. The skilled choice and sequencing of disciplinary content by the teacher in a course, together with the design of activities through which students interact with this content, provide for students the means for developing these competencies.

Caveats

This list of competencies can serve as the nucleus for planning a college curriculum. In doing so, however, several caveats should be noted. First, this list, although representative of what faculties desire for their students, is not exhaustive; each faculty will have its own emphases, greater or lesser, its own degree of desired detail. For example, Quality IV.F.3. "Relates works to their philosophical, historical, and cultural contexts," must be significantly elaborated to specify *which* works and specifically *how* these works are to be handled. Are the works literary or in the performing or visual arts? Which are most important? Answering these questions are faculty responsibilities and prerogatives.

These "qualities" are *skills* in general areas; we have not addressed the specific contents of the areas. The content and instructional activities employed to develop these skills are again the province of faculties and their curriculum committees.

Second, although competency statements should be couched in behavioral language wherever possible, it may not be possible to do so in every case. In difficult cases (see Bowen, 1977, pp. 53–59, for examples), the competency should be stated as clearly as possible in whatever language one can muster. One should avoid trivializing the complex but not assume that complex learning necessarily cannot be stated clearly and in behavioral language. One should attempt to state competencies even if they cannot at this time be measured.

Third, in developing a curriculum, close attention should be given to linguistic precision, clarity, and consistency. The Alverno College materials cited below may serve as useful guides when writing.

Explanation of the Qualities Clusters

Cluster I. Higher-Order Cognitive Skills. The higher-order thinking skills are the means by which we apprehend and control ourselves and our natural and social environment and solve life's problems. These skills constitute the mechanism by which we gain insight into our motivations, consciously shape our behavior, and design our lives. Their practiced use can lead to "wisdom."

The competencies in this cluster are prerequisite to those that follow. They, like the others, are developed through practice, by engaging in abstract problem-solving behavior in many settings, contexts, and situations. The skilled thinker can learn to perform the functions described in the other, succeeding three qualities clusters.

Cluster II. Active Awareness of One's Natural Environment.   We are dependent upon our natural environment for life itself. Our mastery of technology and awareness of its limitations and our understanding and responsible stewardship of our environment are necessary to enable competent decision making that can ensure both the future quality of our own lives and the well-being of other species.

Cluster III. Active Awareness of Oneself.   The aphorism "know thyself" articulates a truth known to reflective men and women since antiquity. Success as a person—becoming a "fully functioning person"—requires substantive insight into one's own self: one's self-identity, emotional dynamics, and values. The central importance of self-awareness in life manifests itself by its strongly enhancing effects on the development of the competencies in the other clusters.

Cluster IV. Awareness of and Effective Action in One's Social and Cultural Environment.   For the developed personality, contact with other people is a major part of daily experience. Understanding others and developing skill in interacting with them is fundamental to achieving one's own goals in life, enjoying other people, and contributing to their lives.

This understanding of others and skill in interacting with them develops through face-to-face practice and reflection and through the use of various media and modes of expression.

Acknowledgments

This description has been developed through an extended review of the professional literature of American liberal arts colleges and the goals they have for their students and the competencies they attempt to develop in them. Of special help were detailed descriptions of the eight "abilities" forming the core of the Alverno College curriculum (see Alverno College Faculty, 1979, 1981; Earley, Mentkowski, and Schafer, 1980; and Loacker, Cromwell, Fey, and Rutherford, 1984) and competencies developed by the Tennessee Higher Education Commission (Branscomb, Milton, Richardson, and Spivey, 1977). In addition, we have drawn on the recently released reports of the National Institute of Education Study Group on the Conditions of Excellence in American Higher Education (Mortimer 1984) and the Association of American Colleges Select Committee of the Project of Redefining the Meaning and Purpose of Baccalaureate Degrees (Curtis 1985).

The following colleagues graciously read various drafts of this description and offered many valuable criticisms, comments, and suggestions: Drs. Michael I. Aissen (Mathematics), Virginia K. Cremin-Rudd (English), Margaret Furcron (Academic Foundations), Patricia A. Gartenberg (English), Jan E. Lewis (History), Marc A. Mappen (Associate Dean, FAS-N), Douglas W. Morrison (Zoology and Physiology, Mary Lou Motto (English), Louis H. Orzack (Sociology), Lillian Robbins (Psychology), Pheroze S. Wadia (Philosophy), and Ann C. Watts (English).

A number of our quality statements are identical to Alverno College ability statements. We thank Sr. Austin Doherty, Vice President for Academic Affairs of Alverno College, for permission to use them here.

Literature Cited

Alverno College Faculty. *Assessment at Alverno College*. Milwaukee: Alverno Productions, 1979. 60 pp.

Alverno College Faculty. *Liberal Learning at Alverno College*. Milwaukee: Alverno Productions, 1981. 42 pp.

Bowen, H. R. *Investment in Learning: The Individual and Social Value of American Higher Education*. San Francisco: Jossey-Bass, 1977. 507 pp. Pages 53–59, "A Catalog of Goals," provides a taxonomy of college goals for student development summarizing 1,500 goal statements in the literature.

Branscomb, H., Milton, O., Richardson, J., and Spivey, H. *The Competent College Student: An Essay on the Objectives and Quality of Higher Education*. Nashville: Tennessee Higher Education Commission, 1977. 20 pp.

Curtis, M. H. (chairman). *Integrity in the College Curriculum: A Report to the Academic Community*. Washington, D.C.: Association of American Colleges, 1985. 47 pp.

Earley, M., Mentkowski, M., and Schafer, J. *Valuing at Alverno: The Valuing Process in Liberal Education*. Milwaukee: Alverno Productions, 1980. 97 pp.

Loacker, G., Cromwell, L., Fey, J., and Rutherford, D. *Analysis and Communication at Alverno: An Approach to Critical Thinking*. Milwaukee: Alverno Productions, 1984. 189 pp.

Mortimer, K. P. (chairman). *Involvement in Learning: Realizing the Potential of American Higher Education*. Final Report of the National Institute of Education Study Group on the Conditions of Excellence in American Higher Education. Washington, D.C.: National Institute of Education, U.S. Department of Education, 1984. 99 pp.

Sample Copyright Agreement

ISBN # _____

COPYRIGHT AGREEMENT

This Agreement is made on _____ 19 _____ between
_____ residing in _____
("Author") and Syracuse University, a not-for-profit educational institution located in
Syracuse, New York ("University").

1. **Recitals**
   (a) Author is the author of certain written materials which were developed with the
       support of the University's Center for Instructional Development ("Center").
   (b) Author desires to have the materials published, and the University is willing to
       publish the materials, all as set forth in this Agreement.
   (c) Author is an employee of the University.
2. **Grant of Rights**
   (a) The Author hereby grants and assigns the University the right to publish and
       sell worldwide the following written work identified by the title:
       _____("Work")

   (b) The University shall publish the Work at its own expense in such style and man-
       ner as it deems appropriate. The University shall have the sole right and author-
       ity to determine the number of issues to be published and the terms and manner
       of the sale of the Work.
   (c) The University is under no obligation to keep the Work in print. In the event
       that all of the printed copies of the Work are sold, the University shall have the
       right to determine, at its own discretion, whether to print additional copies.

(d) The Parties agree that they will jointly promote the sale of the work in such manner as they shall determine. The University shall not be under any obligation to promote the sale of the Work except as otherwise agreed by the parties.

3. **Royalties**

(a) The University shall pay to the Author a royalty of _____ on the retail selling price of every copy of the Work sold by the University, unless rights to royalties are waived by the Author in writing. If more than one author has contributed to the Work, the total royalty shall be split among the contributing authors according to the following schedule:

Principle Author   _____ percent

Author 2 (_____)   _____ percent

Author 3 (_____)   _____ percent

(b) Royalties shall be paid within 60 days after each June 30 and December 31 for the six month period then ended. Royalty payments shall be accompanied by a written statement identifying the number of copies of the Work sold during the period and the total receipts upon which the computation of royalties is based.

(c) The University is authorized to withhold from royalty payments, taxes and other amounts required by law to be withheld.

4. **Manuscript**

The Author authorizes the University to edit and make changes in the manuscript of the Work, provided that all changes in the manuscript are subject to the approval of the Author or, if more than one Author, the approval of the Principal Author.

5. **Copies**

(a) The University shall provide the Author free of charge two copies of the published work, with additional copies to be made available to the Author at the University's cost. One complimentary set of media materials shall also be provided to the Author or, if more than one author, to the senior author.

(b) If the work is a textbook for a University course, the University will also provide one copy of the work to each person with instructional responsibilities for the course.

6. **Commercial Publication**

Notwithstanding the rights granted to the University by this Agreement, either the Author or the University may contract with a commercial publishing house to publish and sell the Work, provided that no such agreement may be entered into without the prior written approval of the other party. In the event an agreement is entered into with a commercial publisher, the royalties payable under that agreement will be divided among the parties as follows, unless otherwise agreed by the parties:

(a) If the commercial publisher requires revisions which, in the sole judgment of the University, will require a minimum of rewriting by the Author, the Author will be entitled to 60 percent of the royalties paid by the commercial publisher and the University will be entitled to the remaining 40 percent.

(b) If the commercial publisher requires revisions which, in the sole judgment of the University, will require major rewriting by the Author, the Author will be entitled to 75 percent of the royalties paid by the commercial publisher, and the University will be entitled to the remaining 25 percent.

7. **Representations and Warranties**

   (a) The Author represent and warrants to the University as follows:

      (i) With the exception of those other authors who contributed to the Work and who have signed a similar agreement with the University, Author is the sole owner of the Work (other than material prepared by the Center and its staff) and of the rights granted by this Agreement;

      (ii) The Author has not granted proprietary rights in the Work to any other party;

      (iii) The Work is an original creation of the Author and does not contain material copyrighted by others, or, if such copyrighted material is included in the Work, the Author has obtained permission to reprint the material in the Work;

      (iv) The Work does not contain any libelous or unlawful matter and does not infringe upon the rights of others.

   (b) The Author will defend with competent counsel, indemnify and hold the University harmless from and against all claims, proceedings, losses, damages, costs, attorneys' fees and expenses arising out of or resulting from the Author's breach of any of the foregoing representations and warranties.

   (c) The University shall be entitled to deduct and offset from royalties to be paid to the Author any damages, costs and expenses, including legal fees, incurred by the University by reason of the Author's breach of any of the foregoing representations and warranties. This remedy shall be in addition to any other remedy provided by law or by this Agreement.

8. **Copyright**

   (a) The parties agree that the University shall own the copyright in the Work and that the Work shall bear a copyright notice in the name of the University upon publication. The University reserves the right to register the copyright in the U.S. Copyright Office but is under no obligation to do so.

   (b) The University shall have the right to, at its own expense, enforce any and all copyrights on the Work, to prosecute any infringement of the copyrights, and to retain the proceeds of any such infringement action.

9. **Terms and Termination**

   (a) This Agreement shall continue in force and effect for the term of the original U.S. copyright of the Work.

   (b) Notwithstanding the foregoing, the parties may terminate this Agreement as follows:

      (i) The Author may terminate this Agreement at any time after five years. Notice of intent to terminate must be in writing.

      (ii) The University may terminate the Agreement at any time it determines there is not sufficient market for the Work to justify continued publication of the Work.

      (iii) Any termination of the Agreement will not affect the rights of the parties to receive royalties from any commercial publishing house publishing the Work pursuant to Paragraph 6.

(iv) In the event of termination, the rights granted to the University shall revert to the Author except as otherwise provided in this Agreement. The Author shall have the right to buy from the University all copies on hand at the University's cost and the University shall have the right to sell or otherwise dispose of all remaining copies of the Work upon such terms as it deems advisable.

10. Instructional Use

The University and its employees shall have the right to use the Work for instructional purposes without payment of any royalty under Paragraph 3, and all sales or free copies of the Work to the University, its faculty and staff shall bear no royalty.

11. This Agreement shall be governed and construed in accordance with the laws of the State of New York.

12. Binding Effect

This agreement shall be binding upon and shall inure to the benefit of the parties and their successors and assigns.

_____	_____
(Signed) Author 1	Social Security #
_____	_____
Address	City, State, Zip
	_____
	Date
_____	_____
(Signed) Author 2	Social Security #
_____	_____
Address	City, State, Zip
	_____
	Date
_____	_____
(Signed) Author 3	Social Security #
_____	_____
Address	City, State, Zip
	_____
	Date
_____	_____
(Signed) for Syracuse University	Date

RESOURCE

Teaching Goals Inventory
Self-Scorable Version

Purpose: The Teaching Goals Inventory (TGI) is a self-assessment of instructional goals. Its purpose is threefold: (1) to help college teachers become more aware of what they want to accomplish in individual courses; (2) to help faculty locate Classroom Assessment Techniques they can adapt and use to assess how well they are achieving their teaching and learning goals; and (3) to provide a starting point for discussions of teaching and learning goals among colleagues.

Directions: Please select ONE course you are currently teaching. Respond to each item on the inventory in relation to that particular course. (Your responses might be quite different if you were asked about your overall teaching and learning goals, for example, or the appropriate instructional goals for your discipline.)

Please print the title of the specific course you are focusing on:

_____

Please rate the importance of each of the fifty-two goals listed below to the specific course you have selected. Assess each goal's importance to what you deliberately aim to have your students accomplish, rather than the goal's general worthiness or overall importance to your institution's mission. There are no "right" or "wrong" answers, only personally more or less accurate ones.

For each goal, circle only one response on the 1-to-5 rating scale. You may want to read quickly through all fifty-two goals before rating their relative importance.

In relation to the course you are focusing on, indicate whether each goal you rate is:

(5) Essential	A goal you always/nearly always try to achieve
(4) Very important	A goal you often try to achieve
(3) Important	A goal you sometimes try to achieve
(2) Unimportant	A goal you rarely try to achieve
(1) Not applicable	A goal you never try to achieve

Rate the importance of each goal to what you aim
to have students accomplish in your course.

	Essential	Very Important	Important	Unimportant	Not Applicable
1. Develop ability to apply principles and generalizations already learned to new problems and situations	5	4	3	2	1
2. Develop analytic skills	5	4	3	2	1
3. Develop problem-solving skills	5	4	3	2	1
4. Develop ability to draw reasonable inferences from observations	5	4	3	2	1
5. Develop ability to synthesize and integrate information and ideas	5	4	3	2	1
6. Develop ability to think holistically: to see the whole as well as the parts	5	4	3	2	1
7. Develop ability to think creatively	5	4	3	2	1
8. Develop ability to distinguish between fact and opinion	5	4	3	2	1
9. Improve skill at paying attention	5	4	3	2	1
10. Develop ability to concentrate	5	4	3	2	1
11. Improve memory skills	5	4	3	2	1
12. Improve listening skills	5	4	3	2	1
13. Improve speaking skills	5	4	3	2	1
14. Improve reading skills	5	4	3	2	1
15. Improve writing skills	5	4	3	2	1
16. Develop appropriate study skills, strategies, and habits	5	4	3	2	1
17. Improve mathematical skills	5	4	3	2	1
18. Learn terms and facts of this subject	5	4	3	2	1
19. Learn concepts and theories in this subject	5	4	3	2	1
20. Develop skill in using materials, tools, and/or technology central to this subject	5	4	3	2	1

	Essential	Very Important	Important	Unimportant	Not Applicable
21. Learn to understand perspectives and values of this subject	5	4	3	2	1
22. Prepare for transfer or graduate study	5	4	3	2	1
23. Learn techniques and methods used to gain new knowledge in this subject	5	4	3	2	1
24. Learn to evaluate methods and materials in this subject	5	4	3	2	1
25. Learn to appreciate important contributions to this subject	5	4	3	2	1
26. Develop an appreciation of the liberal arts and sciences	5	4	3	2	1
27. Develop an openness to new ideas	5	4	3	2	1
28. Develop an informed concern about contemporary social issues	5	4	3	2	1
29. Develop a commitment to exercise the rights and responsibilities of citizenship	5	4	3	2	1
30. Develop a lifelong love of learning	5	4	3	2	1
31. Develop aesthetic appreciations	5	4	3	2	1
32. Develop an informed historical perspective	5	4	3	2	1
33. Develop an informed understanding of the role of science and technology	5	4	3	2	1
34. Develop an informed appreciation of other cultures	5	4	3	2	1
35. Develop capacity to make informed ethical choices	5	4	3	2	1
36. Develop ability to work productively with others	5	4	3	2	1
37. Develop management skills	5	4	3	2	1
38. Develop leadership skills	5	4	3	2	1
39. Develop a commitment to accurate work	5	4	3	2	1
40. Improve ability to follow directions, instructions, and plans	5	4	3	2	1
41. Improve ability to organize and use time effectively	5	4	3	2	1
42. Develop a commitment to personal achievement	5	4	3	2	1
43. Develop ability to perform skillfully	5	4	3	2	1
44. Cultivate a sense of responsibility for one's own behavior	5	4	3	2	1
45. Improve self-esteem/self-confidence	5	4	3	2	1
46. Develop a commitment to one's own values	5	4	3	2	1
47. Develop respect for others	5	4	3	2	1
48. Cultivate emotional health and well-being	5	4	3	2	1
49. Cultivate an active commitment to honesty	5	4	3	2	1

	Essential	Very Important	Important	Unimportant	Not Applicable
50. Develop capacity to think for one's self	5	4	3	2	1
51. Develop capacity to make wise decisions	5	4	3	2	1

52. In general, how do you see your primary role as a
teacher? (Although more than one statement may
apply, please circle one.)

    1 Teaching students facts and principles of their subject matter

    2 Providing a role model for students

    3 Helping students develop higher-order thinking skills

    4 Preparing students for jobs/careers

    5 Fostering student development and personal growth

    6 Helping students develop basic learning skills

1. In all, how many of the fifty-two goals did you rate as "essential"? _____

2. How many "essential" goals did you have in each of the six clusters listed below?

Cluster Number and Name	Goals Included in Cluster	Total Number of "Essential" Goals in Each Cluster	Clusters Ranked— from 1st to 6th— by Number of "Essential" Goals
I Higher-Order Thinking Skills	1–8	_____	_____
II Basic Academic Success Skills	9–17	_____	_____
III Discipline-Specific Knowledge and Skills	18–25	_____	_____
IV Liberal Arts and Academic Values	26–35	_____	_____
V Work and Career Preparation	36–43	_____	_____
VI Personal Development	44–52	_____	_____

3. Compute your cluster scores (average item ratings by cluster) using the following worksheet.

A	B	C	D	E
Cluster Number and Name	Goals Included	Sum of Ratings Given to Goals in That Cluster	Divide C by This Number	Your Cluster Scores
I Higher-Order Thinking Skills	1–8	_____	8	_____
II Basic Academic Success Skills	9–17	_____	9	_____
III Discipline-Specific Knowledge and Skills	18–25	_____	8	_____
IV Liberal Arts and Academic Values	26–35	_____	10	_____
V Work and Career Preparation	36–43	_____	8	_____
VI Personal Development	44–52	_____	9	_____

REFERENCES

Abbott, J., interviewed by T. Marchase. "The Search for Next-Century Learning." *Wingspread Journal* (Johnson Foundation, Racine, Wis.), 1996, *8*(3), 4.

"ADE Statement of Good Practice: Teaching, Evaluation, and Scholarship." *ADE Bulletin*, Spring 1996, *113*, 53–55.

Allen, L. R. "An Instructional Epiphany." *Change*, Mar.–Apr. 1996, *28*(2), 52.

American Historical Association. *Redefining Historical Scholarship.* Washington, D.C.: Ad Hoc Committee on Redefining Scholarly Work, American Historical Association, 1994.

Angelo, T. A. "Developing Learning Communities and Seven Promising Shifts and Seven Powerful Levers." Presentation at a meeting of the Professional and Organizational Development Network in Higher Education, Salt Lake City, Utah, 1966.

Angelo, T. A. *A Teacher's Dozen: 14 Useful Findings from Research on Higher Education.* Washington, D.C.: Phase II Classroom Research Project, American Association of Higher Education, 1993.

Angelo, T. A. "Improving Classroom Assessment to Improve Learning: Guidelines from Research and Practice." *Assessment Update*, Nov.–Dec. 1995, *7*(6), 1–2, 12–13.

Angelo, T. A., and Cross, K. P. *Classroom Assessment Techniques: A Handbook for College Teachers.* (2nd ed.) San Francisco: Jossey-Bass, 1993.

Association of American Colleges and Universities. *Integrity in the College Curriculum: A Report to the Academic Community.* Washington, D.C.: Association of American Colleges and Universities, 1985.

Astin, A. *The American College Teacher.* Los Angeles: Higher Education Research Institute, Graduate School of Education and Information Studies, University of California, Los Angeles, 1991.

Banta, T. "The Power of a Matrix," *Assessment Update*, July–Aug. 1996, *8*(4), 3, 13.

Barr, R. B., and Tagg, J. "From Teaching to Learning: A New Paradigm for Undergraduate Education." *Change*, Nov.–Dec. 1995, *27*(2), 24. Published by Heldref Publications, 1319 Eighteenth Street, NW, Washington, DC 20036–1802.

Batson, T., and Bass, V. "Teaching and Learning in the Computer Age." *Change,* Mar.–Apr. 1996, *28*(2), 44.

Bean, J. C. *Engaging Ideas: A Professor's Guide to Integrating Writing, Critical Thinking, and Active Learning in the Classroom.* San Francisco: Jossey-Bass, 1996.

Bennett, W. J. *To Reclaim a Legacy: Report on the Humanities in Higher Education.* Washington, D.C.: National Endowment for the Humanities, 1984.

Bergquist, W. H., and Armstrong, J. L. *Planning Effectively for Educational Quality: An Outcomes-Based Approach for Colleges Committed to Excellence.* San Francisco: Jossey-Bass, 1986.

Bergquist, W. H., and Sharpe, D. *An Educational Feast.* (Book 1: *Time*; Book 2: *Space*; Book 3: *Resources.*) Point Arena, Calif.: Peter Magnusson Press, 1996.

Bloom, B. S., and others. *Taxonomy of Educational Objectives:* Handbook 1. *The Cognitive Domain.* New York: McKay, 1956.

Bock, D. G., and Bock, E. H. *Evaluating Classroom Speaking.* Urbana: ERIC Center, University of Illinois, 1981.

Bostian, L., and Lunde, J. "Building Writing into Your Course." In J. P. Lunde and others (eds.), *Reshaping Curricula: Revitalization Programs at Three Land Grant Universities.* Bolton, Mass.: Anker, 1995.

Boyer, E. L. *College: The Undergraduate Experience in America.* New York: Harper-Collins, 1987.

Braskamp, L. A., and Ory, J. C. *Assessing Faculty Work: Enhancing Individual and Institutional Performance.* San Francisco: Jossey-Bass, 1994.

Briggs, L. J. *Handbook of Procedures for the Design of Instruction.* Pittsburgh: American Institutes for Research, 1970.

Burstyn, J., and Santa, C. "Complexity as an Impediment to Learning: A Study of Changes in Selected College Textbooks." *Journal of Higher Education,* 1977, *48*(5), 508–518.

Cartwright, G. P. "Technology and Underprepared Students, Part 1." *Change,* Jan.–Feb. 1996a, *28*(1), 45–48.

Cartwright, G. P. "Technology and Underprepared Students, Part 2." *Change,* May–June 1996b, *28*(3), 60–62.

Chickering, A. W., Gamson, Z., and Barsi, L. M. *The Seven Principles for Good Practice in Undergraduate Education: Faculty Inventory.* Milwaukee: Winona State University, 1989.

Clark, R. C. "Authormore, Multimedia and Instructional Methods." In *Taking the Plunge.* San Francisco: Marcomedia, 1995.

Cohen, K. "Report: Pacific Bell External Technology Research Grant." Unpublished, San Jose, Calif., Jan. 1995.

Cohen, K. "Networked Multimedia and On-Line Collaboration: External Technology Report to Pacific Bell." Unpublished, San Jose, Calif., Jan. 1996.

Conference Board of Canada. *Employability Skills Profile: What Are Employers Looking For?* Brochure 1992 E/F. Ottawa: Conference Board of Canada, 1992.

Crouch, M. K., and Fontaine, S. J. "Student Portfolios as an Assessment Tool." In D. F. Halpern and Associates, *Changing College Classrooms: New Teaching and Learning Strategies for an Increasingly Complex World.* San Francisco: Jossey-Bass, 1994.

Davis, B. G. *Tools for Teaching.* San Francisco: Jossey-Bass, 1993.

Deitz, R. "Breaking Down Barriers to Diversity." *Hispanic Outlook,* Mar. 1, 1995, pp. 10–11.

Diamond, R. M. *Preparing for Promotion and Tenure Review: A Faculty Guide.* Bolton, Mass.: Anker, 1995.

Diamond, R. M., and Adam, B. E. (eds.). *Recognizing Faculty Work: Reward Systems for the Year 2000.* New Directions for Higher Education, no. 81. San Francisco: Jossey-Bass, 1993.

Diamond, R. M., and Adam, B. E. (eds.). *The Disciplines Speak: Rewarding the Scholarly, Professional and Creative Work of Faculty.* Washington, D.C.: American Association for Higher Education, 1995.

Dresser, D. L. "The Relationship Between Personality Needs, College Expectations, Environmental Press, and Undergraduate Attrition in a University College of Liberal Arts." Unpublished doctoral dissertation, College of Education, Syracuse University, 1987.

Education Commission of the States. *Transforming the State Role in Undergraduate Education: Time for a Different View.* Denver: Education Commission of the States, 1986.

Eickmann, P., and Lee, R. *Applying an Instructional Development Process to Music Education.* Syracuse, N.Y.: Center for Instructional Development, Syracuse University, 1976.

Evers, F. T., and Rush, J. C. "The Bases of Competence: Skill Development During the Transition from University to Work." *Management Learning,* 1996, *27*(3), 275–299.

Farmer, D. W., and Napieralski, E. A. "Assessing Learning in Programs." In J. G. Gaff, J. L. Ratcliff, and Associates, *Handbook of the Undergraduate Curriculum: A Comprehensive Guide to Purposes, Structures, Practices, and Change.* San Francisco: Jossey-Bass, 1997.

Future Trends in Broadcast Journalism. Washington, D.C.: Radio-Television News Directors Association, 1984.

Gardiner, L. F. *Redesigning Higher Education: Producing Dramatic Gains in Student Learning.* Report 7. Washington, D.C.: Graduate School of Education and Human Development, George Washington University, 1996.

Geoghegan, W. H. *What Ever Happened to Instructional Technology? Reaching Mainstream Faculty.* Norwalk, Conn.: IBM, 1994. [www//:ike.eng.washington.edu].

Gerlach, V. S., and Ely, D. P. *Teaching and Media: A Systematic Approach.* (2nd ed.) Upper Saddle River, N.J.: Prentice Hall, 1980.

Gilbert, S. "Double Vision: Paradigms in Balance or Collision?" *Change,* Mar.–Apr. 1996, *28*(2), 8–9.

Greenwood, A. (ed.). *The National Assessment of College Student Learning: Identification of the Skills to Be Taught, Learned, and Assessed.* NCES #94–286. Washington, D.C.: National Center for Education Statistics, U.S. Department of Education, 1994.

Grunnert, J. *The Course Syllabus: A Learning-Centered Approach.* Bolton, Mass.: Anker, 1997.

Halpern, D. F., and Associates. *Changing College Classrooms: New Teaching and Learning Strategies for an Increasingly Complex World.* San Francisco: Jossey-Bass, 1994.

Hannun, W. H., and Briggs, L. J. *How Does Instructional Systems Design Differ from Traditional Instruction?* Chapel Hill: School of Education, University of North Carolina, 1980.

Hardin, J. H. *Mathematics Prerequisites and Student Success in Introductory Courses: Final Report.* Syracuse, N.Y.: Center for Instructional Development, Syracuse University, 1992.

Hayes, L. S. "Developing Learner Outcomes to Support a Curriculum." In J. P. Lunde and others (eds.), *Reshaping Curricula: Revitalization Programs at Three Land Grant Universities.* Bolton, Mass.: Anker, 1995a.

Hayes, L. S. "Student Portfolios for Academic and Career Advising." In J. P. Lunde and others (eds.), *Reshaping Curricula: Revitalization Programs at Three Land Grant Universities.* Bolton, Mass.: Anker, 1995b.

Jacoby, B. "Bringing Community Service into the Curriculum." *Chronicle of Higher Education,* 1994, *40*(50), B2.

Jones, E. A. *Writing Goals Inventory.* University Park: National Center on Postsecondary Teaching, Learning, and Assessment, Pennsylvania State University, 1994.

Kaufman, R., and English, F. W. *Needs Assessment: Concept and Application.* Englewood Cliffs, N.J.: Educational Technology Publications, 1979.

Keller, F. "Good-Bye Teacher." *Journal of Applied Behavior Analysis,* 1968, *1,* 79–89.

Keller, J. M. *Practitioner's Guide to Concepts and Measures of Motivation.* Syracuse, N.Y.: School of Education, Syracuse University, 1978.

Kemp, J. E. *The Instructional Design Process.* New York: HarperCollins, 1985.

Kemp, J. E. *Designing Effective Instruction.* Upper Saddle River, N.J.: Prentice Hall, 1995.

Kingston-Mann, E. "Multiculturalism Without Political Correctness: The University of Massachusetts/Boston Model." *Boston Review,* May–Aug. 1992, pp. 30–31.

Krathwohl, D. R., Bloom, B. S., and Masia, B. B. *Taxonomy of Educational Objectives: The Classification of Education Goals:* Handbook 2. *Affective Domain.* New York: McKay, 1964.

"Learning Slope." *Policy Perspectives* (Pew Higher Education Program), 1991, *4*(1), 1A–8A.

Levine, J., and Tompkins, D. "Making Learning Communities Work." *AAHE Bulletin,* June 1996, *45*(10), 3–6.

Lough, J. F. "Carnegie Professors of the Year: Models for Teaching Success." In J. K. Ross (ed.), *Inspiring Teaching: Carnegie Professors of the Year Speak.* Bolton, Mass.: Anker, 1996. Used with permission of the publisher.

Lunde, J. P., and others (eds.). *Reshaping Curricula: Revitalization Programs at Three Land Grant Universities.* Bolton, Mass.: Anker, 1995.

Mager, R. F. *Preparing Instructional Objectives.* Belmont, Calif.: Fearon, 1975.

Magruder, J., McManis, M., and Young, C. *The Right Idea at the Right Time: Development of a Transformational Assessment Culture.* Kirksville, Mo.: Office of the President, Truman State University, 1996.

Marchese, T. J. "Third Down, Ten Yards to Go." *AAHE Bulletin,* 1987, *40*(4), 8.

Massey, W. F., and Wilger, A. K. "Productivity in Postsecondary Education: A New Approach." *Educational Evaluation and Policy Analysis,* Winter 1992, *14*(4), 361–376.

McKeachie, W. J. *Teaching Tips: Strategies, Research, and Theory for College and University Teachers.* (9th ed.) Lexington, Mass.: Heath, 1994.

Merrill, M. D. "Content Analysis Via Concept Elaboration Theory." *Journal of Instructional Development,* 1977, *1,* 1.

Milton, O., and Associates. *On College Teaching: A Guide to Contemporary Practices.* San Francisco: Jossey-Bass, 1978.

Molenda, M., Pershing, J., and Reigeluth, C. *Designing Instructional Systems: Training and Development Handbook.* (4th ed.) Alexandria, Va.: American Society for Training and Development, 1996.

Muffo, J. A. "Lessons Learned from a Decade of Assessment." *Assessment Update,* Sept.–Oct. 1996, *8*(5), 1–2, 11.

National Institute of Education. *Involvement in Learning: Realizing the Potential of American Higher Education.* Washington, D.C.: National Institute of Education, 1984.

Pedersen, P. *A Handbook for Developing Multicultural Awareness.* Alexandria, Va.: American Counseling Association, 1988.

Perry, W. G. *Forms of Intellectual/Ethical Development in the College Years: A Scheme.* Austin, Tex.: Holt, Rinehart and Winston, 1970.

Pervin, L., and Rubin, D. "Student Dissatisfaction with College and the College Dropout: A Transactional Approach." *Journal of Social Psychology,* 1967, *72,* 285–295.

Pike, G. A. "The Watson-Glazer Critical Thinking Approach." *Assessment Update,* July–Aug. 1996, *8*(4), 12.

Plater, W. M. "Future Work, Faculty Time in the 21st Century." *Change,* May–June 1995, *27*(3), 23–33.

Popham, W. J., and Baker, E. L. *Establishing Instructional Goals.* Upper Saddle River, N.J.: Prentice Hall, 1970.

Postlethwait, S., Novak, J., and Murray, H., Jr. *The Audio-Tutorial Approach to Learning.* (3rd ed.) Minneapolis: Burgess, 1972.

Prater, E. L., and Smith, M. A. "On Being a Pathfinder on the Information Superhighway: Or How to Lead Your Students a Little Way into the Electronic Frontier." *Journal of Staff, Program and Organizational Development,* 1995–1996, *13*(4), 287–288.

Readon, C. *Critical Adjustments: Tackling Diversity at a Commonwealth College.* New York: Ford Foundation, Winter 1992.

Rogers, S. "Distance Education: The Options Follow the Mission." *AAHE Bulletin,* 1995, *48*(4), 4–10.

Romer, R. *Making Quality Count in Undergraduate Education.* Denver: Education Commission of the States, 1995.

Rothenberg, P. "The Politics of Discourse and the End of Argument." In E. G. Friedman, W. K. Kolmar, C. B. Flint, and P. Rothenberg (eds.), *Creating an Inclusive College Curriculum: A Teaching Sourcebook from the New Jersey Project.* New York: Teachers College Press, 1996a.

Rothenberg, P. "Transferring the Curriculum: The New Jersey Project Experience." In E. G. Friedman, W. K. Kolmar, C. B. Flint, and P. Rothenberg (eds.), *Creating an Inclusive College Curriculum: A Teaching Sourcebook from the New Jersey Project.* New York: Teachers College Press, 1996b.

Rubin, S. "Professors, Students, and the Syllabus." *Chronicle of Higher Education,* 1985, *30*(23), 56.

Russell, J. D., and Johanningsmeir, K. A. *Improving Competence Through Modular Instruction.* Dubuque, Iowa: Kendall/Hunt, 1981.

Schneider, C. "Higher Education and the Contradictions of American Pluralism." In *American Pluralism and the College Curriculum: Higher Education in a Diverse Democracy.* Washington, D.C.: Association of American Colleges and Universities, 1995.

Shaelwitz, J. A. "Capstone Courses: Are We Doing Assessment Without Realizing It?" *Assessment Update,* July–Aug. 1996, *8*(4), 4, 6.

Shapiro, W., Roskos, K., and Cartwright, G. P. "Technology—Enhanced Learning Environments." *Change,* Nov.–Dec. 1995, *27*(6), 67.

Simmons, S. R. "Using Discussion Cases in a Capstone Course." In J. P. Lunde and others (eds.), *Reshaping Curricula: Revitalization Programs at Three Land Grant Universities.* Bolton, Mass.: Anker, 1995.

Soderberg, D. J. "Using the Worldwide Web for Teaching and Learning." *Focus on Teaching and Learning,* Winter 1996, pp. 8–9.

Speech Communications Association. *Criteria for the Assessment of Oral Communication.* Annandale, Va.: Speech Communications Association, 1990.

Spotts, T. H., and Bowning, M. "Faculty Use of Instructional Technologies in Higher Education." *Educational Technology,* Mar.–Apr. 1995, 56–63.

Stark, J. S., and Lattuca, L. R. *Shaping the College Curriculum: Academic Plans in Action.* Needham Heights, Mass.: Allyn & Bacon, 1997.

State of New Jersey College Outcomes Evaluation Program Advisory Committee. *Report to the New Jersey Board of Higher Education from the Advisory Committee to the College Outcomes Evaluation Program.* Trenton: Board of Higher Education, State of New Jersey, 1987.

Stern, G. *People in Context.* New York: Wiley, 1970.

Terenzini, P. T., and Pascarella, E. T. *How College Affects Students: Findings and Insights from Twenty Years of Research.* San Francisco: Jossey-Bass, 1991.

Terenzini, P. T., and Pascarella, E. T. "Living with Myths: Undergraduate in America." *Change*, Jan.–Feb. 1994, *26*(1), 32.

University of Northern Iowa. *Project Group in the Qualities of an Educated Person: An Initial Report for Opening a University-Wide Conversation.* Cedar Falls: Center for Enhancement of Teaching, University of Northern Iowa, Oct. 4, 1996.

Useem, M. *Liberal Education and the Corporation: The Hiring and Advancement of College Graduates.* Hawthorne, N.Y.: Aldine de Gruyter, 1989.

Useem, M. "Corporate Restructuring and Liberal Learning." *Liberal Education,* Winter 1995, pp. 19–23.

Walker, C. J. "Assessing Group Process: Using Classroom Assessment to Build Autonomous Learning Teams." *Assessment Update,* Nov.–Dec. 1995, 7(6), 4–5.

Watson, G. "What Psychology Can We Feel Sure About?" *Teachers College Record,* 1960. Reprinted as a separate pamphlet, *What Psychology Can We Trust?* New York: Bureau of Publication, Teachers College, Columbia University, 1961.

Weingartner, R. *Undergraduate Education: Goals and Means.* Phoenix: Oryx Press, 1993.

Wittich, W., and Schuller, C. *Instructional Technology: Its Nature and Use.* (6th ed.) New York: HarperCollins, 1979.

Wlodkowski, R. J., and Ginsberg, M. B. *Diversity and Motivation: Culturally Responsive Teaching.* San Francisco: Jossey-Bass, 1995.

NAME INDEX

SUBJECT INDEX

A

Academic priorities, 34–37
Accountability, 4–6
Accreditation criteria, 75
Alverno College, 53, 73, 120, 142, 221, 247–249, 296
American Academy of Religion, 7
American Assembly of Collegiate Schools of Business, 7, 35, 75
American Association of Higher Education, 6, 76
American Chemical Society, 7
American Historical Association, 6, 7
American Sociological Association, 7
"Assessing Learning in Programs" (Farmer and Napieralski), 151
Assessment: of classroom, 150; for course design, 140–150; group form for, 144; and matching to objectives, 126–128; questions for, 241–246; references for, 152; sequence for, 11; of specific goals, 144–145
Association of American Colleges and Universities, 3
Association of American Geographers, 7
Association for Education in Journalism and Mass Communication, 7
Audiotutorial approach, 165

B

Basic design sequence, 10
Basic planning inputs. *See* Data gathering and analysis

Basic skills needed for managers, 218
Behavioral objectives, 129–130
Bentley College, 120
Boulder, Colorado, 287
Brigham Young University, 120
"Bringing Community Service into the Curriculum" (Jacoby), 162
British Open University, 120
Brochure 1992 E/F (Conference Board of Canada), 53

C

California State University, 178, 179
Capstone courses, 215
Carnegie Foundation for the Advancement of Teaching, 6
Carnegie-Mellon Institute of Technology, 120
Carolinians Creed (University of South Carolina), 204
Change, 76
Civilization (Clark), 178, 182
Classroom Assessment Technique (CAT) (Walker), 142, 150
College of Agriculture at the University of Minnesota, 71, 72, 131, 159, 223
College: The Undergraduate Experience in America (Boyer), 13
Colorado, 139
Communications design, first semester, 81–82
Community: and institutional assessment culture, 284–285; role of, in learning experience 162–163
Compact (Syracuse University), 204

Conference Board of Canada, 53
Content modification. *See* Data gathering and analysis
Content options, 164–165
Copyright agreement, sample of, 299–302
Core competencies, ensuring the acquisition of, 93–96
Council of Administrators of Family and Consumer Sciences, 7
Course Syllabus, The: A Learning-Centered Approach, 191
Course and curriculum design: data gathering for, 59–77; and delivery of instruction, 3–4; determination of objectives in, 125–137; and development of syllabus, 191–202; difference between, 107–108; and diversity goals, 203–214; evaluation of, 217–225; ideal sequence design for, 79–102; implementation and revision of, 215–234; initial design meeting for, 43–48; instruments and procedures for evaluation of, 139–152; learning-centered approach to, 1–12; operational sequence for, 107–124; project selection in, 49–58; system model for, 13–29
Course description: of Introductory School of Management Care, 95; for second part of Cost-Effectiveness in Instruction and Training, 92
Course management options, 165–167
Course projects: and decision to begin project, 37–39; establishing

317

Students: attitudes of, 62; entering level competence of, 60–61, 277–282; and information gathering, 63; input from, 59–60; and introductory Microeconomics course case study, 64; and introductory course in Religion case study, 122–124; long range goals of, 63; older age of, 63; priorities and expectations of, 62–63; references on assessment of, 152; research and, 118–119

Support staff, 27. *See also* Team approach

Syllabus: content and style of, 195–197; cost of production of, 200–201; learning-centered approach to, 191–202; obtaining permission to reproduce copyrighted material in, 198–199; on-line version of, 201; production of, by outside publisher of printer, 199; royalties and copyright for, 201; uses of, 193–195

Syllabus, 187

Syracuse University, 6, 36, 47, 60, 61, 62, 71, 74, 86, 91, 93, 98, 134, 163, 165, 197, 201, 204, 226–227, 233, 257–259, 265–275, 277, 299

System model: advantages of, 15–18; characteristics of, 18–27; options for, 27–28; and political sensitivity, 27; and team approach, 23–27; and thinking in the ideal, 18–19; and use of data, 23; and use of diagrams, 19–23

Systematic change, 8–11

Systematic design, 13–28

Systems theory, 16

T

Task Force on the Student Experience of the Faculty of Arts and Sciences at Rutgers University, 131

Teaching: questionnaire for effectiveness of, 232; research findings on good practice in, 84; in team, 116

Teaching Goals Inventory (TGI), 303–307

Teaching Tips: Strategies, Research, and Theory for College and University Teachers (McKeachie), 119

Team approach: and curriculum development, 2; and evaluators, 27; and facilitators, 25–27; and support staff, 27; and system model, 23–27

Team membership, 43–45

Technology: and Art History case study, 177–181; basic uses of, 170–171; design and field testing of materials in, 182–183; electronic sources of, 186–187; locating and evaluating existing materials in, 181–182; logistics of, 183–186; low varieties of, 176–177; MINI-QUEST questionnaire for student evaluation of materials, 184; print sources in, 187; selection of, 173–176; specific applications of, 171–173; top forty websites in, 188–189; transition to, 169–170

Testing, 143

Time factors, 77, 113–114, 277–282

Tools for Teaching (Davis), 119, 155

Trade-offs, 165. *See also* Instructional formats

Transforming the State Role in Undergraduate Education (Education Commission of the States), 139

Truman State University, 127, 283–287

U

Undergraduate education, 158

Undergraduate Education: Goals and Means (Weingartner), 3

United States Copyright Office, 301

United States Department of Education, 145

University College at the University of Maryland, 120

University of Colorado at Boulder, 120

University of Guelph, 120

University of Hawaii, 120

University of Maryland, 193

University of Massachusetts at Boston, 208, 209–213

University of Memphis, 73

University of Miami, 16, 120

University of Massachusetts case study in diversity goals, 209–210

University of Northern Iowa, 239

University of Rhode Island, 280–282

University of South Africa, 120

University of South Carolina, 204

Utah State University, 120

W

Washington State University, 173

Who Is Going to Run General Motors? (Seymour), 94

William Paterson College, 173

Winona State University, 155

Work flow by time, 18

Writing goals inventory, 145, 146–149. *See also* Evaluation instruments and procedures

Writing objectives: and categorizing, 132–134; and grading process, 135; inventory for, 146–148; of process, 134; samples of, 135–136; and specification, 134–135. *See also* Objectives